COURAGEOUS HUMILITY

COURAGEOUS HUMILITY

Reflections on the Church, *Diakonia*, and Deacons

WILLIAM T. DITEWIG

Foreword by Gerald F. Kicanas,
Bishop Emeritus of Tucson

Paulist Press
New York / Mahwah, NJ

The Scripture quotations contained herein are from the New Revised Standard Version Bible: Catholic Edition, copyright © 1989, 1993 National Council of the Churches of Christ in the United States of America. Used by permission. All rights reserved worldwide.

Cover image: *He Washed Their Feet*, copyright © 2012 by John August Swanson, serigraph, 16" x 20", www.JohnAugustSwanson.com
Cover design by Sharyn Banks
Book design by Lynn Else

Library of Congress Cataloging-in-Publication Data
Names: Ditewig, William T., author.
Title: Courageous humility : reflections on the church, diakonia, and deacons / William T. Ditewig ; foreword by Gerald F Kicanas, Bishop Emeritus of Tucson.
Description: New York ; Mahwah, NJ : Paulist Press, 2022. | Includes index. | Summary: "This book offers a spiritual reflection on the nature of the Church and very practical recommendations for approaching the future needs of the Church"—Provided by publisher.
Identifiers: LCCN 2021055213 (print) | LCCN 2021055214 (ebook) | ISBN 9780809155712 (paperback) | ISBN 9781587689703 (ebook)
Subjects: LCSH: Church. | Catholic Church—Doctrines. | Deacons—Catholic Church.
Classification: LCC BX1746 .D573 2022 (print) | LCC BX1746 (ebook) | DDC 262/.02—dc23/eng/20220128
LC record available at https://lccn.loc.gov/2021055213
LC ebook record available at https://lccn.loc.gov/2021055214

ISBN 978-0-8091-5571-2 (paperback)
ISBN 978-1-58768-970-3 (e-book)

Published by Paulist Press
997 Macarthur Boulevard
Mahwah, New Jersey 07430
www.paulistpress.com

Printed and bound in the
United States of America

To my wife, Diann
For fifty years of love and adventure
With all my love

CONTENTS

FOREWORD

Deacon Bill Ditewig has spent much of his ministerial life studying, writing, and living out passionately the diaconate. His latest work begins with a reflection on the Church and the call to live its mission with courageous humility. The first three chapters are a call to become a humble, courageous Church, and the final chapters show how that can be lived out through the diaconate. The book has much to offer for those seeking a renewed understanding of the Church and the role of deacons.

Diane Coutu, a writer for the *Harvard Business Review*, once wrote about resilience and why some institutions faced with crisis bend or break while others bounce back. She cites the Catholic Church as an institution that has bounced back time and time again. Ditewig is convinced that the way back now is for a humbler, more engaged Church, a Church on the way not yet arrived.

Faced with scandals that have broken trust from within and without the Church, Ditewig's appeal for a humble Church is exactly the call that is needed the most today. He refers to "courageous humility" as "one that takes risks, investing the talents and strengths God has given us for the good of others." That is the way the Lord Jesus lived and how he has called his followers to live. "The Church is humble because our God is humble."

Ditewig then turns to the *Rule of St. Benedict*, which is permeated with the virtue of humility, with Benedict devoting a whole chapter to it. This *Rule* can guide the Church and its ministers to ascend into a deeper relationship with God by descending from pride and self-sufficiency. While the idea of obedience as opposed to one's personal freedom is unpopular today, Benedict sees it as the virtue that can bring true freedom. Ditewig's focus on the heart of the *Rule of St. Benedict* and his reference to one of the great Church leaders, Archbishop John Quinn, who, faced with his own challenges and weaknesses, approached his ministry with humility, help us understand how the Church can live out its ministry with courageous humility. He addresses directly the challenge of how we can be a humble Church, yet one grounded on the rock of Peter. He reflects on Archbishop Quinn's work in reenvisioning how we can live out humility in the institutional structure of the Church and explores how we can be both a bold and faithful Church, a call given us by Pope Francis.

This beautiful reflection on ecclesiology leads seamlessly into a fuller understanding of deacons as "icons of the Church's humility." Here the work speaks in a refreshing and insightful way for a renewal in understanding the diaconate. Deacons serve as Christ served. While all in the Church are called to serve, Ditewig sees deacons as icons of Christ the Servant, constantly reminding the Church of the centrality of service.

Finally, drawing upon the great canonist Rev. James H. Prevost, Ditewig offers some helpful and extensive recommendations for the revision of canon law and its implied understanding of the diaconate and its relationship to the Church. In addition, he offers some interesting suggestions for a liturgical renewal of the rite of ordination for deacons.

This comprehensive work is valuable for all in the Church but most especially for bishops who identify, support, and ordain deacons; for deacons themselves, so often misunderstood; for their co-workers; and for the communities where they serve.

Gerald F. Kicanas
Bishop Emeritus of Tucson

PREFACE

In 2017 the universal Church celebrated the fiftieth anniversary of the 1967 promulgation of St. Pope Paul VI's *Sacrum Diaconatus Ordinem*, reestablishing the diaconate as a "stable and permanent" order of ministry. In 2018, the Church in the United States marked the occasion when, in 1968, it had requested and received permission to renew the diaconate in our country. In a landmark gathering in New Orleans, some three thousand bishops, deacons, presbyters, religious, and laity reflected on the past, present, and future of the diaconate. As one of the speakers addressing the future of the diaconate, I began the current project as an extended reflection on the future of the Church and its deacons.

However, we cannot inquire about the diaconate (or any other Church ministry) in a vacuum. As Edward Kilmartin wrote decades ago, the Church's ministries derive from its nature and needs, which means our reflections on the diaconate must necessarily begin with considering the future of the Church itself.[1] That, too, is an impossible task, for who can chart that course with any accuracy? Imagine living a century ago and trying to predict the past one hundred years! So, instead of beginning with the "future of the diaconate," I began to think about the future of the Church. Specifically, what will we carry into the future? No matter what happens, what must remain constant if we are to remain the Catholic Church? In other words, there are certain things, ideas, truths that we must have if we are to remain Christian: our core belief in the Trinity, for example, and the sacramental nature of the one, holy, catholic, and apostolic Church along with its participation in Christ's threefold ministry of priest, prophet, and servant-king. Only then can we turn our attention to specific questions related to the renewed diaconate.

Facing the future, we must not strike out blindly and haphazardly. Instead, in humility, we must consider carefully and honestly where we are in terms of our institutions, processes, attitudes, and visions. I wish to briefly outline three fundamental points that will recur throughout this project. First, we examine how we Christians in general, and Catholic Christians in specific, confront crises and "reveal our hearts," to use Pope Francis's phrase.[2] Second, following St. Paul in his letter to the Philippians, we explore how we "put on the mind of Christ" and how that "attitude adjustment" is reflected in ecclesial structures. Third, we will consider the implications of facing the future emboldened by courageous humility.

These reflections are offered just as Pope Francis has summoned the Church to a two-year synodal process, a Synod on Synodality.[3] He understands this time to be a "season of grace" for the Church, and I agree with many observers that this process has the potential to be the most significant event of reform and renewal since the Second Vatican Council. The pope cautions against three risks. The first is *formalism*, which could focus only on external appearances, "like admiring the magnificent facade of a church without ever actually stepping inside." The second risk is *intellectualism*, which "would turn the Synod into a kind of study group, offering learned but abstract approaches to the problems of the Church and the evils in our world. The usual people saying the usual things, without great depth or spiritual insight, and ending up along familiar and unfruitful ideological and partisan divides, far removed from the reality of the holy People of God and the concrete life of communities around the world." The third risk mentioned by the pope is that of *complacency*, "the attitude that says: 'We have always done it this way.'" The pope describes this attitude as "poison for the life of the Church."

This current project should be seen as a respectful contribution to this synodal process.

A Humble and Humbled Church Confronts Crisis: "Revealing Your Heart"

We face the future through the overlapping lenses of crisis. For years, we have dealt with the travesty and criminality of sexual abuse and coverup by clergy, religious, and other ministerial leadership. Coupled with this, but not restricted to it, is the loss of credibility in our teachings and our episcopal leadership. Cases of institutional and financial corruption continue to occur at the parish, diocesan, and international levels. On top of all this, a pandemic forced us to find new ways to meet people's needs in light of social distancing and other public health requirements.

Crisis (κρίση) is a medical term that marks a tipping point: either the patient will begin to improve, or she will continue to sicken further and die. The decisions we make at a crisis point are often determinative. Pope Francis has written that it is through a crisis that we find out who we are.

> The question is whether you're going to come through this crisis, and, if so, how. The basic rule of a crisis is that you don't come out of it the same. If you get through it, you come out better or worse, but never the same....In the trials of life, you reveal your own heart: how solid it is, how merciful, how big or small. Normal times are like formal social situations: you never have to reveal yourself. You smile, you say the right things, and you come through unscathed, without ever having to show who you really are. But when you're in a crisis, it's the opposite. You have to choose. And in making your choice, you reveal your heart.[4]

Much of what we will consider in this project begins with personal spirituality but goes further. On a personal level, my response to crisis reveals my own heart: "how solid it is, how merciful, how big or small." But our mark of catholicity takes us beyond personal piety to an ecclesial identity. It is not merely how *I* respond to crisis but how *we*—the people of God, mystical body of Christ, and temple of the Holy Spirit—respond to crisis. What does our response to crisis teach us of the heart of our Church? How solid, how merciful, how big or small is that heart?

What are some factors of the crises we face? First, there seems to be, among some Catholics, a sense of denial. They acknowledge that there are challenges to be met, but they are the surrounding culture's failings. Once the "culture wars" have been won, these Catholics seem to hold, there can be a return to the *status quo ante*. There's nothing wrong that prayer can't fix, and then we can go back to the way we were. When

I was serving on the senior staff of the USCCB, I received a phone call from a lady who asked if I could get a message to the bishops: "I want the bishops to know just how much we love and appreciate our deacons!" Naturally, it was wonderful to have such affirmation, and I assured her the bishops would get her message. We had an enjoyable conversation, but then the topic turned to the sexual abuse crisis, among other things. "Oh, Deacon, won't it be wonderful when all of these problems go away? And then, we won't need you deacons anymore!" For this wonderful lady, the only reason for the Church to have deacons and to have expanded the role of laypersons in the Church was to meet the demands of crisis. Once the troubles were over, the Church could go back to a time in which priests and sisters took care of everything.

But as Pope Francis says, we don't come out of a crisis the same, even if we refuse to admit it. Like an ill patient who has received a bad diagnosis, we have to acknowledge not only that a crisis exists; we must confess further that it will change us forever. We are dealing with anger resulting from seemingly endless sexual abuse, collapsing moral authority and credibility, mixed messaging from hierarchical leadership, fading attendance and participation in the Church's sacramental life (even before COVID-19), and widespread lack of agreement with Church teaching, all within the context of a global pandemic and crisis of faith in government. It seems that a growing number of people no longer believe in the Church, its teachings, or its ministers, nor do they experience it as a credible moral presence in the world. Nothing the Church has to say seems to have any relevance to their lives. And yet, over fifty years ago, in *Gaudium et Spes*, the world's bishops taught us that "in language intelligible to each generation, [the Church] can respond to the perennial questions which men ask about this present life and the life to come, and about the relationship of the one to the other. We must therefore recognize and understand the world in which we live, its explanations, its longings, and its often-dramatic characteristics."[5] It seems clear that the Church has failed in finding that "language" and that our answers no longer respond to the questions people have. We have not successfully recognized and understood the world in which we live. Many of us may think we know the world, but the truth is that we would be far more effective in responding to it if we actually did.

We face these crises as a humbled Church, a Church no longer seen as a credible pillar of society. Today, most people, including many Catholics, no longer seek out the Church's opinion or teaching on any topic in their decision-making. They see the Church as tangential, irrelevant, tone deaf, and out of touch with their lives. Observers in the media and even those involved in the entertainment industry portray people of faith as abusive, rigid, reactionary, or as a punchline. The days of *Going My Way* and *Bells of St. Mary's* are long gone, and they are not coming back.

But crisis opens the door to healing, growth, and conversion. One might approach crisis in fear and dread, or as an opportunity, a "new *Kairos*."[6] The decisions we make and the actions we take will determine our ecclesial health in the years ahead. Specifically, our responses must be immediate, practical, substantive, and other focused. Navigating these challenges will require commitment, creativity, and—most significantly—humility in facing the unknown. Where is the Church in the face of global mistrust of the Church, its institutions, and its ministers? What can we do to regain credibility? How does a humbled Church speak of God and proclaim God's reign? How does a humbled Church "carry forward the work of Christ under the lead of the befriending Spirit"?[7] The answer is to imitate Christ, who came not to be served but to serve and give his life as a ransom for many (Matt 20:28). In short, we must be a humble, as well as a humbled, Church. Humility is not merely an aspect of individual spirituality; it is the foundational attitude of our ecclesial identity. Yves Congar, in a monograph written during the conciliar debates on the nature of the Church, wrote, "Because the Church is a form of Christ's presence in the world, she must reproduce Christ's image as perfectly as possible and in her visible as well as her hidden life. The poverty that is the sign of the Incarnation must be the sign of the Church too."[8] This insight forms the core of the current project. To survive the current crises and face the unknown future, we must first have an "attitude adjustment."

"Attitude Adjustment": Putting on the Mind of Christ

During my lengthy Navy career, I learned some essential leadership truths. One was simple: attitude influences performance. For example, for several years, I served at sea in submarines. Even in "normal" operations, putting over one hundred people in a steel tube, submerging that tube hundreds of feet in salt water while also having various weapons and electrical systems onboard, is never routine, safe, or normal. All officers and sailors who serve in submarines are volunteers. Missions can last many weeks or months, all at sea with no time ashore. On some missions, the submarine never goes to the surface, remaining submerged and using the periscope as necessary. One novelist referred to submarine duty as weeks of boredom punctuated by seconds of sheer terror. Under such conditions, it can be easy to become overwhelmed, frightened, and claustrophobic. No matter what one encounters, no matter how frightened one might get, there is no getting off the ship during the mission. Sometimes you just have to *will* yourself to get over whatever the challenge is. One's attitude in meeting every challenge makes all the difference. While a positive attitude may not guarantee a successful result, a negative attitude will undoubtedly lead to disaster and failure. Leaders often refer to the need for an "attitude adjustment" to improve operational morale, health, and performance.

What should be the attitude of the Church? How do we, individually and communally, view the world? We have all seen this in our lives. One person might see everything around them negatively, sarcastically, or fearfully; her decisions and life choices will follow suit. Another person might see life positively, optimistically, or courageously; likewise, his decisions and life choices will follow suit. This insight applies equally to institutions and leadership. An organization's morale led by competent people with enthusiasm, optimism, and courage is markedly different from one led by fear and pessimism. The Church, in its institutional dimensions, is affected in the same way. Attitude influences performance. Over the centuries, the Church has adopted different attitudes toward itself and the world around it.

What is the "attitude" for the Christian? St. Paul states it clearly, in a quotation that inspires this entire project. Writing from prison to the Christian community in Philippi, he entreats them, "Do nothing from selfish ambition or conceit but in humility regard others as better than yourselves. Let each of you look not to your own interests, but to the interests of others. Let the same mind be in you that was in Christ Jesus" (Phil 2:3–5). Paul completes his exhortation by describing precisely the "mind of Christ" through the words of the great christological hymn describing the kenosis of Christ. The attitude of the one who follows Christ must have the same kenotic humility: an emptied vessel poured out in the "interests of others" who are "better than ourselves." Such an attitude affects our view of the world and how the world views us. Our point of view determines how we interpret life and interact with God and with each other and the world—an attitude that Vatican II invited us particularly to embrace.

St. Pope John XXIII called the Church's bishops to a new and daring approach to contemporary life and ministry, best expressed in his famous opening address on October 11, 1962. He spoke of the balance between the "sacred deposit of Christian doctrine" and its relationship to the changing demands of the contemporary world.

> In order, however, that this doctrine may influence the numerous fields of human activity, with reference to individuals, to families, and to social life, it is necessary first of all that the Church should never depart from the sacred patrimony of truth received from the Fathers. But at the same time she must ever look to the present, to the new conditions and new forms of life introduced into the modern world, which have opened new avenues to the Catholic apostolate....The substance of the ancient doctrine of the deposit of faith is one thing, and the way in which it is presented is another.[9]

The bishops responded to the pope's words and made them their own:

> The Church has always had the duty of scrutinizing the signs of the times and of interpreting them in the light of the Gospel. Thus, in language intelligible to each generation, she can respond to the perennial questions which men ask about this present life and the life to come and about the relationship of the one to the other. We must therefore recognize and understand the world in which we live, its explanations, its longings, and its often dramatic characteristics. (*GS* 4)

The bishops were not naïve. While they recognized the positive dimensions of the contemporary world, they acknowledged the challenges ahead:

> Today, the human race is involved in a new stage of history. Profound and rapid changes are spreading by degrees around the whole world. Triggered by the intelligence and creative

> energies of humanity, these changes recoil upon them, upon their decisions and desires, both individual and collective, and upon their manner of thinking and acting with respect to things and to people.…As happens in any crisis of growth, this transformation has brought serious difficulties in its wake. (*GS* 4)

Reading the signs of the times in light of the gospel and doing so "in language intelligible to every generation" demanded a new approach to confronting contemporary pastoral issues, and Pope St. Paul VI began to refer to this new approach as a *novus habitus mentis*, usually translated as "a new way of thinking." He first used this expression on Saturday, November 20, 1965 (while the Council was still in session), when he addressed the commission revising the Code of Canon Law. Although focused in this instance on the revisioning process of the Code, its effect is much broader. The revised Code would have to mirror, enable, and empower the servant Church as described by Vatican II. "Now, however, with changing conditions…canon law must be prudently reformed; specifically, it must be accommodated to a new way of thinking proper to the second ecumenical council of the Vatican, in which pastoral care and new needs of the people of God are met."[10]

This "new way of thinking" is no mere cognitive process. Nor is it merely a legal principle. Instead, this "new habit of mind" has the practical end of concrete pastoral care and meets God's people's needs. Canonist Ladislas Orsy has written that *novus habitus mentis* may be understood in a variety of ways: most literally as "new habit of mind," "new habit of the mind," or even "a mind with a new disposition," "a new mentality" or "a new mind." "The point is that the pope asked for a change in the mind itself."[11] Orsy pushes us even further: "To acquire a new disposition of the mind means to enter into a new field of vision; that is, into a new horizon."[12]

Just what is this new horizon for the Church? How do we stay on course toward that horizon? It is easy for a ship to drift off course due to tides, winds, poor navigation decisions, and even accidents and equipment failures. While affirming the hierarchical structures of the Church, the Second Vatican Council emphasized its most fundamental character as that of sacrament, pilgrim, and servant. As I have frequently stressed, Paul VI summarized the whole work of Vatican II as proclaiming the Church as servant:

> All this rich teaching is channeled in one direction [The Latin original has *huiusmodi divitem doctrinae copiam eo unite spectare*, so perhaps it might also be translated as "all this rich teaching has one point of view"], that it may serve humanity [*ut homini serviat*], of every condition, in every weakness and need. The Church has declared herself the handmaid of humanity [*Ecclesia quodammodo se professa est humani generis ancillam*]....Indeed, the exercise of service is its principal purpose [*immo vero ministerii exercendi propositum reapse praecipuum obtinuit locum*].[13]

Following Pope Paul, the Church must continuously recognize that "service" is not merely something the individual Christian (lay, religious, or ordained) "does" for someone else; it is precisely who we are. Service is not an activity as much as it is a state of being and a frame of reference, a *habitus mentis*. Servanthood is the distinguishing characteristic of what it means to be the Christian Church in the world. The servant Church must have a different way of looking at, and interacting with, the world around us. It must have, in the words of Paul VI and John Paul II, a *novus habitus mentis*, a new horizon of meaning, the eyes, hands, heart, and soul of a servant.

This project's central theme is that it is only through the courageous humility of the servant that the Church might regain its credibility and be more effective in its mission of evangelization. As we shall examine throughout this project, the virtue of humility has been and continues to be the cornerstone of faith. If we approach the world with pride or with an attitude that "we have all the answers," then we will continue to fall. As the proverb teaches, "When pride comes, then comes disgrace; but wisdom is with the humble" (Prov 11:2).

Early Christians quickly understood and accepted the truth that humility was the heart of Christian discipleship. St. Augustine wrote in a letter to a student that "humility is the foundation of all the other virtues; hence, in the soul in which this virtue does not exist, there cannot be any other virtue except in mere appearance." The way to follow Christ is all about humility, humility, and humility:

> This way is first humility, second humility, third humility, and however often you should ask me, I would say the same [*Ea est autem prima, humilitas; secunda, humilitas; tertia,*

> *humilitas: et quoties interrogares hoc dicerem*], not because there are no other precepts to be explained, but, if humility does not precede and accompany and follow every good work we do, and if it is not set before us to look upon, and beside us to lean upon, and behind us to fence us in, pride will wrest from our hand any good deed we do while we are in the very act of taking pleasure in it.[14]

Humility serves as a lens through which the Church regards the world and its place in it. Humility serves as a measure to judge the Church and its human institutions. Humility serves as both the hallmark of individual disciples and an evident characteristic of the Church itself, a *communio* of disciples who have in them the same "mind of Christ" and therefore "in humility regards others as better than yourselves."

The Second Vatican Council adopted a new approach to understanding the Church. *Lumen Gentium* describes the Church as a people on "their pilgrimage toward eternal happiness."[15] In doing so, the Council rejected the *perfecta societas* model of prior years. As Richard Gaillardetz has observed, "Vatican II didn't just say we're a church of pilgrims; it said we're a pilgrim church. The Church itself is on the way. It hasn't arrived....Once you've admitted this, once you've begun to imagine a church that makes mistakes, you have the beginning of a humble church."[16] Gaillardetz suggests three characteristics of humility to be of particular value to building a humble Church:

1. humility and magnanimity as a kind of twofold virtue oriented toward honest self-assessment;
2. humility as an intrinsically relational and other-centered virtue, eager to celebrate the greatness of God and the gifts of others;
3. humility as a fundamental ground for the proper exercise of power.[17]

Subsequent chapters will refer to these three characteristics in dealing with specific ecclesial contexts.

Humility means to be grounded. The origins of the word itself lie in the Latin *humus* (earth). Humble people see themselves as they are, not as something better or, conversely, something worse than they are. To be humble means to see oneself as a creature of a loving Creator and as radically equal to all other creatures. It also means not seeing oneself as anything *less* than a beloved creature of the loving Creator. Humility is balanced, honest, and realistic.

Humility, like *diakonia*, is other-directed. *Humility* is the point of view—the *habitus mentis*—of our relationship with God and with others; *diakonia* is the way we live out those relationships. The "humble servant" connects people, serving the *communio* that is the Church. But the Church is more than a community of like-minded disciples who act humbly. The Church itself, in its very nature, is a humble and diaconal Church. The earliest Christians understood this identity clearly. We have already alluded to St. Augustine's "humility, humility, humility." He was not alone. St. Benedict of Nursia, the father of Western monasticism, made humility the cornerstone of his community's spirituality, devoting an entire chapter to that single virtue in his *Rule*. We will consider the *Rule* and Benedict's twelve steps of humility in a subsequent chapter. But the reason humility is essential goes beyond personal spirituality.

Humility is foundational, not because of who or what we are, but because of who God is. Facing the challenges of a new millennium, John Paul II put it this way:

> The very heart of theological inquiry will thus be the contemplation of the mystery of the Triune God....From this vantage point, the prime commitment of theology is seen to be the understanding of God's *kenosis*, a grand and mysterious truth for the human mind, which finds it inconceivable that suffering and death can express a love which gives itself and seeks nothing in return.[18]

In short, we are humble because God is humble: pouring forth in creation, self-emptying to save, and strengthening, sanctifying, and providing for all of creation out of love and for the good of creation. God has proclaimed, "See, I am making all things new" (Rev 21:5). Through sacramental initiation, we are immersed into a participation in that divine humility, to cooperate with God by pouring ourselves out for the good of others. As deacons pray when adding water to the wine at the Eucharist, "Through the mystery of this water and wine, may we come to share in the divinity of Christ, who humbled himself to share in our humanity."

Finally, let me offer a word on what I mean by "courageous humility." One of the most common phrases found in Hebrew Scripture is "Be strong and courageous!" (חזק ואמץ—*chazak v'emats*). Used more than forty times in Hebrew Scripture, this phrase remains a common expression within the Jewish Tradition today. One of the more dramatic passages is found in the first chapter of the Book of Joshua. Moses is dead. God has come to Joshua and extended the covenant made with Moses to him: "As I was with Moses, so I will be with you; I will not fail you or forsake you" (v. 5). God pounds home the message: "Be strong and courageous"; "be strong and very courageous"; "I hereby command you: Be strong and courageous; do not be frightened or dismayed, for the Lord your God is with you wherever you go" (vv. 6–9).

Strength and courage. In Hebrew, *chazak* and *emats* go together. *Chazak* is the strength that comes from being bound to someone else, and in this case, being bound to God. Because of this relationship, it is God's strength, not Joshua's; it is God's strength, not ours. This acknowledgment of the primacy of God's power is the foundation of humility. *Emats*, on the other hand, is the courage to *act* with that strength; it is a willingness to take action. Consider a person with significant physical, spiritual, or emotional strength. What if that person never uses those strengths? Hebrew thought reminds us that having strength is not enough; our covenant with God demands that we act according to the strength God has given us. In Joshua's case, he was to "be strong and courageous" in leading the people into the promised land. He, too, was facing an unpredictable future, and God reminds Joshua that, in humility, he is to be strong in God and to use this strength to serve and to lead.

God exhorts us with the same message: "Be strong and courageous!" In November 2020, Pope Francis preached on the parable of the talents. "In the Gospel, good servants are those who take risks. They are not fearful and overcautious; they do not cling to what they possess but put it to good use. It is significant that fully four times those servants who invested their talents, who took a risk, are called 'faithful.'" He concludes, "If you do not take risks, you will end up like the third servant: burying your abilities, your spiritual and material riches, everything."[19]

Courageous humility, then, is a humility that takes risks, investing the talents and strengths God has given us for the good of others. The following reflections revolve around that call. "Be strong and courageous!" Chapter 1 grounds the project in the Trinity, the core dogma of the Church. From the earliest days of the Church, humility has been seen as the heart of Christian communal life, so chapter 2 examines the classic insights on humility from St. Benedict and his groundbreaking *Rule*.

Humility should be the foundation of all the various external structures we create to support our mission of evangelization. Chapter 3 offers some suggestions on ecclesial structural reform. Building on these foundational chapters, the succeeding chapters focus on the diaconate within this context of ecclesial humility. Chapter 4 discusses the sacramentality of the diaconate. Chapter 5 suggests revisions to the Code of Canon Law vis-à-vis the diaconate, and chapter 6 recommends developments in the liturgy of diaconal ordination. Chapter 7 responds to some of the recurring issues of the diaconate, and chapter 8 discusses how the Church may tap the full potential of the renewed diaconate.

On his recent apostolic visit to Slovakia, Pope Francis remarked that "the church is not a fortress, a stronghold, a lofty castle, self-sufficient and looking out upon the world below." Rather, he continued,

> How great is the beauty of a humble church, a church that does not stand aloof from the world, viewing life with a detached gaze, but lives her life within the world....Living within the world means being willing to share and to understand people's problems, hopes and expectations.
>
> This will help us to escape from our self-absorption, for the center of the church is not the church! We have to leave behind undue concern for ourselves, for our structures, for what society thinks about us.[20]

I feel I should end this preface with a personal note. Any time we ponder the unknowns of the future, we risk claims of presumption. None of us can know the future and the challenges it holds. So to suggest certain courses of action that might help face that future is at a minimum curious and at most perhaps even foolhardy. Beginning with chapter 5, we will consider a wide variety of issues related to the future of the diaconate: canon law, the rite of ordination, and other recurring questions. In my reflections on these issues, I offer certain proposals and suggestions. I want to make it clear as crystal that these are made as a faithful deacon seeking to serve the Church. There is no sense of rebellion here, but questions of "what if?" It is a book of personal reflections, and I find myself recalling the famous words of Robert Kennedy: "Some men see things as they are, and say why. I dream of things that never were, and say why not?" Or, as St. Peter reminded his listeners on that first Pentecost, quoting from the prophet Joel,

COURAGEOUS HUMILITY

In the last days it will be, God declares,
that I will pour out my Spirit upon all flesh,
    and your sons and your daughters shall prophesy,
and your young men shall see visions,
    and your old men shall dream dreams. (Acts 2:17)

I am not too old to see visions, and not too young to dream dreams.

ABBREVIATIONS

AG	*Ad Gentes*
AS	*Acta Synodalia Sacrosancti Concilii Oecumenici Vaticani II*
CCC	*Catechism of the Catholic Church*
CCEO	*Code of Canons of the Eastern Churches*
CCL	*Code of Canon Law*
EG	*Evangelii Gaudium*
EN	*Evangelii Nuntiandi*
ES	*Ecclesiam Suam*
FT	*Fratelli Tutti*
GIRP	General Instruction of the Roman Pontifical
GS	*Gaudium et Spes*
LG	*Lumen Gentium*
OS	*Ordinatio Sacerdotalis*
RB 1980	*The Rule of St. Benedict* (Liturgical Press 1980)
SDO	*Sacrum Diaconatus Ordinem*
SO	*Sacramentum Ordinis*

CHAPTER ONE

A HUMBLE CHURCH AS ICON OF THE HUMBLE TRINITY[1]

To love another person and to be loved in return is an act of humility. The most common example of this reciprocal loving is a marriage. Applying that same standard, we can find that humility at work in the Church. The humble loving of Father, Son, and Holy Spirit within the one triune God overflows in the loving kenosis of God, who comes to love, to serve, and not be served. In response to this divine love, we respond in kind to God and our neighbor. To be loved by God and to love that God Who-Is-Love in return is an act of humility. In this chapter, we will reflect on the humble nature of the triune God through the lens of the Creed. I hope to sketch an outline of how the Church's creedal profession of love and faith in God reflects an understanding of both God and Church as essentially grounded in humility: God's humility in loving us and the Church's humility in loving God and neighbor.

"Who Is God?"

Attending Catholic grade school in the 1950s, we studied religion from the venerable *Baltimore Catechism*. Promulgated by the United States' bishops at the Third Plenary Council, held in 1885 in Baltimore, the *Catechism* was the standard religion textbook through the mid-1960s. The *Catechism* covered a wide range of topics in a series of hundreds of short questions and answers. Our homework assignments generally were to memorize a handful of those questions and answers for the next day. Sister would walk up and down the rows of students with her clipboard and call on us one at a time and check off our names as we answered each question. The very first question was "Who made the world?" with the answer, "God made the world." That led to the second question: "Who is God?" Answer: "God is the Creator of heaven and earth, and of all things." No matter how many decades have passed, any Catholic school kid of that era can still answer the question, "Why did God make you?" "God made me to know Him, to love Him, and to serve Him in this world, and to be happy with Him forever in the next."

The simple and easy phrasing of these questions belies the profound human struggle to express who God is and our relationship with God. Humanity has asked similar questions for thousands of years in every culture. Judeo-Christian Scriptures record a gradual unfolding of God's self-revelation along with the nature and course of that relationship over many centuries—slowly, not always methodically, but always mysteriously. We understand this quite readily because it is analogous to the way we learn about each other. Couples married for decades will often say the same thing: that they are still getting to know each other, even after all the years of living and loving together. Every day is a new revelation about the beloved *other*. We are mysteries gradually being revealed to each other. Given this human experience, it is no wonder that God is mystery to us. The accumulated experience of humanity with God has been expressed in countless ways by philosophers, artists, religious, and spiritual leaders.

Who is God? No one has captured the reality better than the author of the First Letter of John: "God is love, and those who abide in love abide in God, and God abides in them" (1 John 4:16). God's love is eternal, universal, and absolute. Love is always focused on the other, and Christians soon described the Father's love for the Son and the Son's love for the Father. That love—so eternal, universal, and absolute—is the Spirit. Theologians for centuries have written extensively on the nature of God and the relationships among Father, Son, and Spirit. In this chapter, we will focus on the implications of God's interior life on those who, abiding in love, "abide in God." Abiding in the Love who is God affects everything: who we are, whom we are becoming, and how we live our own lives in love.

Immersion into the sacred waters of baptism plunges a person into the living heart of the Trinity, and it is there that we find the very identity of the Church. St. John Paul II wrote, "The Church is mystery because the very life and love of the Father, Son, and Holy Spirit are the gift gratuitously offered to all those who are born of water and the Spirit and called to relive the very communion of God and to manifest it and communicate it in history" (*Pastores Dabo Vobis* 12).[2] He then wrote a statement that has been used by the Holy See ever since in a variety of ecclesial documents on the laity, priests, and deacons: "It is within the Church's mystery, as a mystery of Trinitarian communion in missionary tension, that every Christian identity is revealed" (no. 12). The twofold mention of communion and mission is critical. God's love is not a "closed loop" between Father, Son, and Spirit. The eternal, universal, and absolute Love between the Divine Persons overflows through creation and providence for that creation. In that way, we come to the mystery of incarnation and the kenosis of God.

One theologian has written that God's kenosis is "an attribute of God's love disclosed in the compassionate existence of Jesus."[3] This self-emptying of God is not about Christ surrendering or forsaking his divine nature but expressing the divine nature most fully. Kenosis is at the heart of "who God is." Reflecting beautifully on the temptations of Christ, Johann Baptist Metz wrote,

> Satan wants to make Jesus strong, for what the devil really fears is the powerlessness of God in the humanity that Jesus has assumed. Satan fears the Trojan horse of an open human heart that will remain true to its native poverty, suffer the misery and abandonment that is humanity's, and thus save humankind. Satan's temptation is an assault on God's self-renunciation, an enticement to strength, security, and spiritual abundance; for these things will obstruct God's saving approach to humanity in the dark robes of frailty and weakness.[4]

Hans Urs von Balthasar was even more explicit, writing that "it is precisely in the *kenosis* of Christ (and nowhere else) that the inner majesty of God's love appears, of God 'who is love' (1 John 4:8) and a 'trinity.'"[5] Von Balthasar focuses on the Trinity within the celebration of the paschal mystery, especially as celebrated by the Church during the Triduum. The paschal mystery is both redemptive and revelatory: God's nature is being revealed through it.[6] Here we find "not only a sublime *metaphor* of eternal love but Eternal Love itself."[7] John Paul II, who esteemed von Balthasar greatly, wrote that "God's *kenosis* [is] a grand and mysterious truth for the human mind, which finds it inconceivable that suffering and death can express a love which gives itself and seeks nothing in return."[8] God is love, and love, at its core, is kenotic. The one who loves always focuses on the other, the beloved; the lover pours himself or herself out for the beloved, without reservation or limit. True, total self-giving love, known so well through our own human experience of lifelong, committed, covenant love, reflects the very nature of God. Lucien Richard is correct: God's kenosis demands a reevaluation of how we think about God, and von Balthasar completes the thought. Our God is most powerful, most creative, most redemptive, and most life giving precisely because God is continuously self-emptying. In creating the Other, saving the Other, illuminating and vivifying the Other. Kenosis is not merely something that God—Father, Son, and Spirit—does; it is who God is. God is "absolute letting-be, self-giving, self-spending. *Kenosis* is the way God relates to the world."[9]

God creates all of humanity in God's image and likeness. Through sacramental initiation, we are immersed into this divine mystery of the humble and kenotic God. We are to breathe with the very breath of God, living as God does: bringing life to others, reconciling, healing, and following the teaching of St. Paul, who wrote, "In humility regard others as better than yourselves. Let each of you look not to your own interests, but to the interests of others. Let the same mind be in you that was in Christ Jesus" (Phil 2:3–5). Christ, the Second Person of the Trinity, shows us the way we are to live and to love, not only in imitation of him but in imitation of Father and Spirit as well. In Christ, we discover divine love is not some abstract, otherworldly, pie-in-the-sky, greeting card kind of love. To say "God is Love" does not equate to "love is God." Consider a few examples.

After the Last Supper, Jesus washed the feet of his disciples. He told them that this was a model (*hypodeigma*) to follow, a model of sacrificial death, a model that they must follow if they are to have fellowship with him. Jesus models a Messiah who is the opposite of the mighty warrior-king many of the Jews were expecting. Jesus came "not to be served but to serve, and to give his life a ransom for many" (Mark 10:45). Jesus heals, and he feels power going out from him (Luke 8:46). Peter correctly identifies Jesus as the Messiah and is given the keys to the kingdom. But then, "Jesus began to show his disciples that he must go to Jerusalem and undergo great suffering at the hands of the elders and chief priests and scribes, and be killed, and on the third day be raised." Peter objects and Jesus turns on him, calling him a *satan*, a stumbling block. "You are setting your mind not on divine things but on human things" (Matt 16:21–23). Time after time, Jesus teaches and exemplifies a radically different type of Messiah, a new way of understanding God and God's Anointed, God's humble servanthood. St. Augustine, preaching on St. Paul, outlines this reality well: "Who is the Lord? Christ crucified. Where there is humility, there is majesty; where there is weakness, power; where there is death, life. If you seek those things, do not spurn these."[10]

Who is God? John's answer remains the best, and it is an answer anyone who has ever truly loved or been loved can understand. "God is love, and those who abide in love abide in God, and God abides in them" (1 John 4:16).

The Creed of a Humble Church: Profession of Love

"I give you my heart." Words from the heart, never spoken lightly. Think of the times a person might use that expression; not very often. We can give time; we can give a suggestion; we can give an idea. But to give our heart? That is a profound notion. "I give you my heart" is reserved for the deepest gift of love we are capable of giving to another person. It is the kind of love that we want to scream from the rooftops so everyone can share in the joy of our love. In this context, consider this remarkable fact: we literally "give our hearts" every time we celebrate Sunday Eucharist. It happens when we proclaim the Creed, the *Credo*. The roots of humility run deep into the very core of our being, and we don't simply "recite" the Creed or even "pray" the Creed. We profess before all, and in all humility, the Divine Mystery who loves us, and to whom we now profess our love. It is upon this foundation of humble love that the Church is built.

Although we usually translate *credo* as "I believe," the term's Latin roots are much richer. *Credo* derives from *cor* (heart) and *do* (I give): literally, "I give my heart." We are proclaiming before all our unconditional love for God: "I give my heart to God, the Father Almighty," "I give my heart to Jesus Christ His only Son, Our Lord," "I give my heart to the Holy Spirit, the Lord and Giver of life." We do not casually make such a profession even in human terms. When we make this profession to another person, our lives are changed forever, and we attempt to live out in concrete terms the demands of that relationship. The same applies to our relationship with God. The bishops of the Second Vatican Council explain it this way:

> The fundamental basis of human dignity lies in a person's call to communion with God. From the very circumstance of human origin, a person is already invited to converse with God. For we would not exist were we not created by God's love and constantly preserved by it, and a person cannot live fully according to truth unless he freely acknowledges that love and devotes himself to His Creator. (*GS* 19)

My wife and I have been married for more than fifty years. We professed our love publicly and gave our hearts to each other more than five decades ago. That was just the beginning. The children came, and so did the constant moving and occasional family separations of a Navy career, living in foreign lands and cultures, the constant worry over the children and having enough money to provide for them, and all the other challenges of life. The profession of our love was translated into the language of everyday life. This is something everyone who has enjoyed a long loving relationship recognizes: ultimately, their love has been a mystery. We could not know on our wedding day fifty years ago all the challenges, tragedies, joys, excitement, and adventures that followed over the years. When you ask jubilarians to talk about their spouses or their secrets for a long-married life, you will not get an academic lecture, technical language, or jargon. You will hear—through tone of voice, gestures, and simple, direct, heartfelt words, even good-natured banter and teasing—the love that has sustained them throughout their lives together. They have lived their love so long and so profoundly that the expressions flow from the heart as well as the head.

Art and theology have always been partners in expressing the truth. I can think of few contemporary examples more illustrative of this point than the musical *Fiddler on the Roof.* The theology of *Fiddler* is wonderfully expressed in any language, and it has been translated and performed in dozens of languages around the world. The milkman Tevye and his intimate relationship with God capture so much at the heart of the Judeo-Christian Tradition. One of the songs, in particular, expresses artistically the relationship we are describing. Tevye approaches Golde, his wife of twenty-five years and the mother of their daughters, with the question, "Do you love me?" Her responses capture the truth and the consequences of giving our heart in love. First, she can't believe Tevye has to ask in the first place: "Do I what?" When Tevye persists, Golde responds by listing twenty-five years of concrete acts of love: washing clothes, cooking meals, cleaning the house, giving birth to their children, and even milking the cow. She has "lived with him, fought with him, starved with him," and shared her bed with him.

It seems ludicrous to Golde that Tevye needs her to confess her love for him. Over twenty-five years, she has lived that love in concrete ways every second of the day: "If that's not love, what is?" We find the same kind of dialogue in the Gospel of John when Jesus repeatedly asks Peter, "Peter, do you love me?" (John 21:15–17). Many have written about the various meanings of this passage, and I will not review them here. My point is simple: Christ repeatedly asks a question that Peter felt did not need to be asked, any more than Golde understood why Tevye was asking the same thing. However, in both cases, the answer, "I love you," is carried out by action: "Feed my lambs. Feed my sheep." No one, on any level, can say that they love another without acting in service of that love.

A Trinitarian Church: People of God, Mystical Body of Christ, Temple of the Holy Spirit

To reiterate how we began this chapter: to love another person and to be loved in return is an act of humility. The lover's focus on the beloved puts others' needs and expectations ahead of one's own. Once we have given our heart to God as Father, Son, and Holy Spirit—one God—we must act on that fact. The study of theology has traditionally been separated into the broad categories of dogmatic theology ("God's call") and moral theology ("our response"). In reflecting on the humility of lovers, one cannot escape the realization that it is not only the human person who is humble in the face of God's love, but that God-as-Love is also humble. Understanding humility as essentially relational and other directed allows us to see our creative and kenotic God as Humility itself. God is the perfect model of humility.

Our "Three-Personal God" (to borrow from C. S. Lewis) is Love and therefore always other focused: Father loving Son and Spirit, Son loving Spirit and Father, Spirit loving Father and Son. This absolute love overflows into all God has created, and all three Persons are involved in the act of creation. The triune God is Creator, the sole Creator, beginning all that exists. The Word is, of course, present at Creation, and "all things came into being through him, and without him not one thing came into being" (John 1:1–3). In Christ, "all things in heaven and on earth were created, things visible and invisible, whether thrones or dominions or rulers or powers—all things have been created through him and for him" (Col 1:16–17). The Creed affirms the Holy Spirit as "Lord and Giver of life," while the hymn *Veni, Creator Spiritus* sings of the "creator Spirit." Each of the Persons burst forth out of love into creation, withholding nothing and seeking nothing from the beloved creation except *communio*: "The Church is in Christ like a sacrament or as a sign and instrument both of a very closely-knit union with God and the unity of the whole human race" (*LG* 1). The first two chapters ("The Mystery of the Church" and "On the People of God") of *Lumen Gentium* were initially crafted as a single chapter. It is essential to keep this in mind because it would be a mistake to see "the mystery" as distinct from "the people of God." The chapters, in that sense, are complementary, "two ends of the same thought."[11]

The climax of chapter 2 concludes with chapter 17, describing the Church's mission of evangelization. "As the Son was sent by the Father, so He too sent the Apostles, saying: 'Go, therefore, make disciples of all nations, baptizing them in the name of the Father and of the Son and of the Holy Spirit, teaching them to observe all things whatsoever I have commanded you....In this way the Church both prays and labors in order that the entire world may become the People of God, the Body of the Lord and the Temple of the Holy Spirit" (*LG* 17).

The Humble People of God

Many have written on the topic of "the people of God." Our task here is not to review that considerable literature. Instead, we want to examine some distinguishing aspects of the notion of the people of God, especially in light of the humility of the Church. First, "You did not choose me but I chose you" (John 15:16). The assembling of the people is God's call. No one really "joins the Church" on their own initiative: they are called into the *communio* by God. It is, in a very literal sense, a vocation. In humility, we realize our total dependence upon God. In particular, it is not merely as individuals that we are humble; it is the whole *communio* that is humble, "a chosen race, a royal priesthood, a holy nation" (1 Pet 2:9).

Second, once called by God, we enter the *communio* through sacramental initiation and rebirth in water and the Spirit. We come to the font freely, where we are—quite literally—plunged (*baptizein*) into a new life in the Trinity. We insist upon the trinitarian formula for sacramental validity. Baptism is not about one or another Person of the Trinity but all three Persons of the one God. Baptism is immersion into the community of Divine Persons. Third, the Trinity exists and acts *ad intra* and *ad extra*, and so must the Church. *Ad intra*, God-is-Love Eternal between Father, Son, and Spirit. The Persons are one in love, distinct in Person. The classic description of the Trinity's interior life shows that "God is Father, Son, Spirit, but that Father is not Son, Father is not Spirit; Son is not Father, Son is not Spirit; Spirit is not Father, Spirit is not Son." *Ad extra*, God's kenosis into human nature pours out divine love into creation, especially humanity. God seeks to be one with God's creation: God-Love is always creative, kenotic, and theotic. We experience this at Mass in a short ritual whose theological significance is often overlooked. During the preparation of the gifts, the deacon adds "a little water" to the wine in the chalice. He prays "in a low voice" a prayer that was originally part of the Roman Christmas liturgy, "By the mystery of this water and wine may we come to share in the Divinity of Christ who humbled Himself to share in our humanity." Just as the water is inseparable from the wine, so too we pray to be inseparable from our Lord God, offering ourselves with Christ to the Father through the power of the Holy Spirit.

The Body of Christ

The Christ, the Anointed One, is the Head of the people of God. Throughout his public ministry, Jesus stressed the intimate and life-giving bond between the disciples and himself. For example, "Abide in me as I abide in you. Just as the branch cannot bear fruit by itself unless it abides in the vine, neither can you unless you abide in me. I am the vine; you are the branches. Those who abide in me and I in them bear much fruit because apart from me you can do nothing" (John 15:4–5). The Anointed One, the Vine, through the paschal mystery, pours out his anointing on the people. As an anointed people, all participate in Christ's threefold *munus* of Priest, Prophet, and King. St. John Newman wrote,

> When our Lord went up on high, He left His representative behind Him. This was Holy Church, His mystical Body and Bride, a Divine Institution, and the shrine and organ of the Paraclete, who speaks through her till the end comes. She, to use an Anglican poet's words, is "His very self below," as far as men on earth are equal to the discharge and fulfillment of high offices, which primarily and supremely are His.
>
> These offices, which specially belong to Him as Mediator, are commonly considered to be three; He is Prophet, Priest, and King; and after His pattern, and in human measure, Holy Church has a triple office too... three offices, which are indivisible, though diverse.[12]

Overall, as part of the Body of Christ, and in each of the threefold *munera* of Christ, we imitate the kenotic Christ. We are a priestly people (see 1 Pet 2:9), and the principle distinguishing task of any priest is to offer sacrifice. We offer ourselves completely—"joys, hopes, griefs, and anxieties" (*GS* 1)—to God, especially during the Eucharist. Likewise, there is an obligation to serve "as a leaven and as a kind of soul for human society as it is to be renewed in Christ and transformed into God's family" (*GS* 40). As prophets, we are all called to evangelize, to spread the good news to the people around us. The Council is very specific:

> Incorporated in the Church through baptism, the faithful...must confess before all the faith which they have received from God through the Church. They are more perfectly bound to the Church by the sacrament of Confirmation, and the Holy Spirit endows them with special strength so that they are more strictly obliged to spread and defend the faith, both by word and by deed, as true witnesses of Christ. (*LG* 11)

Participating in Christ's ruling, or kingly, office, all the baptized are called to leadership according to their state of life. Lay Christians, for example, should exercise their rightful leadership within the community. The ruling office, however, is exercised in imitation of the kenotic leadership of Christ. St. Ambrose of Milan expressed it well: "That man is rightly called a king who makes his own body an obedient subject and, by governing himself with suitable rigor, refuses to let his passions breed rebellion in his soul, for he exercises a kind of royal power over himself."[13]

The Temple of the Holy Spirit, Soul of the Church

The Holy Spirit, we proclaim, is "the Lord, the giver of life," the Advocate and Revealer of all truth. The Holy Spirit is "adored and glorified, and spoke through the prophets." Jesus introduced the Spirit to the disciples as their Advocate, who would remain with them forever. John describes the Spirit further: "This is the Spirit of truth, whom the world cannot receive because it neither sees him nor knows him. You know him, because he abides with you, and he will be in you. But the Advocate, the Holy Spirit, whom the Father will send in my name, will teach you everything and remind you of all that I have said to you" (John 14:17, 26). A few centuries later, St. Augustine preached that "what the soul is to the human body, the Holy Spirit is to the Body of Christ, which is the Church."[14] His insight that the Holy Spirit is the very soul of the Church has remained a touchstone of Catholic teaching on the Spirit.

In 1897, for example, Pope Leo XIII promulgated the encyclical *Divinum Illud Munus*, on the Holy Spirit. In a section on the Holy Spirit and the Church, he wrote,

> On [Pentecost], the Holy Spirit began to manifest His gifts in the mystic body of Christ, by that miraculous outpouring already foreseen by the prophet Joel (2:28–29), for the Paraclete "sat upon the apostles as though new spiritual crowns were placed upon their heads in tongues of fire."[15] Then the apostles "descended from the mountain," as St. John Chrysostom writes, "not bearing in their hands tables of stone like Moses, but carrying the Spirit in their

> mind, and pouring forth the treasure and the fountain of doctrines and graces." (no. 5)

And then, after discussing the role of the Holy Spirit in the ordination of bishops, Pope Leo concludes by quoting Augustine: "What the soul is in our body, that is the Holy Spirit in Christ's body, the Church" (no. 6).

In 1943, Pope Pius XII also wrote about the Holy Spirit in his encyclical *Mystici Corporis*. "To this Spirit of Christ, also, as to an invisible principle is to be ascribed the fact that all the parts of the Body are joined one with the other and with their exalted Head; for He is entire in the Head, entire in the Body, and entire in each of the members…by His grace He provides for the continual growth of the Church." He then includes Leo XIII's quote from Augustine: "Let it suffice to say that, as Christ is the Head of the Church, so is the Holy Spirit her soul" (no. 57).

Pope Francis echoes his predecessors (and Augustine): "The Holy Spirit is the soul of the Church. He gives life, he brings forth different charisms which enrich the people of God, and, above all, he creates unity among believers: from the many, he makes one body, the Body of Christ. The Church's whole life and mission depend on the Holy Spirit; he fulfills all things."[16]

But really? Is that the way many Christians think of the Holy Spirit? The Holy Spirit, especially in the Latin West, is particularly mysterious to many people. Franciscan theologian Dan Horan describes a problem he calls "Holy Spirit atheism."

> By this, I do not mean that most Christians outright reject the divinity of the Spirit. Rather, I have a sense that many Christians think and act as if the Holy Spirit did not exist and therefore, this phenomenon is largely implicit.
>
> For example, it is easy for most people to pray to "God the Creator" or "God the Father," and it is likewise inescapable to reflect on and pray to the incarnate word in Jesus Christ, but where does the Holy Spirit factor into our prayer lives? Each Sunday we proclaim the spirit is "the

> Lord, the giver of life" whom we "adore and glorify," but do we *really* believe in the Holy Spirit?[17]

I think Father Horan's observation resonates with many of our own experiences, including that of Pope Francis. The pope said, in the same homily,

> The temptation is always within us to resist the Holy Spirit because he takes us out of our comfort zone and unsettles us; he makes us get up and drives the Church forward. It is always easier and more comfortable to settle in our sedentary and unchanging ways. In truth, the Church shows her fidelity to the Holy Spirit in as much as she does not try to control or tame him....He is freshness, imagination, and newness....
>
> The Church, flowing from Pentecost, is given the fire of the Holy Spirit, which does not so much fill the mind with ideas, but enflames the heart; she is moved by the breath of the Spirit which does not transmit a power, but rather an ability to serve in love, a language which everyone is able to understand. In our journey of faith and fraternal living, the more we allow ourselves to be humbly guided by the Spirit of the Lord, the more we will overcome misunderstandings, divisions, and disagreements and be a credible sign of unity and peace, a credible sign that our Lord is risen and he is alive.[18]

The Church must recover this appreciation of the Holy Spirit as our very soul. Moving into the future, we must recognize the "freshness, imagination, and newness" offered by the Spirit. On the one hand, institutional structures and leadership tend to conserve and protect themselves by claiming a sense of stability, a professed desire not to disrupt communion, and, sometimes, through just plain inertia. Respecting Sacred Tradition (along with Sacred Scripture) as an invaluable source of revelation does not mean that the Church's structures, processes, and ecclesiastical laws cannot—and should not—change. Breathing with the very breath of God, the Holy Spirit, we cannot and must not succumb to the temptation to resist the workings of the Spirit. Only in this way can we indeed be the temple of the Holy Spirit.

Marks of Humility: One, Holy, Catholic, Apostolic

The Nicene Creed identifies the Church as having four marks or characteristics: one, holy, catholic, and apostolic. "These four characteristics, inseparably linked with each other, indicate essential features of the Church and her mission. The Church does not possess them of herself; it is Christ who, through the Holy Spirit, makes his Church one, holy, catholic, and apostolic, and it is he who calls her to realize each of these qualities" (*CCC* 811). As we reflect briefly on each of these marks, or notes, of the Church, we want to keep in mind *Lumen Gentium*'s description that the Church "is in Christ like a sacrament or as a sign and instrument both of a very closely-knit union with God and of the unity of the whole human race" (*LG* 1).

In the fifth century, St. Augustine described a sacrament as "an outward and visible sign of an inward and invisible grace." As the Church continued to reflect on the nature of sacrament, several elements remained constant: that a sacrament consisted of an outward sign, was connected to the person and ministry of Christ, and was effective. For example, the definition many of us learned as children was that "a sacrament is an outward sign, instituted by Christ, to give grace." The *Catechism of the Catholic Church* 1131 states, "The sacraments are efficacious signs of grace, instituted by Christ and entrusted to the Church, by which divine life is dispensed to us." *Lumen Gentium* captures these three elements by referring to the Church as a sacrament, being (1) in Christ, (2) a sign, and (3) an instrument.

The Church is one. This mark refers to a unity of faith while affirming diversity of practice. For example, some of this legitimate diversity is found in the beautiful and varied traditions of the Eastern as well as the Western Churches of the Catholic Church. We must not confuse unity with uniformity. It is difficult to refer to the Church as one in today's fractious world and fractured Church. Perhaps the Church has never been more divided, more polarized.

Whether talking about divisions between various Churches or the divisions within a Catholic parish, "unity" is an elusive thing. Frequently, efforts to promote unity have focused on ecumenism and interfaith ministries. However, internal divisions within the Church also threaten the Church's unity.

Claiming that the Church is one seems untenable. Looking at the human members of the Church, it would be impossible. However, Christ is the Head of the Church, and so our unity is anchored to the unity of the Trinity in which we have been immersed. God is one. The Church is to be an "outward sign" of that unity, to be "signs of the cross" ("In the name of the Father, and of the Son, and of the Holy Spirit") in the world. However, while perfect in the Trinity, this unity is still imperfect among the members of the Church. In that way, then, the Church is to be an "instrument" always working for perfect unity. Thomas Aquinas taught that "sacraments of the New Law are both cause and signs," referring to the expression that sacraments "effect what they signify."[19] We are both a sign of perfect divine unity and an instrument working to perfect human unity. As Christ prayed at the Last Supper, "I ask not only on behalf of these, but also on behalf of those who will believe in me through their word, that they may all be one. As you, Father, are in me and I am in you, may they also be in us, so that the world may believe that you have sent me" (John 17:20–21).

What specific actions might we take as a Church—both *ad extra* and *ad intra*—to perfect the unity to which we are called? How do we contribute to healing divisions in the parish and diocese as well as between Christian Churches? Working for interpersonal unity requires humility, an openness to the other that affirms our common bonds and stresses areas that unite us over those that divide us.

The Church is holy. To claim that we are holy is perhaps even more difficult to accept than our claim of unity. First, we are all aware of our failings and sinfulness. Second, reports of financial and other crimes in the Church, including at the Vatican, have escalated. Third, and most egregious, are the unspeakable crimes by Church ministers, ordained, religious, and lay, against our youth and vulnerable adults. Long before the *Boston Globe* broke the story of clergy sexual abuse on a massive scale in the Archdiocese of Boston in 2002, researchers documented crimes of sexual abuse worldwide. Recently, an independent study concluded that since 1950 as many as ten thousand children and other vulnerable people were abused in France alone. How do we have the audacity to call ourselves holy?

The Second Vatican Council acknowledges this reality. "Already the final age of the world has come upon us and the renovation of the world is irrevocably decreed and is already anticipated in some kind of a real way; for the Church already on this earth is signed with a sanctity which is real although imperfect" (*LG* 48). Once again, as with unity, we may claim some measure of holiness because our God is holy, and God is always with us. In Christ, we may serve as a sign of the holiness we aspire to while continually working to perfect our state of holiness, as individuals and as Church. It is only "by the grace of God we acquire holiness" (*LG* 48).

In humility, we acknowledge our sinfulness and responsibility for reconciliation. As the people of God, we must do the same. Reconciliation demands justice as well as charity, and our ecclesial examination of conscience must be honest and thorough. We must eliminate all sources of institutional sinfulness related to clericalism, racism, xenophobia, and abuse of power and authority. As necessary, institutions must be evaluated and changed or even eliminated if they no longer proclaim the gospel effectively. Just as we expect humility in ourselves as individuals, we should expect no less in ourselves as members of the people of God, mystical body of Christ, and the temple of the Holy Spirit. Humility involves seeing ourselves with honesty.

The Church is catholic. The Church is universal (the fundamental meaning of *catholic*) because Christ, the Messiah, is the Head of the Church, the source of all communion. As St. Ignatius of Antioch wrote, "Where there is Christ Jesus, there is the Catholic Church."[20] This universality—this catholicity—is found in obedience to Christ's command: "Go therefore and make disciples of all nations, baptizing them in the name of the Father and of the Son and of the Holy Spirit, and teaching them to obey everything that I have commanded you. And remember, I am with you always, to the end of the age" (Matt 28:19–20; cf. Mark 16:15; Acts 1:8).

God's call to communion is universal because God's love is universal. God excludes no one from God's love. In John Paul II's words, the Church's identity is a mystery within the "mystery of Trinitarian communion in missionary tension." Just as the communion of Divine Persons is complete and inclusive, so is God's call to all people. One theologian captured this relationship well when she wrote,

> Our baptism into the paschal mystery of Jesus immerses us into a God who is not the poverty of aloneness, God as an isolated individual, but God as the richness of trinitarian communion. Nowhere else is there such absolute oneness and yet such utterly unique personhood. Nowhere else does the mystery of human persons called to both autonomy and communion find its source and goal than in the infinite uniqueness and communion of the persons who are God. And precisely in not running away from the price of our own personhood, we begin to discover that the proclamations central to the Christian message are not simply doctrines to be believed, but reality that can be experienced, reality that can transform experience.[21]

Once again, we act not merely in obedience to God's command but because of who God is and who we are in Christ. "Trinitarian communion in missionary tension": we do not hoard the good news or only share it with a select few. The mission is universal. The questions for the future are varied. How "catholic" are we? What can we do to reach more people and introduce them to Christ? Are there people now being excluded in any way from our outreach? In our highly polarized society, some Catholics judge other people, including other Catholics, as "too sinful" to be "faithful Catholics." Their attitude is frequently, "These public sinners are unwelcome to fellowship with us until they accept our teachings fully. Until then, they are Catholic in name only." Some even go so far as to say they are no longer Christian or Catholic at all! This propensity to pass judgment on the state of another's sinfulness (or virtuousness) is itself against Church teaching; only God knows the depths of a person's soul. In humility, we must each acknowledge that we all are sinners and fall short of the ideal of perfect virtue.

The good news of God's love is total, unconditional, and available to all. Indeed, all of us struggle to reform our lives accordingly, and this is not limited to some people and not others. Our mission is to proclaim the good news to all. Pope Francis is fond of speaking of accompanying people on their faith journey, even those with whom we disagree. Accompaniment demands humility, not judgment.

The Church is apostolic. The Church's mission to make disciples by proclaiming the good news to all, baptizing them into the Trinity, bridges the marks of being catholic and apostolic. The Greek *apostolos* means "one who is sent": a messenger, an ambassador, an envoy. There is a dynamism to the term that suits the mission. The Church is apostolic in that it is continuously sent forth as God's messenger, commissioned by Christ himself. Scripture distinguishes the unique missionary role of the apostles from the life of Christ's disciples. Apostles are disciples who have received a specific mission from the risen Christ.

The Church has always revered its apostolic foundation, beginning with the early Church's accounts in the Acts of the Apostles. The *Catechism* lists three ways the Church is apostolic: (1) It was founded and remains built on the apostles, the witnesses chosen and sent on a mission by Christ himself. (2) With the assistance of the Holy Spirit, the Church keeps and hands on that teaching. (3) It continues to be taught, sanctified, and guided by the apostles until Christ's return, through their successors in pastoral office: the college of bishops (*CCC* 857). Nevertheless, undergirding these three "ways" from the *Catechism*, I believe we need always to emphasize the dynamic role of apostolicity. Understood in this way, the Church is always "on the move," in every place, culture, and time, preserved in its mission by the Holy Spirit.

Thus, we return to John Paul II and his "Trinitarian communion in missionary tension." During an address to a eucharistic congress held in the Diocese of El Paso, Texas, Cardinal Roger Mahony, former Archbishop of Los Angeles, shared his conviction that "it is not so much that the church has a mission; it is rather more that the mission has a church."

> What is this mission? It is none other than that of Jesus, Christ, the Word, and of the Holy Spirit, the gift of God's love dwelling in our hearts. Jesus' mission is to announce the time of God's favor, the coming of the reign of God. Jesus proclaimed the reign of God as the fulfillment of God's

> hope, desire, and intention for the world now and to come. In God's reign, truth, holiness, justice, love, and peace will hold sway forever. Jesus established the Church to continue and further this mission....This mission is so central to the word and work of Jesus that the Second Vatican Council affirmed and emphasized that *mission* defines the Church. The Church in every dimension of its life and practice exists for mission: to proclaim in word and deed the reign of God to people in every culture, time, and place.[22]

Conclusion

We have tried in this chapter to review some fundamental aspects of our Church, suggesting how they may be seen and experienced through the lens of humility. The bottom line is that the Church is humble because our God is humble. The Second Vatican Council adopted a new approach to understanding the Church. *Lumen Gentium* describes the Church as a people on "their pilgrimage toward eternal happiness" (no. 21). As we saw in the preface, Richard Gaillardetz has observed, "Vatican II didn't just say we're a church of pilgrims; it said we're a pilgrim church. The Church itself is on the way. It hasn't arrived....Once you've admitted this, once you've begun to imagine a church that makes mistakes, you have the beginning of a humble church."[23]

Gaillardetz suggests three characteristics of humility to be of particular value to building a humble Church:

1. Humility and magnanimity as a kind of twofold virtue oriented toward *honest self-assessment*
2. Humility as *an intrinsically relational and other-centered virtue*, eager to celebrate the greatness of God and the gifts of others
3. Humility and the proper exercise of power[24]

I am indebted to Dr. Gaillardetz for his insights, and they will be most helpful in the succeeding chapters.

CHAPTER TWO

ECCLESIAL 12-STEP PROGRAM

Humility in the Rule of St. Benedict

Introduction: Benedict and His *Rule*

Benedict of Nursia was born in the year 480 and died in 547. Studying in Rome during the empire's decline, young Benedict soon rejected what he encountered there and relocated to Subiaco to live the simple, spiritual life of a hermit. Others began to approach him for spiritual advice and support. These associations soon led to the formation of religious communities inspired by his moderate and balanced spirituality. These communities would eventually cover Europe and, over the course of centuries, spread throughout the globe.[1] Foundational to this movement's success was an extraordinary document now referred to as the *Rule of St. Benedict* (*Regula Sancti Benedicti*). When I teach courses on the classics of Christian literature and spirituality, I have found that Benedict's *Rule* invariably captures most students' attention. Its brevity, moderation, and wisdom remain intriguing even after so many centuries, still providing a rich source of inspiration and spiritual depth for the people of our own time. Written around 529, the *Rule* consists of a prologue and seventy-three brief chapters covering both spiritual foundations (especially chapters 1—7) and monastic regulations (chapters 8—73).[2]

The *Rule* was not the first of its kind, but it quickly emerged as one of the most influential texts in the Christian Tradition. One commentator has written about Benedict,

> While he was aware of the forms of monastic life that had preceded him in both East and West and drew copiously upon their literature, *he saw that a new beginning had to be made to meet the needs of the times. His moderation, his emphasis upon a stable community life in opposition to individualism, and his encouragement of civilizing work ensured that the institute he founded would become a powerful force in fashioning a Christian Europe out of the ruins of the barbarian invasions.* He may even have been commissioned by the Pope to reform Western monasticism; in any case, his work was a contribution of extraordinary originality and foresight, that makes him tower above his predecessors and contemporaries. (*RB 1980* 70, emphasis added)

It is this insight that I believe reveals once again the contribution of the *Rule* for our purposes. The fact that Benedict was seeking a particular response to the needs of his own time suggests its applicability to our own. Benedict's balanced and moderate approach, grounded in humility, has inspired the Church for more than fifteen hundred years; it will continue to do so.

The virtue of humility permeates many of the chapters of the *Rule*, but he devotes an entire chapter to it, detailing twelve steps of humility. Humility is fundamental to his approach to communal life, and his insights take us outside monastic walls. In this chapter, we shall examine how the Church of the future may continue to appropriate and adapt Benedict's twelve steps to its own time. Speaking of humility in the *Rule*, Sr. Joan Chittister notes that "the Twelve Steps of Humility are the centerpiece of this book [the *Rule*], in fact. Not because they are old but because they model a way to the freedom of heart and soul which we seek."

Best of all, they are sure proof that such freedom is possible in a world where demagoguery is the new political brand, where narcissism is too often misunderstood to be leadership, where pathological individualism in the name of freedom and independence is confused with healthy personal development and spiritual maturity. This entire document is about growing into the consciousness of God. But the key to this quest lies, Benedict says, in "humility." These twelve steps are explicit and basic to any group, any relationship, any search for God in life.[3]

With that in mind, then, we turn to Benedict's twelve steps, looking at them not only as applicable to our personal spirituality but as foundations for a genuinely humble Church. We take as our inspiration *Gaudium et Spes* 40:

> Thus the Church, at once "a visible association and a spiritual community," goes forward together with humanity and experiences the same earthly lot which the world does. She serves as a leaven and as a kind of soul for human society as it is to be renewed in Christ and transformed into God's family. That the earthly and the heavenly city penetrate each other is a fact accessible to faith alone; it remains a mystery of human history, which sin will keep in great disarray until the splendor of God's children, is fully revealed.

Preface: Benedict's Ladder (*RB 1980* 191, 193)

St. Benedict begins by citing Luke's Gospel that "whoever exalts himself shall be humbled, and whoever humbles himself shall be exalted" (see Luke 14:11). He tells his brothers (and us) that "we must set up that ladder on which Jacob in a dream saw *angels descending and ascending* (Gen 28:12)" and that we will descend through pride and ascend through humility. (Although not a connection made in the *Rule*, it is interesting to note that the author of John's Gospel connects Genesis to Christ: "And he said to him, 'Very truly, I tell you, you will see heaven opened and the angels of God ascending and descending upon the Son of Man'" [John 1:51].[4]) Benedict explains, "The ladder erected is our life on earth, and if we humble our hearts, the Lord will raise it to heaven. We may call our body and soul the sides of this ladder, into which our divine vocation has fitted the various rung of humility and discipline we must climb."[5] We now turn our attention to the twelve rungs of the ladder.

Step 1: The Fear of God (*Timor Dei*)

> The first step of humility, then, is that a person keeps the *fear of God* always *before his eyes* (Ps 36:2) and never forgets it. (*RB 1980* 193)

We should pay particular attention to this step precisely because it is the first. As Psalm 111 has it, "The fear of the Lord is the beginning of wisdom; all those who practice it have a good understanding" (v. 10). The rest of the steps build on this one; it behooves us to get it right.

Indeed, the notion of "fearing God" is a challenging first rung on the ladder. I remember memorizing the "gifts of the Holy Spirit" in Catholic grade school in the 1950s, and no one bothered to explain it very well. "Fear of the Lord" conveyed precisely what we children thought it did: our God is an awesome, all-powerful God, sitting in judgment, ready to punish any transgression. Of course, as one's spiritual quest deepens, it becomes clear that our God does not want us to be afraid of him! On June 11, 2014, during his general audience, Pope Francis explained that this "fear" is the

> joyful awareness of God's grandeur and a grateful realization that only in him do our hearts find true peace. It does not mean being afraid of God: we know well that God is Father, that he loves us and wants our salvation, and he always forgives, always; thus, there is no reason to be scared of him! Fear of the Lord, instead, is the gift of the Holy Spirit through whom we are reminded of how small we are before God and of his love and that our good lies in humble, respectful, and trusting self-abandonment into his hands. This is fear of the Lord: abandonment in the goodness of our Father who loves us so much.

> This is why we need this gift of the Holy Spirit so much. Fear of the Lord allows us to be aware that everything comes from grace and that our true strength lies solely in following the Lord Jesus and in allowing the Father to bestow upon us his goodness and his mercy. To open the heart so that the goodness and mercy of God may come to us. This is what the Holy Spirit does through the gift of fear of the Lord: he opens hearts.[6]

Since the expression "fear of God" is found frequently in the Hebrew Scriptures, let's look more closely at the original Hebrew. There are two principal words for "fear." First is יִרְאָה (*yir'ah*), used forty-five times in the Old Testament. Its root is the adjective יָרֵא (*yare'*), used sixty-four times. Second is the Word פַּחַד (*pachad*). *Pachad* is the kind of fear that is "imagined" or "projected" into a situation. There's a sense of panic to this kind of fear. Some English words that capture its meaning include *irrational fear*, *dread*, *panic*, and *terror*. Imagine those times in life when we have been worried about an upcoming event and how that fear felt. In my own life, two examples come to mind. In the weeks leading up to my reporting for Navy boot camp, I grew increasingly full of *pachad*. I had no idea what to expect, there was no Google to find out more about it, and the chief petty officer who recruited me simply said, "Nothing to worry about, son. When you get there, a chief like me is going to take you by the hand and lead you to the promised land." This did not assuage my *pachad*. The second example is similar. I was on my first mission at sea, and we were about to cross the equator. Those of us who had never "crossed the line" before would be put through a day-long hazing to turn us into "trusty shellbacks" worthy to transit the realm of King Neptune. Once again, *pachad* filled me since I had no idea what to expect; it dissipated once the initiation was over.

Now we turn to *yir'ah*, the term associated with "fear of the Lord" and "fear of God." This word has a different sense. One rabbi has said that it is "the fear that overcomes us when we suddenly find ourselves in possession of considerably more energy than we are used to, inhabiting a larger space than we are used to inhabiting. It is also the feeling we feel when we are on sacred ground." This notion of feeling is important here, and *yir'ah* captures that sense of emotion, awe, and reverence. If you have ever been so overwhelmed by something that you could feel it physically as well as emotionally and spiritually, that was *yir'ah*. Rudolf Otto's famous description of the Holy as *mysterium tremendens et fascinans* captures this feeling of *yir'ah* well.[7] I remember the first time we traveled by car through the mountains of the West and Southwest and being physically overcome by the power and majesty of the landscape; indeed, it was "sacred ground." Driving the long, twisting highway, with very little other traffic around us, we would suddenly come across an even higher mount and an even more overwhelming view. Was there "fear" involved? Yes, but it was a reverential and majestic fear; it was *yir'ah* fear. This, then, is the "fear of the Lord" we are being called to by St. Benedict. And we are called to this fear of the Lord both as individual believers and as a Church.

One practical effect between a *pachad* Church and a *yir'ah* Church, a Church responding to God out of fear, on the one hand, or a Church responding to God out of reverential awe, on the other hand, is captured well by Sr. Joan Chittister. She recounts a conversation with a friend who had left the Catholic Church, who told Sister, "I left the Church because if I stayed there, I never could be anything but a failure." Sr. Joan asks, "What kind of spirituality was this? And what kind of God were we dealing with? Where was the greatness of the spiritual life?"[8]

A humble Church stands in awe of God. God is the overwhelming power, the awe-inspiring presence, the One that loves and is love. Ours is not a *pachad* fear of divine judgment but a *yir'ah* fear that always stays focused, immersed, and enfolded by God. Simply put, we need to keep always in our hearts that we need to "do justice, and to love kindness, and to walk humbly with your God" (Mic 6:8). The implications for the life of the Church are profound. When people encounter us, do they meet a people overwhelmed, overcome, and immersed in the love of God? Not only in our liturgy but in our conversation, in our hopes and dreams for the future, in the way we treat strangers and newcomers, in the way we put God first in every dealing and in every plan we make? What about our tweets, our Facebook posts, and our blog essays? Even the way we handle things like parish administration and record keeping: When people come to us, do we communicate, even unintentionally, that we are more interested in getting the paperwork correct than we are in the people involved? Do we make people feel like Sr. Joan's friend, that no matter what they do, they will always be a failure, or do we serve as a bridge of faith, hope, and love between them and God? In short, when they encounter us, do they see through us and find God? As Victor Hugo wrote so beautifully, "To love another person is to see the face of God."

Step 2: Doing the Will of God

> The second step of humility is that a man loves not his own will nor takes pleasure in the satisfaction of his desires; rather, he shall imitate by his actions that saying of the Lord: I have come not to do my own will, but the will of him who sent me (John 6:38). Similarly we read, "Consent merits punishment; constraint wins a crown."

Benedict does not say that we should not have our own free will, just that we do not see that will as supreme. We are to surrender that will to the greater will of God. It is no coincidence that the earliest references to Christian initiation use the technical term *sacramentum* to refer to it. Christian initiation, they said, is a *sacramentum*, the solemn and sacred oath made by a recruit entering Roman military service. While military analogies are not always helpful in understanding the Church, this particular connection happens to be rich with symbolism.

As I've already mentioned, I entered the Navy as a young man and headed off to basic training. Boot camp has one goal: to take individuals—women and men who up to that point had been "doing their own thing"—and turn them into a team. Immediately upon arrival, recruits realize that they are in a new and different world. Everything is communal. There is no privacy, very little personal space, and almost no time to oneself. Civilian clothes are removed, boxed up, and sent home. Uniforms are issued. There is no longer any personal preference for clothing or identity.

Everyone wears the same thing, and one's uniform tells the world a lot about where the recruit fits into the organization, what the recruit will do, and how the recruit relates to others. Then there's the haircut, with the classic question from the barber to the young recruit: "Do you want to keep your hair?" When the recruit answers yes, the barber tosses the cut hair into the recruit's lap. The recruit loses nearly every vestige of individuality. Recruits tackle tasks that can only be accomplished as a team. In short, boot camp trains recruits to put their individual wills aside and execute the will of others. By the end of boot camp, the neophyte sailors have put on a new identity. They wear the uniform with pride, and they know precisely how they "fit" into the bigger scheme of things in the service. There is a new authority over their lives. All of this because they have sworn a *sacramentum*, a solemn oath to preserve, protect, and defend something bigger than themselves: the Constitution and the people of the United States.

Sacramental initiation is analogous. Proclaiming before all the *sacramentum* of faith in Father, Son, and Spirit, neophytes strip off the old life of individualism and sin, put on the new white garment ("uniform") of the Christian *communio*, and are led forward to the eucharistic table. No longer individual believers, no longer "solo practitioners," they are immersed into the life of the Tri-Personed God and part of the community of faith, under the headship of Christ. As St. Paul writes to the Galatians, "It is no longer I who live, but it is Christ who lives in me. And the life I now live in the flesh I live by faith in the Son of God, who loved me and gave himself for me" (Gal 2:20). Just as the recruit's life was no longer her own, the new Christian accepts the supreme authority of God. Our will is to serve God's will. But how do we come to know God's will? How do we hear God's Word?

Step 3: Obedience to Superiors

> The third step of humility is that a person submits to the superior in all obedience for the love of God, imitating the Lord of whom the Apostle says: "He became obedient even to death" (Phil 2:8).

The word *obedience* derives from two Latin words *ob* and *audire*: to act upon what one hears. One hears something and then acts accordingly. On one level, of course, this can be the common understanding of being given an order to do something and then carrying it out. Taken to the extreme, we find "blind obedience": to do whatever a superior orders with no questions asked. What is this obedience to which St. Benedict refers? Are we simply to follow whatever orders we receive from people in authority in the Church? It certainly seems that sometimes people are tempted to approach religion in that way. If someone else can tell us what decision to make, we can avoid the sometimes-painful process of deciding for ourselves. There are three aspects of obedience to consider: listening, acting accordingly, in humility.

First, listening. It's the first step of obedience, and it's the first word of the *Rule*. We have already seen the etymological root of obedience as the Latin *ob audire*, to act because of what we hear. The *Rule* begins with *Obscülta* (or, in some manuscripts, *Ausculta*): "Listen carefully."[9] The preferred text (*obsculta*) even has that particle *ob* again. To "listen" goes beyond just hearing something; it implies active listening, listening that leads to action. Even more ancient, of course, is the *Shema* in the Jewish Tradition, often called the most fundamental prayer of Judaism. Its opening line is drawn from Deuteronomy, "Hear [*Shema*], O Israel: The Lord our God is one Lord." How do we hear the Word of God?

Our relationship with God and our ability to hear what God wants to say to us—revelation—comes through many means. As detailed in *Dei Verbum*,

> The invisible God out of the abundance of His love speaks to us as friends and lives among us, so that He may invite and take us into fellowship with Himself. This plan of revelation is realized by deeds and words having an inner unity: the deeds wrought by God in the history of salvation manifest and confirm the teaching and realities signified by the words, while the words proclaim the deeds and clarify the mystery contained in them. By this revelation then, the deepest truth about God and human salvation shines out for our sake in Christ, who is both the mediator and the fullness of all revelation. (*DV* 2)

Ultimately God speaks through mediation: through God's creation, through the prophets and martyrs, through the holy women and men of the Tradition, and most definitively through the Christ of God, the incarnate Word. In humility, we realize that God speaks through others in our lives and not solely to "me" alone. In our relationships, we come to know the others we encounter in life and how God may be speaking to us through them. We frequently proclaim that we are created in the image and likeness of God: recognizing the "image and likeness of God" in others can be challenging and humbling. For members of a monastic community, an essential voice is that of the superior. For those of us secular clergy who make a solemn promise of obedience to our diocesan bishops, there is an appreciation that we too rely on the same Holy Spirit. The bishop and the ordinands acknowledge the Spirit's presence in the other, as all are seeking to carry out God's plan. The humility comes in realizing that none of us has all of the answers to life's problems or a direct line to knowing God's will.

Step 4: Obedience in the Face of Suffering

> The fourth step of humility is that in this obedience under difficult, unfavorable, or even unjust conditions, his heart quietly embraces suffering and endures it without weakening or seeking escape. For Scripture has it: Anyone who perseveres to the end will be saved (Mt 10:22) and again, Be brave of heart and rely on the Lord (Ps 27:14).

For the middle part of my twenty-two-year Navy career, I served in a number of submarines for two- to-three-month patrols. These patrols involved diving when we left port and not surfacing again until the patrol was over. Hour after hour, day after day, week after week, month after month, 120 men (and today, both men and women) live, work, eat, and sleep in a metal tube, hundreds of feet underwater. Constant machinery noise, assorted odors, confined space with little privacy were a way of life, and a third of the crew slept and lived in the torpedo room, and that meant they were sleeping literally next to a torpedo.

Living under such conditions requires considerable adjustment.

Submarine service is voluntary, and every volunteer goes through psychiatric testing before making their first deployment. After all, if there's a problem underway, you can't just walk off the ship and quit; all of that is out of the crew's control. You either adapt or go crazy. Everyone develops certain routines, and the everyday rituals of shipboard life can be helpful. But the bottom line is that this community of sailors is bound together in both boredom and terror. Every moment, every person's life depends on another. Each crew member comes to accept the fact that they must accept the situation and get on with their duties just as they would ashore; only now, they're doing it four hundred feet underwater.

Acceptance and patience, regardless of the challenges, see them through. And this is the message of the fourth rung of the ladder of humility. In living out the word of God in humility, we are often in situations out of our control; we can't just leave. The demands of religious life, married life, and the single life all challenge us with matters outside of our control. Other conditions of life are even more challenging: going through illness, abuse, societal upheaval. Through it all, there is a degree of acceptance and patience. Even when things are overwhelming, God remains with us. However, there is a dark side, hinted at above.

Sr. Joan Chittister puts it well. "Why call for patience even if this obedience is 'under difficult, unfavorable, or even unjust conditions'? The answer demands serious consideration. What is the place of endurance in situations of abuse like bad marriages, demeaning professional environments, institutional oppression, and systemic injustice?"[10] Are there legitimate boundaries for patience? Should one be expected to persist within an abusive situation? At what point does a person legitimately reach a point where enough is more than enough? This applies in specific interpersonal relationships and systemic wrongs such as slavery, sexism, and racism. Patience and humble obedience do not mean that people must remain within such injustices; in fact, it is never God's will that one suffers indignity, violence, and abuse. Neither Scripture nor the Church expects anyone to remain in abusive relationships. The fundamental truth is that this rung of humility involves being obedient to the word of God, despite all hardships. However, God never wills anything that violates essential human dignity. We condemn all institutional abuse and systemic evil and work for their elimination.

This rung of humility is about obedience to the word of God even in the face of suffering, but abuse and systemic evil go beyond pain and suffering. Abuse and evil offend the very idea of the human being as an image and likeness of God. Furthermore, obedience to the word of God includes being coresponsible for the human dignity of all. Therefore, those suffering abuse are obeying God's will when they escape from such evil and assist others in doing so.

Step 5: Opening of the Heart

> The fifth step of humility is that a man does not conceal from his abbot any sinful thoughts entering his heart, or any wrongs committed in secret, but instead confesses them humbly.

Modern psychology has generated considerable study of the nature and benefits of self-disclosure to develop intimate relationships. "Few areas of psychological investigation have attracted people from as many disciplines as the study of self-disclosure. Social psychologists, clinical and counseling psychologists, specialists in interpersonal communication, and others have all examined this topic."[11] Everything from scholarly journals to self-help books explore the importance of self-disclosure to relationships of growing intimacy. At the heart of effective self-disclosure is honesty.

Here we turn to our relationship with God. For the moment, let us leave aside the participation of the abbot. Benedict tells us to conceal nothing about ourselves, especially matters of "sins and wrongs." No secrets, no prevarication, no deceit. As Sr. Joan Chittister observes, we are to "acknowledge faults and strip away masks."[12]

The relationship involved, of course, is with God. Can we be honest with ourselves in the relationship? As a priest-pastor friend likes to tell people, "You can always lie to yourself and me, but you can't lie to God." As we have already seen, humility is a virtue of honesty, groundedness, knowing who we are and how we relate to God and each other. Before we can be humble and honest to others in our self-revelation, we must begin first with ourselves.

Of course, God does not need our self-revelation, knowing us better than we can ever know ourselves. Our self-knowledge, especially of our limitations, sinfulness, and weakness, permits us to grow in humility. Within the Tradition, Christians have long valued the blessings of the sacrament of reconciliation, in which we confess humbly to God, and to our sisters and brothers of the Church, through the ministry of our confessors. There is a communitarian nature to this rung of humility, which ultimately strengthens the entire *communio*. I remember talking with a recent convert who was simply in love with going to confession. He said that he felt comfortable confessing his sins directly to God in his days as a Protestant. However, his experience with sacramental confession showed him that he was still confessing to God, but now he could actually hear the consoling words of God's mercy and forgiveness.

The Church's theology has always maintained that the effects of sacramental confession are both "horizontal" and "vertical." There is the ("vertical") healing of the penitent's relationship with God and the ("horizontal") healing of the penitent's relationship with the people of God. It is this horizontal healing that often gets overlooked or shortchanged. The humility of accepting responsibility for one's sins and their effect on the community is one level of relationship; another is the institutional humility of accepting our corporate sins and their impact on the community. The example of recent popes begging forgiveness for past sins acknowledges the problem, although one can still question whether asking for forgiveness is enough. There is a need to repair the damage caused ("reparation"). Additional questions remain. How might a local community such as a parish confess its sins and shortcomings and, equally important, make reparations?

There is a longstanding liturgical Tradition that offers, I believe, a rich opportunity to express personal and communal acknowledgment of our sinfulness and need for God's mercy and forgiveness. For many centuries, before the postconciliar liturgical changes, the Mass of the Roman Rite included preparatory prayers known as the "Prayers at the Foot of the Altar." They involved the priest and the altar servers; the servers represented the people and spoke on their behalf. Often, the priest and servers were the only people present at the Mass. Even on Sundays, with greater numbers of the laity present, they were silent; it was still the servers who spoke the prayers on their behalf. With the priest and servers praying antiphonally (in Latin, of course), the prayers consisted of two major groups of prayers: first, Psalm 43 (*Introibo ad altare Dei*), and second, the *Confiteor*. Today, in the reformed liturgy, we still have the option of praying a shortened form of the *Confiteor* as part of the Penitential Rite at Mass; however, the former practice was much more expressive.

At the end of Psalm 43, the priest bowed with a "profound bow" and began the *Confiteor*. It is a fuller, richer form of the prayer:

> I confess to Almighty God, to blessed Mary ever Virgin, to blessed Michael the Archangel, to blessed John the Baptist, to the holy Apostles Peter and Paul, to all the Saints, and to you, my brothers [*et vobis, fratres*], that I have sinned exceedingly, in thought, word and deed: through my fault, through my fault, through my most grievous fault. Therefore I beseech blessed Mary ever Virgin, blessed Michael the Archangel, blessed John the Baptist, the holy Apostles Peter and Paul, all the Saints, and you, brothers [*et vos, fratres*], to pray to the Lord our God for me.

The "brothers" to whom the priest is speaking are the servers. When he refers to them (twice), the priest—still bowing—rotates to each server in turn. As soon as the priest finished the *Confiteor*, the servers immediately prayed, "May Almighty God have mercy upon you, forgive you your sins, and bring you to life everlasting." The priest then stood upright, and the servers took their turn, bowed profoundly, and prayed the same *Confiteor*, only this time referring to the priest (*et tibi, Pater* and *et te, Pater*), rotating toward him as he had toward them. When the prayer was complete, the priest offered the same prayer that the servers had prayed for him: "May Almighty God have mercy upon you, forgive you your sins, and bring you to life everlasting."

I have provided this detailed description to apply it, with some modification, to our Mass today. Of course, today, we celebrate the Ordinary Form of the Mass in the vernacular; there is no need to change that. Similarly, in the past, the priest and servers were facing *ad orientem*. Today the Ordinary Form is usually celebrated *versus populum*, and this would continue. My suggestion works most powerfully if bishops, presbyters, deacons, and other ministers face the people and vice versa. Finally, the servers will no longer speak for the assembly; the assembly will speak for themselves.

Here's my suggestion. The Mass begins as customary. The presider then invites the assembly to penitence, as we do now. However, after the invitation, the clergy (any and all bishops, presbyters, and deacons) would bow profoundly toward the altar (representing Christ) and the people (also a sign of Christ's presence), praying the full, older version of the *Confiteor*. When the clergy have finished, and while they are still bowing, the whole assembly would pray over them: "May Almighty God have mercy upon you, forgive you your sins, and bring you to life everlasting." (For anyone concerned about laypersons and deacons offering this prayer, I would simply point out that it was the young altar servers who offered it for centuries!) Then the clergy would stand upright while the assembly bows profoundly and pray the full, older *Confiteor* in turn, with the priest praying for God's mercy when they are finished. In today's world, such an act of mutual confession and plea for God's mercy would be a powerful and much-needed form of reconciliation.

Step 6: Be Content with the Lowest Place

> The sixth step of humility is that a monk is content with the lowest and most menial treatment, and regards himself as a poor and worthless workman in whatever task he is given, saying to himself with the Prophet: *I am insignificant and ignorant, no better than a beast before you, yet I am with you always* (Ps 73:22–23).

Cardinal Wilton Gregory, the archbishop of Washington, DC, was asked about the evil of clericalism. He gave an excellent illustration in response. He mentioned those times when he would visit a parish for confirmation. Often, parishioners reserve a parking space near the Church for his use. He joked that he always appreciated that gesture, especially as he has gotten older. But having a reserved parking space for the archbishop is not a sign of clericalism. The archbishop continued that if he began *demanding* or *expecting* that reserved space, that would be clericalism. He is echoing St. Benedict, who reminds us that it is not the "lowest and most menial treatment" that is key to this rung. It is the attitude toward that treatment that matters.

I believe the key to this rung rests in the word *content*. The monk is to be "content" with the lowest and most menial treatment. The Latin root carries a sense of "containment" of having everything enclosed in one space. Even in the context of "the lowest and most menial," God is with us—and we have everything we need. Such an attitude is a challenge today. We are barraged by messages that we must have the latest gadget, the best clothes, and the next promotion. One could argue that we need to do whatever we can to support ourselves and our families, and that involves acquiring certain things and positions: a construction laborer gets promoted to foreman on a job; a clerk in a shop, through frugality and planning, can buy her own establishment; a soldier earns a promotion to sergeant; a monk is elected to serve as prior or abbot. All of these are good in and of themselves. So, are these people expected to ignore this rung of humility and jump onto the next one?

Attitude is the answer. If we approach such things as something we are entitled to, or ways to lord ourselves over others, or the power of a title, then we miss the point and slip off the rung. Some of the humblest people I have known have also been senior Church officials, high-ranking military officers, and corporate giants. Extending this thought to an ecclesial spirituality, what is our attitude toward others? Do we present ourselves as having all truth and authority over others? Do our structures project power without mercy, pride without self-sacrifice, position without risk or vulnerability? Have some of our structures grown to such a degree that we have forgotten that we exist to serve others, especially those with nothing?

Step 7: Heartfelt Humility and "Regard[ing] Others as Better than Yourselves" (Phil 2:3)

> The seventh step of humility is that a monk not only admits with his tongue but is also convinced in his heart that he

> is inferior to all and of less value, humbling himself and saying with the Prophet: "I am truly a worm, not a man, scorned by men and despised by the people" (Ps 22:7).

This step embodies a Scripture we have considered before, Philippians 2:3–4: "Do nothing from selfish ambition or conceit, but in humility regard others as better than yourselves. Let each of you look not to your own interests, but to the interests of others." We must walk the walk and not just talk the talk. The focus of this rung of the ladder is on this integrity of humility. I must not only *say* that I am the servant of others; I must hold that in my heart and express it in my actions.

In thinking about this step, I thought immediately of Uriah Heep, the slimy, fawning, and dishonest character in Charles Dickens's *David Copperfield*. This groveling "humble" clerk, a devious, manipulative villain, is a classic example of someone who has not reached this rung of humility! Old Uriah was proclaiming humility "with his tongue" without being "convinced in his heart." Humility should reflect our fundamental relationship with God and, as a result, with others. Just as the Second Person of the Trinity emptied himself radically into human nature for our salvation, we too must have "the mind of Christ" and empty ourselves for the good of "the other." Regardless of any position of authority one might hold, that authority is exercised in the service of others.

Once again, we find ourselves asking how self-giving we are in our own lives. That is a necessary first step. Then we apply that same question to the Church. How self-giving are we as Church? Do all of us, regardless of position, office, or order, do more than just proclaim our commitment to others with our tongues? Does our integrity shine through? Do we proclaim and act on what is in our hearts? Or are we, and our structures, guilty of the sin of Uriah Heep, talking a good and humble game but harboring pride and self-interest in our hearts? Among other things, there lies the cancer of clericalism. The truth is that clericalism is the opposite of "regard[ing] others as better than ourselves," and it eats away at every aspect of Church life.

Step 8: Acting for the *Communio*

> The eighth step of humility is that a monk does only what is endorsed by the common rule of the monastery and the example set by his superiors.

This step seems benign enough: follow along with everyone else and follow the rules. But that seems too simplistic. What if the time has come for changes to the "common rule" or if "the example of our superiors" is not worthy of emulation? Consider the renewal of the diaconate as one example. When St. Paul VI implemented the Council's decision about the diaconate in 1967 with the promulgation of *Sacrum Diaconatus Ordinem*, the 1917 Code of Canon Law was still in effect in the Latin Church. Under those canons, bishops could not ordain married men, nor could they ordain a man to any order without a reasonable expectation that he could eventually be ordained to the presbyterate. That was the "common rule" of the time. Those laws had to be changed so that these new deacons, most of them married, could be ordained to a permanent exercise of the diaconate. So, at what point in our spiritual quest for humility does "Do it this way because this is how we've always done it" give way to a new way? In her reflection, Sr. Joan Chittister offers a beautiful distinction between *Tradition* and *traditionalism*.

> Tradition is vital, but traditionalism is nothing more than its weak shadow sister. Traditionalism repeats the past; it considers the past impeccable, and so suppresses the development of a bona fide tradition in the present. The distinction between those two approaches stuck for my entire life.[13]
>
> More specifically:
>
> Tradition is what constitutes the heart and soul of an institution, its purpose and reason for being, its highest vision of itself, and its deepest dreams. Traditionalism includes all the tiny little customs and practices, laws, and explanations that reflect the insights important to maintain-

> ing that Tradition in every particular age that succeeds it. Tradition lives and thrives on the energy and clarity of its vision and its dreams, its purpose and goals. Traditionalism stands to smother the Tradition under an avalanche of times-bound practices that served one generation well but have little spiritual nourishment or meaning to offer the next.[14]

Humility seeks to discern the difference between Tradition and traditionalism. In normal times (if those exist), we need things in our lives that help us connect the dots, finding meaning. Those symbols of Tradition connect our past to our present and help us face the future. In times of crisis, we turn to these symbols to help us find a measure of stability and continuity. Life in black and white can be so much more comfortable than the gray in which we usually live. Sometimes the lived experience of faith becomes detached from its external expressions, and once that happens, those outward expressions can become traditionalisms. Consider a few examples.

From the earliest days of Christianity, disciples found ways to symbolize their faith, such as using the shape of a fish (after the Greek ιχθύς) providing an acronym for "Jesus Christ, Son of God, Savior." Another example is the Sign of the Cross, in which we express our fundamental relationship with the Trinity. And yet, in both these cases, as profound as they are, we see them used so often in a manner that suggests mere reification or superficial gesture. We find the fish on keychains, refrigerator magnets, and tailgates, as well as in churches and art. Athletes make the Sign of the Cross before sporting events.

On a deeper level, consider the preconciliar *Missale Romanum*. The rubrics required the priest to make the Sign of the Cross thirty-three times during the Mass, one for each year of Christ's life. The priest blessed himself, the gifts (several times), the incense, the people, and so on. Since the Mass was celebrated *ad orientem*, most of these gestures were unseen by the assembly. Giving the general principles for the reform of the liturgy, Vatican II's *Sacrosanctum Concilium* 34 directed that "a noble simplicity should distinguish the rites; they should be short, clear, and unencumbered by useless repetitions; they should be within the people's powers of comprehension, and normally should not require much explanation."

To be clear, I am not judging anyone's motives or spirituality by citing these examples, nor am I denigrating the older form of the Mass of the Roman Rite. Countless priests undoubtedly performed the ancient rites with integrity and faith. Sports figures making the Sign of the Cross before a competition might be raising a heartfelt prayer. For some families, that refrigerator magnet of the ichthys might be an opportunity to call to mind God's presence in their busy day. What I am saying, however, is that there is the possibility of taking Tradition and turning these outward signs into acts of traditionalism. If such gestures are made merely out of habit, without thought, without intentionality, they risk being empty and devoid of significance.

From the time of the ancient catechumenate up to our contemporary experience of the RCIA, the community "hands over" (*traditio*) the symbols of Christian faith: the Creed and the Lord's Prayer, usually during the period of purification and enlightenment (Lent). Although it is customary in some places today to hand the elect the prayers printed on fancy scrolls, the ancient practice and the current rite presume that these symbols are handed over orally by the presider and the assembly. In this way, we stress the living character of the essential elements of faith, especially as professed liturgically: *lex orandi, lex credendi*. In my opinion, merely handing the elect a scroll runs the risk of reifying the Tradition. If that were to happen, the "Tradition" of handing over the symbols of faith could become a ritual devoid of meaning, an act of traditionalism. A symbol that needs explanation is no symbol.

Consider one final example. From at least the time of the Pastoral Letters, such as 1 Timothy, Christian communities referred to their leaders as "overseers," in Greek, *episkopoi*, coming down to us in English as "bishops." In a Tradition that goes back to the earliest synods in the patristic era, bishops were married to their communities while at the same time being co-responsible for the larger *communio*. This Tradition of two millennia is seen in Vatican II's *Lumen Gentium* 22:

> Just as in the Gospel, the Lord so disposing, St. Peter and the other apostles constitute one apostolic college, so in a similar way, the Roman Pontiff, the successor of Peter, and the bishops, the successors of the apostles, are joined together. Indeed, the very ancient practice whereby bishops duly established in all parts of the world were in communion with one another and with the Bishop of Rome in a bond of unity, charity, and peace, and also the councils assembled together, in which more profound issues were settled in common, the opinion of the many having been prudently considered, both of these factors are already an indication of the collegiate character and aspect of the Episcopal order; and the ecumenical councils held in the course of centuries are also manifest proof of that same character.

Bishops and their people are one, and that ancient Tradition remains. However, one challenge that emerged in the late Middle Ages was the emergence of "titular" sees. Imagine a priest living in Rome in 1595 during the papacy of Clement VIII. He comes to the pope's attention, who selects the priest to take over a senior office in his curia. Clement ordains him a bishop, but there's a problem. The new bishop will be residing and working in Rome, so there is no diocesan church for the new bishop. The solution (arrived at long before Clement) is to appoint such a bishop to a diocese, but a diocese that no longer exists. These former dioceses exist worldwide (even here in the United States), and this practice continues today. A large diocese may have a diocesan bishop, assisted by several auxiliary bishops. The diocesan bishop holds the "title" of the diocese; the auxiliary bishops, however, all hold one of those "titular" sees. As Richard Gaillardetz has observed,

> Consider that approximately half of today's bishops—every ordained church diplomat, many Vatican bureaucrats, and every auxiliary bishop—is assigned to a titular see, that is, a diocese that once existed but no longer does today. So, technically, every bishop is ordained to serve a local church, even if that local church has no living members!

> How can such a custom not trivialize the bishop's relationship to the local church?[15]

The relationship of the bishop and the people he oversees and serves is foundational. To divorce the bishop from the people risks turning the sacramental ordination of a bishop not serving a living diocese into an act of traditionalism rather than an exercise of the Tradition. In this case, the office (of the bishop) has become more important than the Church. What are those traditions that we will carry forward with us into the future, and what traditionalisms do we discard? On this rung of the ladder, we seek the common good and others' example in discerning the direction God is leading the *communio*.

Step 9: Silence; Step 10: Seriousness and Respect; Step 11: Gentle and Modest Speech

There is a consistency to these three rungs that suggests we treat them together.

> The ninth step of humility is that a monk controls his tongue and remains silent, not speaking unless asked a question....The tenth step of humility is that he is not given to ready laughter, for it is written: "Only a fool raises his voice in laughter" (Sir 21:23)....The eleventh step of humility is that a monk speaks gently and without laughter, seriously and with becoming modesty, briefly and reasonably, but without raising his voice.

I left home for the seminary when I was thirteen years old (if you think that is young, Angelo Roncalli, the future St. Pope John XXIII, entered the seminary when he was only eleven!). It was 1963, and the Second Vatican Council was beginning its second session. The seminary was a six-year institution: the four years of high school and the first two years of college. The system then was a 6-1-6 model: You would attend the first six years in one school, and then the candidates for religious life would go off for their novitiate year. Then came another school for the next six years: the final two years of college and the four years of theology. There were some 250 students across the six years, ranging in age from thirteen to twenty. A couple of weeks into the academic year, all of us entered into a week-long silent retreat. Completely silent. Completely. Silent. The only words spoken were words of prayer. Even after the retreat, our schedule involved silence. Every night following Compline, there was the Grand Silence, which extended throughout the night and until after Mass and breakfast the following morning. Silence was a fundamental component of seminary life. Silence permits us to hear God's voice with clarity and without interference.

What do we speak about during any given day? And how are we saying it? Are we gossips? Do we address others with contempt? Do we find ourselves entering into every argument, every conversation, every debate? Just as we know that effective human communication demands that we listen to others before responding, so too in our relationship with God, we must listen. The sixteenth-century mystic, St. John of the Cross, once wrote, "God's first language is silence." In commenting on this insight, the late Trappist monk Thomas Keating, in his book *Invitation to Love*, said, "Everything else is a poor translation. To understand this language, we must learn to be silent and to rest in God." Sr. Joan Chittister describes her own growth in silence:

> Silence is the key to everything. First, silence teaches us to go down inside ourselves to find real life rather than to reach for it always and forever outside ourselves. Second, silence provides us with the harrowing ground of the soul. It breaks up the clods of our lives, it roots out the weeds, it levels the rocky ground in which we've grown. Most of all, it is in silence that we hear our own cries of fear and pain and resistance, which only in silence can really be addressed. In silence, we come to know ourselves.
>
> Then, we are ready to disengage ourselves from the thickets that block the way beyond ourselves where light is and growth is and God is. Silence, I knew now, confronts us with the hardest question of all. What are we hiding from that our flight into noise holds at bay?[16]

Sr. Joan's questions invite us to turn to the possibilities silence might offer to a humble Church confronting the future, just as we have been doing as we pursue the other steps of humility throughout this chapter. The Church, and in a particular way its ministers—lay, religious, and ordained—need not attempt to have something to say about everything. A humble Church journeys with other people, listening to their "joys and hopes, griefs and anxieties" (*GS* 1). Sometimes our most powerful proclamation of God's love is through simple accompaniment—being there, or as several writers have put it: to exercise a ministry of presence. Silence opens the door to the other, putting their needs before our own. When a bishops' conference decides to issue a statement about a particular topic, they should (and in many cases, but not all, they do) first ask if people genuinely need such a statement. Yes, bishops are teachers in faith. But good teachers don't always lecture; great teachers listen first and engage their students in various ways. In the case of episcopal teaching statements, the bishops should first have listened deeply to the people. Only then should they decide if such a statement is needed and how it will be received. *Being received* is a technical term, and it means much more than simply writing a text that is popular. It means that the text is seen to be coherent, consistent with experience, and something people can make their own. Far too often, bishops' conference statements are seen as little more than political posturing and given the lack of credibility of the Church and its leadership, they are often derided and disregarded as so much "noise." More often than not, people want to be listened to, not condescended to.

Step 10 instructs that the monk is "not given to ready laughter, for it is written, 'Only a fool raises his voice in laughter' (Sir 21:23)." When I first read this step years ago, my first reaction was to conclude that Benedict must be joking! I spent nearly eight years in the seminary, and humor was always a crucial part of our communal life. After all, as de Chardin once wrote, joy is an infallible sign of God's presence. Are we Christians supposed to be not only silent but glum, humorless individuals as well? What is Father Benedict trying to convey to us?

The distinction, of course, is that laughter is not the same as humor or joy. Benedict seems to be reminding us that an attitude that "life is just a joke" is not to be part of our spiritual life. The meaning of life is nothing to be taken lightly. One who laughs at everything and everyone, or who ridicules everyone and everything, is a fool (explaining Benedict's citation from Sirach). Joy does not minimize others or find satisfaction at someone else's expense. As a humble Church, we are not to exclude, mock, ridicule, or judge. Just as we examine our individual consciences, so too must we critique our collective structures, processes, and even the ways and terms we use to express our teachings.

When dealing with other people, are people hurt by our words and actions while we maintain that "we're just joking"? When we're questioned when teaching, do we respond that "we have all the answers, and you're just not able to understand them"? Do the terms we use (e.g., "objectively disordered") intentionally or unintentionally carry such baggage that a reasonable reader will find them hurtful and offensive? The question of whether something is hurtful, confusing, or offensive rests with the person being addressed, not with the one commenting. Remember that as a servant, our concern always rests with the one being served. Consider the field of education. If all the students in my class miss the same question on an exam, the fault lies with me, not with them. It was a poorly framed question in the first place. That's my responsibility, not theirs. The same applies here. A humble and servant Church serves and is not served.

The teaching role of the Church is not in question. But as St. John XXIII taught, "The substance of the ancient doctrine of the deposit of faith is one thing, and how it is presented is another. And it is the latter that must be taken into great consideration with patience if necessary, everything being measured in the forms and proportions of a magisterium which is predominantly pastoral in character."[17] In short, teaching must respect those receiving it. Do we do that in our daily exercise of ministry? In our zeal for truth, we must find ways of expressing that truth "with patience" and pastoral sensitivity.

"The eleventh step of humility is that a monk speaks gently and without laughter, thoughtfully and with becoming modesty, briefly and reasonably, but without raising his voice." A humble person is concerned not only with what they say but how they say it. In the seminary, I studied Latin (six years!) and French. Later, in the Navy,

I studied Hebrew (both modern and biblical) and later, Russian. The approach to learning Hebrew and Russian was intense. Each course was nearly a year long. We spent eight to ten hours a day in the classroom, with teachers who were all native speakers. Class sizes were small, and in the case of the Hebrew course, there were more teachers than students: we would rotate among them to experience different dialects and accents. We ate lunch together with our instructors, and informal learning continued over the meal. Every evening, we had a minimum of four hours of memorization and homework.

Language emerged as so much more than merely learning words and writing them down. The tone of voice, the use of gestures, vocal inflections, and facial expressions were all critically important. How we spoke the words affected our ability to communicate effectively. The same skills apply to ministry. As humble servants of God, we speak gently, respectfully, humbly, quietly, and thoughtfully. And, like language school—and subsequent service as a linguist—taught me, it's not just the words we use in our speaking, writing, and teaching. To communicate, one needs first to listen so we can know how to respond.

In his encyclical *Fratelli Tutti*, Pope Francis offers some beautiful insights that seem drawn from this rung of humble dialogue. "Approaching, speaking, listening, looking at, coming to know and understand one another, and to find common ground: all these things are summed up in the one word 'dialogue.' If we want to encounter and help one another, we have to dialogue....Unlike disagreement and conflict, persistent and courageous dialogue does not make headlines, but quietly helps the world to live much better than we imagine" (*Fratelli Tutti* 198).[18] Francis further describes dialogue: "Dialogue between generations; dialogue among our people, for we are that people; readiness to give and receive while remaining open to the truth" (*FT* 199). In remaining open to the truth, we admit our own frailty and limitations; in short, that what we are saying, or how we are saying it, just might be wrong.

This dialogue, of course, is complex in today's cultural climate. "The media's noisy potpourri of facts and opinions is often an obstacle to dialogue since it lets everyone cling stubbornly to his or her own ideas, interests, and choices, with the excuse that everyone else is wrong. It becomes easier to discredit and insult opponents from the outset than open a respectful dialogue to achieve agreement on a deeper level" (*FT* 201). Today's Church is subject to the virulent, violent, and vicious discourse that has infected the whole culture. To be countercultural and communicate in a Christ-like manner demands patience and humility. This is particularly true if we hope to change cultural discourse in the future.

Step 12: Talking the Talk, Walking the Walk

> The twelfth step of humility is that a monk always manifests humility in his bearing no less than in his heart, so that it is evident at the Work of God, in the oratory, the monastery or the garden, on a journey or in the field, or anywhere else.

We now arrive at the twelfth rung of humility, and its charge is simple. Humility is not a mere matter of being humble interiorly. We must be humble in deed as well as in our hearts. When this becomes a way of life ("at all times"), and in every human activity, we reach the last rung of humility. "Now, therefore, after ascending all these steps of humility, the monk will quickly arrive at that perfect love of God which casts out fear. Through this love, all that he once performed with dread, he will now begin to observe without effort, as though naturally, from habit, no longer out of fear of hell but out of love for Christ, good habit and delight in virtue."

Humility demands integrity. Integrity means having high moral principles and living up to them to the best of our ability. Integrity also means wholeness, completeness. For example, one can speak of the "integrity" of a wall or a building (as in, "the army breached the integrity of the walled city"). Integrity is all about a unity of purpose: what we say is what we do.

As a young Navy officer, I was assigned to a large communications command overseas. My boss had been in the Navy for quite a while, but I had only recently been commissioned. A common requirement throughout the Navy is the periodic "zone inspection." As the term implies, the ship or base is divided into zones. An officer is assigned to inspect every part of her designated zone, primarily for health, cleanliness, and safety issues. Shortly after I reported to the command and assumed my regular duties, I was assigned as inspecting officer for a zone that included my own division.

As I made my way through the zone, I directed the clerk who was assisting me to note any and all problems: a broken electrical cover, equipment not stowed properly, and so on. I turned in the paperwork after the inspection, believing I had done an excellent job. My boss, however, was furious! "How could do you that?" he screamed. "You put our own division on the spot by these findings. Whoever heard of such a thing! You should just have made note of the problems privately, and we would have taken care of them." From his standpoint, there was no need to "embarrass" our division—we could have fixed any problems on our own.

I struggled with this criticism for a while. Was my supervisor correct? Indeed, his approach would have been easier. But I concluded that he was wrong, and I maintain that judgment even today. I had been assigned to conduct the inspection. I applied the same standards to my division as I did to others. The fact that I found discrepancies in my division was unfortunate, but integrity demanded that I treat the whole matter with consistency and honesty. It was also a humbling experience to acknowledge shortcomings in my own division.

So it is with our spiritual and ecclesial lives. As we examine our own lives and actions, we must do so with consistency, honesty—and humility. Many of the crises we face in the Church come from the fact that we do not consistently examine ourselves, our Church, and our ecclesial institutions with humility. We often want to handle our problems "on our own," just as my supervisor wanted to do so many years ago. Consider the struggles to establish lay-led review boards to examine cases of abuse, the recurring problems involving Church finances, and so on. Not long ago, a bishop was encouraged to implement a performance review system for the clergy of the diocese. The deacons took it in stride since they were used to such reviews as part of their secular jobs, occupations, and professions. While most of the priests were also amenable, a few of them raised objections, telling the bishop, "No one is qualified to assess our performance—no one can understand priests except other priests." Unfortunately—in my opinion—the bishop backed down and dropped all plans for the performance review.

The final rung of humility carries us into this realm of integrity. As a Church, we proclaim our love for God and our neighbor. Do our actions bear out that claim? Are we appropriately self-critical, honestly assessing our actions in light of our words? As a Church, are we as transparent as we ask others to be? This demands, above all, humility.

As the Church moves into the future, we have a choice. We can move forward with faith, hope, and charity, or we can retreat from the unknown in fear. In my judgment, the believer has only one course to take, which is to face the future with courageous humility. Christ has shown us that his way lies ahead of us, not behind us. Calling again on St. John XXIII, we hear his words about the "prophets of gloom" who "are not endowed with too much sense of discretion or measure."

> In these modern times, they can see nothing but prevarication and ruin. They say that our era, in comparison with past eras, is getting worse, and they behave as though they had learned nothing from history, which is, nonetheless, the teacher of life. They behave as though at the time of former Councils, everything was a full triumph for the Christian idea and life and for proper religious liberty.[19]

"Prophets of gloom" seem even more prevalent today than in 1962 when St. John uttered those words. They look to the past, seeking a model of Church that they believe to be more "pure" or "faithful" than where we are today. They seem to suggest that the best way forward is to restore a mythical past that never existed.

Our reflection on St. Benedict's *Rule*, especially his chapter on humility, is not attempting to turn all Christians into monastics or turn the clock back to the sixth century. I see the *Rule* as a piece of classical music. In the case of music, a composer wrote down the music, sometimes centuries ago. Every musician who picks up that music will play it in her own way while remaining faithful to the composer's original vision. And every time a musician plays that music, it will be slightly different each time. The music of the *Rule* is not for the monastery alone; its beauty resounds over the walls into the community surrounding it. The *Rule* gives us the notes, but it is the Spirit who helps us interpret the music today and tomorrow. Just as music penetrates the musician's heart, it also nurtures, inspires, and builds up the people who hear it.

CHAPTER THREE

RENEWING STRUCTURES FOR A HUMBLE AND DIACONAL CHURCH

In Tribute to John Quinn

Introduction

The Church, like Christ, is one. This one Church, like Christ, has two natures: the divine and the human. The world's Catholic bishops stressed this point in *Lumen Gentium*:

> Christ, the one Mediator, established and continually sustains here on earth His holy Church, the community of faith, hope and charity, as an entity with visible delineation through which He communicated truth and grace to all. But, the society structured with hierarchical organs and the Mystical Body of Christ, are not to be considered as two realities, nor are the visible assembly and the spiritual community, nor the earthly Church and the Church enriched with heavenly things; rather, they form one complex reality which coalesces from a divine and a human element. For this reason, by no weak analogy, it is compared to the mystery of the incarnate Word. As the assumed nature inseparably united to Him, serves the

> divine Word as a living organ of salvation, so, in a similar way, does the visible social structure of the Church serve the Spirit of Christ, who vivifies it, in the building up of the body. (*LG* 8)

Having reflected on some of the spiritual elements of the Church, we turn now to aspects of its "visible assembly." In particular, our focus is on the need for, and the process of, ongoing reform of the various "hierarchical organs" established by the "human element" of the Church. This chapter will consider foundational issues and general principles related to structural reform in the Church.

In his classic text *Models of the Church*, Avery Dulles describes the need of the Church, to perform its mission, has "stable organizational features," "responsible officers," and "properly approved procedures." The history of the Church shows it has always had "recognized ministers, accepted confessional formulas, and prescribed forms of public worship."[1] He makes the valuable distinction that "all this is fitting and proper. It does not necessarily imply institutionalism, any more than papacy implies papalism, or law implies legalism, or dogma implies dogmatism." One crosses the line from a proper understanding of the Church's institutional dimension into institutionalism when the institution becomes the primary or principal focus of attention.

> From the point of view of this author, institutionalism is a deformation of the true nature of the Church—a deformation that has unfortunately affected the Church at certain periods of its history, and one that remains in every age a real danger to the institutional Church. A Christian believer may energetically oppose institutionalism and still be very much committed to the Church as institution.[2]

Such a Christian believer and a significant contributor to the contemporary conversation on ecclesial structural reform was the late John R. Quinn, archbishop emeritus of San Francisco. Quinn (1929–2017) was a native Californian who became one of the youngest bishops in the United States when he was ordained and assigned as auxiliary bishop of San Diego in 1968. In 1971 he became bishop of the Diocese of Oklahoma City–Tulsa; when the diocese split into the Archdiocese of Oklahoma City and the Diocese of Tulsa, he became the first archbishop of Oklahoma City. Five years later, in 1977, Quinn became the archbishop of San Francisco and remained in that office until his retirement in 1995. During his years of active ministry, he earned a doctorate in sacred theology and served a three-year term as president of the United States Conference of Catholic Bishops. Following his retirement, Archbishop Quinn received a visiting fellowship at Campion Hall, Oxford. On June 29, 1996, he delivered the Centennial Lecture on "The Claims of the Primacy and the Costly Call to Unity" in response to Pope John Paul II's request that bishops and theologians address the reform of the Petrine ministry in *Ut Unum Sint*. Upon returning to the United States, he developed that lecture into a significant book entitled *The Reform of the Papacy: The Costly Call to Christian Unity*. In his second book, *Ever Ancient, Ever New: Structures of the Communion in the Church*, he continued his research into institutional reform in 2012.[3]

In these two major works, the archbishop covered topics such as the papacy and its reform, collegiality, the appointment of bishops, the reform of the Roman curia, the ancient synodal process, the metropolitan structure, the patriarchal structure, and "the preeminent structures of communion," that is, the Church's councils. Through it all, several significant needs recur: the need for decentralization, greater and more effective collegiality, a truly functional and practical exercise of subsidiarity, substantive reform of the Roman curia, and greater diversity in participation and decision-making. The next logical step is to extend these insights to other structures such as parishes, deaneries, dioceses, the associated pastoral councils related to these structures, and the various regional episcopal conferences and their structures. Such a task is beyond this project's scope; however, later in the chapter, we do consider a series of elements that can serve as essential in any structural reform. While not a checklist per se, they are undoubtedly crucial factors to be considered. Before developing those factors, we first lay a foundation for Church institutional reform.

Foundations of Church Institutional Reform

Sociologically, a structure refers to how component parts of something are arranged or organized to accomplish a specific purpose. Applied to the Church, we proceed teleologically: considering the "end," or purpose, of the Church, how do we structure the Church to accomplish that end? The purpose of the Church is evangelization, to introduce and nurture the relationship of individual believers and the entire ecclesial *communio* with Christ. Therefore, ecclesial leadership should design and create structures to carry out that mission. A recent *Instruction* from the Congregation for the Clergy encourages such efforts. Entitled "The Pastoral Conversion of the Parish Community in the Service of the Evangelizing Mission of the Church," it begins,

> The ecclesiological reflection of the Second Vatican Council, together with the considerable social and cultural changes of recent decades, has resulted in various Particular Churches having to reorganize the manner in which the pastoral care of Parish communities is assigned. This has made it possible to initiate new experiences, enhancing the dimension of communion and implementing, under the guidance of pastors, a harmonious synthesis of charisms and vocations at the service of the proclamation of the Gospel, which better corresponds to the demands of evangelization today.[4]

While this a good and reasonable contribution to the process of structural reform, I would suggest that Church members conduct analogous operations at every level of ecclesial life. Many parishes and dioceses already use pastoral planning processes, but current canon law often limits the full range of possible pastoral responses. In the future, diocesan bishops and other ecclesial leaders will need the ability to adapt structures themselves and the canonical framework that supports them. In a later chapter, for example, we examine the canonical structures related to the exercise of the diaconate.

Another aspect of reform involves institutional change and how one approaches it. Many people fear change and seek to do everything possible to avoid it. Others accept change as a part of life. Most Christians seek a balance between change and stability, readily accepting the fact of life that some things are changeable while others are not. It takes courage, trust, and wisdom to discern the difference. Our process of ongoing conversion, ever deepening our relationship with Christ, is a form of change. The Church is also subject to the same constant conversion. Change has always been and will continue to be an integral part of the Church.

We do many things today in the Church that the first generations of the Church would not recognize. St. Peter never wore liturgical vestments and didn't have a curia around him, nor did he assume all authority for decision-making. St. Paul would not have known what a Christian "cardinal" was, and Mary did not speak Latin. St. Stephen would not know what a "church" building was, other than the temple in Jerusalem. Until Constantine, the Church had no dioceses, parishes, or deaneries. There were no clerical collars or even any distinctive clerical dress. The question is not really about ecclesial change but about how we deal with that change. As stated so well by St. John Henry Newman, "In a higher world it is otherwise, but here below to live is to change, and to be perfect is to have changed often."[5]

Ecclesial reform involves not only changes to structures but also within the hearts of believers. But an internal reform that does not result in structural reform is sterile. A humble heart in a servant's soul is not merely expressed by an individual; given the unicity and *communio* of the Church, humble service is a function of the whole Church. This demands that our structures resonate with the same vision. Yves Congar gives the example of the Latin word *reformatio* used by Jean of Limoges in the mid-thirteenth century as "a regular activity of an abbot with respect to his monks, without the word meaning exclusively a purely interior or moral reform." Once again, the wisdom of monastic life has applicability outside the monastery. For example, a diocesan bishop or pastor can benefit from the *Rule*'s guidance to the abbot.

Congar's reference to *reformatio* as a word not meaning "exclusively a purely interior or moral reform" is essential. A "purely moral" reform is not enough: reform, in both monastery and diocese, must have external, practical, and applied consequences. Congar offers several points that can serve as a "hermeneutical norm" for reform: affecting structural causes of a problem, affecting the conditions in which people live, and using the world's structures.

1. "A purely moral reform is insufficient because it does not affect the structural causes that underlie the problem and so fails to put into effect dynamic means that will change history."
2. "There can be no realization of an evangelical spirit in the religious context without an evangelical spirit that also affects the conditions (even external and economic) of the way people live." Although written some seventy years ago, this point finds a contemporary echo in the papal magisterium, especially that of Pope Francis. Evangelization, the identity and mission of the Church, is more than a purely spiritual (Congar's "purely moral") reality; it can only be truly effective when it has practical effects.
3. "There will be no full adaptation or renewal unless the church, sustained by the impulse of the Gospel as its source, generously agrees to attune itself to the structures of the emerging world and of a renewed society—which it also needs to baptize."[6] Congar here anticipates Vatican II: that the Church, in light of the gospel, not only reads the signs of the times but adapts ("attunes") to cultural structures and takes advantage of those structures of the contemporary world, while concurrently working to reform what needs reform in that society itself.

Vatican II and the papal magisterium of John XXIII, Paul VI, and all their postconciliar successors convey similar insights, perhaps showing the influence of Congar. The recent document from the Congregation for Clergy owes its origin to those sources. Consider a few examples. Opening the Second Vatican Council, John

XXIII famously emphasized that "the substance of the ancient doctrine of the deposit of faith is one thing, and the way in which it is presented is another. And it is the latter that must be taken into great consideration with patience if necessary, everything being measured in the forms and proportions of a magisterium which is predominantly pastoral in character."[7]

In its Decree on Ecumenism (*Unitatis Redintegratio*), the Council proclaimed,

> Christ summons the Church to continual reformation as she sojourns here on earth. The Church is always in need of this, in so far as she is an institution of men and women here on earth....There are ecclesial structures which can hamper efforts at evangelization, yet *even good structures are only helpful when there is a life constantly driving, sustaining, and assessing them.* Without new life and an authentic evangelical spirit, without the Church's "fidelity to her own calling," any new structure will soon prove ineffective. (no. 6 [emphasis added])

During the Council's development of the Dogmatic Constitution *Lumen Gentium*, Pope Paul promulgated his first encyclical, *Ecclesiam Suam.*[8] "The aim of this encyclical will be to demonstrate with increasing clarity how vital it is for the world, and how greatly desired by the Catholic Church, that the two [the world and the Church] should meet together, and get to know and love one another" (*ES* 3). To this end, Paul continued,

> We are convinced that the Church must look with penetrating eyes within itself, ponder the mystery of its own being, and draw enlightenment and inspiration from a deeper scrutiny of the doctrine of its own origin, nature, mission, and destiny....A vivid and lively self-awareness on the part of the Church inevitably leads to a comparison between the ideal image of the Church as Christ envisaged it...and the actual image which the Church presents to the world today....Hence the Church's heroic and impatient struggle for renewal: the struggle to correct

> those flaws introduced by its members which its own self-examination, mirroring its exemplar, Christ, points out to it and condemns. (*ES* 9–11)

More than a decade later, following the 1974 Synod on Evangelization, Pope Paul wrote the landmark apostolic exhortation *Evangelii Nuntiandi*. He proclaimed,

> Evangelizing is in fact the grace and vocation proper to the Church, her deepest identity. She exists in order to evangelize, that is to say, in order to preach and teach, to be the channel of the gift of grace, to reconcile sinners with God, and to perpetuate Christ's sacrifice in the Mass, which is the memorial of His death and glorious resurrection.[9]

Pope Paul has taken us to new depth: our constant efforts at ecclesial reform are made for the precise reason that we must be able to evangelize more effectively. The Church exists to evangelize, and evangelization is the "deepest identity" of the Church. Evangelization (mission) is not simply what we do; it is who we are as Christians. John Paul II would later echo Pope Paul when he wrote, "All renewal in the Church must have mission [evangelization] as its goal if it is not to fall prey to a kind of ecclesial introversion."[10] The goal of reform is always outward directed, never to elevate or even maintain the status quo. Reform must help us evangelize more effectively and with no other purpose.

Finally, we turn to Pope Francis. In the early days of his papacy, Pope Francis promulgated his first apostolic exhortation, *Evangelii Gaudium* (*The Joy of the Gospel*), officially the concluding document to the 13th Ordinary Synod of Bishops on the New Evangelization convened by his predecessor, Pope Benedict XVI. Pope Francis made this document the launching pad for his entire papacy. "In this Exhortation, I wish to encourage the Christian faithful to embark upon a new chapter of evangelization marked by this joy while pointing out new paths for the Church's journey in years to come" (no. 1).[11]

Dreaming of a "missionary impulse capable of transforming everything," Pope Francis proposes that "the Church's customs, ways of doing things, times and schedules, language and structures can be suitably channeled for the evangelization of today's world rather than for her self-preservation" (*EG* 27). This lens of evangelization, which in itself calls for interior conversion, allows us to focus on making all of our structures "more mission-oriented, to make ordinary pastoral activity on every level more inclusive and open, to inspire in pastoral workers a constant desire to go forth and in this way to elicit a positive response from all those whom Jesus summons to friendship with himself" (*EG* 27).

Pope Francis has drawn heavily from Pope Paul VI. For example, after recalling Pope Paul's *Ecclesiam Suam*, cited above, Francis continues,

> The Second Vatican Council presented ecclesial conversion as openness to a constant self-renewal born of fidelity to Jesus Christ....There are ecclesial structures which can hamper efforts at evangelization. Yet, even good structures are only helpful when there is a life constantly driving, sustaining, and assessing them. Without new life and an authentic evangelical spirit, without the Church's "fidelity to her own calling," any new structure will soon prove ineffective. (*EG* 26)

The trajectory from Vatican II to the present is clear. The conciliar and postconciliar popes have challenged the Church to live up to our identity as evangelizers. We must reform and conform all of our institutional structures accordingly. Opening that door, we return to 1995 and *Ut Unum Sint*.

John Paul II issued this encyclical letter, a landmark document on Christian unity, in May 1995. He wrote,

> Christ ardently desires the full and visible communion of all those Communities in which, by virtue of God's faithfulness, his Spirit dwells. I am convinced that I have a particular responsibility in this regard...in heeding the request made of me to find a way of exercising the primacy which, while in no way renouncing what is essential to its mission, is nonetheless open to a new situation. (*Ut Unum Sint* 95)[12]

He then requested that bishops and their theologians

> engage with me in a patient and fraternal dialogue on this subject, a dialogue in which, leaving useless controversies behind, we could listen to one another, keeping before us only the will of Christ for his Church and allowing ourselves to be deeply moved by his plea "that they may all be one…so that the world may believe that you have sent me"? (*UUS* 96)

Pope Francis has made a similar plea in *Evangelii Gaudium*: "I too must think about a conversion of the papacy. It is my duty, as the Bishop of Rome, to be open to suggestions which can help make the exercise of my ministry more faithful to the meaning which Jesus Christ wished to give it and to the present needs of evangelization" (*EG* 32). He mentions John Paul II's earlier appeal but concludes rightly, "We have made little progress in this regard." He also opens the lens of reform to "the central structures of the universal Church," which also need "pastoral conversion." Finally, Pope Francis notes that the Council had declared,

> Episcopal conferences are in a position "to contribute in many and fruitful ways to the concrete realization of the collegial spirit." Yet this desire has not been fully realized since a juridical status of episcopal conferences which would see them as subjects of specific attributions, including genuine doctrinal authority, has not yet been sufficiently elaborated. Excessive centralization, rather than proving helpful, complicates the Church's life and her missionary outreach. (*EG* 32, citing *LG* 23)

Ultimately, ecclesial reform is born out of a process of discernment, both individual and ecclesial. Discernment is a keystone of Ignatian spirituality. St. Ignatius often referred to the "motions of the soul." These interior movements consist of thoughts, imaginings, emotions, inclinations, desires, feelings, repulsions, and attractions. Spiritual discernment involves becoming sensitive to these movements, reflecting on them, and understanding where they come from and where they lead us. Section 23 of the *Spiritual Exercises* includes "The First Principle and Foundation," and Jesuit David Fleming offers the following translation:

> The goal of our life is to live with God forever. God, who loves us, gave us life. Our own response of love allows God's life to flow into us without limit.
>
> All the things in this world are gifts of God, presented to us so that we can know God more easily and make a return of love more readily. As a result, we appreciate and use all these gifts of God insofar as they help us develop as loving persons. But if any of these gifts become the center of our lives, they displace God and so hinder our growth toward our goal.
>
> In everyday life, then, we must hold ourselves in balance before all of these created gifts insofar as we have a choice and are not bound by some obligation. We should not fix our desires on health or sickness, wealth or poverty, success or failure, a long life or a short one. For everything has the potential of calling forth in us a deeper response to our life in God.
>
> Our only desire and our one choice should be this: I want and I choose what better leads to God's deepening his life in me.[13]

One concrete example of this discernment in practice is the daily (or twice daily) examen. Here one is alone with God, reviewing the events of the day thus far and discerning moments where things had gone well and where things might have gone better, forming a resolve to improve the relationship with God and others. In 2017, Pope Francis described discernment as a way "to go out of the world of one's convictions and prejudices to open oneself to understand how God is speaking to us, today, in this world, in this time, in this moment, and how He speaks to me, now."[14] His insight works in the plural and the singular; we are discerning how God is speaking to us now. This is the doorway both to personal conversion and institutional reform.

What follows are seven essential elements of institutional reform suggested, developed, and adapted from Archbishop Quinn's work. For example, he writes, "Looking into the New Testament, we see that there were three factors involved in settling the problem [of the admittance of non-Jewish converts]: pastoral experience, the appeal to scripture, and the Jerusalem meeting of the leaders. No one of these three factors alone determined the solution; they were all interrelated."[15] These three factors are at the core of the following elements, and they are framed by additional factors related to ecclesial structural reform and decision-making. This is a *first-level* reflection that might apply to ecclesial structures at every level. The seven elements are the following: (1) Approaching God, *alpha* and *omega*; (2) Courageous humility, where we fall short; (3) Subsidiarity, authority, and delegation; (4) "Structures of Communion" (Quinn): Unity and diversity in governance; (5) Pastoral experience; (6) Appeal to Scripture; (7) Synodal response.

Element One. GOD: The *Alpha* and the *Omega*, the Beginning and the End

Before anything else, we are living and acting in God. As we have discussed in earlier chapters, it is God's will we seek to discern, both for us as individuals as well as for the Church universal. All of our grand ideas, proposals, goals, objectives, and metrics will be for nothing if we forget the One calling us to be Church to one another.

One of the great blessings of my life was studying Hebrew and serving as a Hebrew linguist in the United States Navy. When our teachers found out that I had spent eight years (high school and college) studying for the priesthood, they decided that we would take a couple of hours each day to study biblical Hebrew in addition to modern Hebrew. Soon we were looking at the word for "truth": אֱמֶת (*eh-meht*). The word consists of three characters (reading right to left): *alef*, *mem*, *tav*. The significance of this word, as our teachers stressed to us, lies in the fact that *alef* is the first character of the Hebrew alphabet, *mem* is in the middle, and *tav* is the final character: it, quite literally, covers the whole range of the alphabet and, symbolically, the whole of human life and experience. אֱמֶת is more than simply "truth" as the opposite of "false"; instead, it is the beginning, middle, and end of life. "Truth" is God's presence and action throughout the whole of life. And, appropriate to our theme, St. Bernard of Clairvaux associates pride with falsehood, humility with truth: about ourselves, relationships with others, and God.[16]

In Scripture, we read passages such as Isaiah 44:6:

> Thus says the LORD, the King of Israel,
> and his Redeemer, the LORD of hosts:
> *I am the first and I am the last*;
> besides me there is no god.

Hebrew wisdom understood the one God to be the God of the whole of life. In the Christian Tradition, we find Revelation 21:5–6: "And the one who was seated on the throne said, 'See, I am making all things new.' Also, he said, 'Write this, for these words are trustworthy and true.' Then he said to me, 'It is done! I am the Alpha and the Omega, the beginning and the end.'" And then 22:12–13: "See, I am coming soon; my reward is with me, to repay according to everyone's work. I am the Alpha and the Omega, the first and the last, the beginning and the end."

The mission of the Church can be seen within this larger context. Consider the Great Commission: "And Jesus came and said to them, 'All authority in heaven and on earth has been given to me. Go therefore and make disciples of all nations, baptizing them in the name of the Father and of the Son and of the Holy Spirit, and teaching them to obey everything that I have commanded you. And remember, I am with you always, to the end of the age'" (Matt 28:18–20). Our God, who is Truth, who is be all and end all, first and last, commands us to spread the good news, to immerse others into a relationship with God. That's our mission, to be—in the words of *Lumen Gentium* 1, "in Christ like a sacrament or as a sign and instrument both of a very closely-knit union with God and of the unity of the whole human race." Therefore, our institutions, organizations, and structures need to be designed to facilitate that mission.

Some years ago, a pastor with his parishioners designed a pastoral plan in which the mission of the parish—evangelization—was to be the prime commitment of every aspect of parish life: sacramental, religious education, finance, administration, social justice, and even maintenance. Each group's budget and planning focused on evangelization, with intentional collaboration between various areas as much as possible. When discussing this approach with others, the pastor would give the parish maintenance staff as an example. The employees had decided that their part of the plan for the coming year would be accessibility: making sure that all entrances were ADA compliant, that the parking lots and other parts of the grounds were as free of obstacles as possible, anything and everything possible so that all people could have more manageable and ready access to all parts of the campus.

Element Two. Courageous Humility: Where We Fall Short

Once the vision is clear, it becomes easier to see where matters stand and where improvements are necessary. Through ongoing discernment, gaps become apparent: the gap between who we are and who we are called to be, between where we are and where we should be, and between what we are doing and what we should be doing. We must acknowledge those gaps and do all we can to close them. An essential element of ecclesial reform is courageous humility. This can be displayed in many ways, including the humble acceptance that we might not have all the answers to life's questions and situations. The Church has a reputation among many people for being arrogant, exclusive, and judgmental. I am not suggesting that we do not have an incredible intellectual and theological heritage. However, our prime concern must be introducing others to Christ and helping to nurture that relationship. I once served with a wonderful priest who shared his view of ministry. "I see our ministry as being like the lenses in eyeglasses. We are invisible; people should be able to look through us and focus on Christ." John Paul II, explicitly addressing the human formation of priests, offers advice that applies to all Christians:

> Of special importance is the capacity to relate to others....This demands that the priest not be arrogant, or quarrelsome, but affable, hospitable, sincere in his words

> and heart, prudent and discreet, generous and ready to serve, capable of opening himself to clear and brotherly relationships and of encouraging the same in others, and quick to understand, forgive and console. People today are often trapped in situations of standardization and loneliness, especially in large urban centers, and they become ever more appreciative of the value of communion. Today this is one of the most eloquent signs and one of the most effective ways of transmitting the Gospel message. (*Pastores Dabo Vobis* 43)[17]

In both *Ut Unum Sint* and *Evangelii Gaudium*, we find John Paul II and Francis, two very different men, acknowledging to themselves and the whole world that things are not what they should be. To paraphrase the words of St. John XXIII, they affirmed that while the truth and substance of something (e.g., Petrine primacy) is one thing, how that primacy is exercised is another. It is significant that in both cases, neither John Paul II nor Francis spoke about the Petrine primacy in a detached, objective way: they both "own" their personal engagement in the process of reform. For most people, the hardest thing in the world to do is to ask for help. Such an act is both courageous and humble. The challenge continues when assistance, feedback, and analysis are offered; will they be accepted and acted upon? Will recommended changes be made?

Element Three. Subsidiarity, Authority, and Delegation

One of the principles of Catholic social teaching is *subsidiarity*, usually described as a principle by which nothing should be done at a higher level that can be done as well or better at a lower level. Finding the lowest appropriate level based on participation and overall effectiveness is a challenge and decision that needs to be made early in the process of reform. This applies in macro terms when considering whether a decision should be made by the federal government or a town council. Similarly, should certain Church decisions be made by the Holy See, or at the parish, deanery, or diocesan level? Sometimes it is asserted that subsidiarity is simply "making decisions at the lowest level," but that is simplistic and incorrect. The *Catechism of the Catholic Church* describes subsidiarity as a principle in which "a community of a higher order should not interfere in the internal life of a community of a lower order, depriving the latter of its functions, but rather should support it in case of need and help to coordinate its activity with the activities of the rest of society, always with a view to the common good" (*CCC* 1883). A higher level of authority should not arrogate to itself those tasks, decisions, and judgments more appropriate to a lower level; the higher level "should not interfere" in such matters. Subsidiarity gives responsibility to individuals and local communities to work toward the common good.

Yves Congar offers further insight in his discussion of "The Center and the Periphery": "Often enough, it is not the hierarchy that takes the initiative....Initiatives often start at the periphery."[18] He points out that "not one single religious order" has ever been established by the central power; all were from the periphery. For example, neither the Holy See nor even the bishop of Assisi founded the Franciscans. They owe their origins directly to the conversion of the young Francesco of Assisi. In the twenty-first century, therefore, what initiatives for mission and reform are already in existence and operating at the periphery? Subsidiarity does not mean solely looking up and down a vertical structural ladder, but to the horizontal fringes as well.

The historical process of the reform of the diaconate began as an exercise in subsidiarity. Throughout the nineteenth and twentieth centuries, discussions and initiatives related to the diaconate took place primarily among the laity. The notion found particular resonance during and following the Second World War. Bishops and other ecclesial leaders did not begin to support the proposal until the late 1950s. On the eve of the Council, more than one hundred proposals regarding a renewed diaconate were submitted by bishops, with additional support developing during the Council itself.[19] The bishops of Vatican II completed their work on a renewed diaconate during the third session (1964).[20] For voting purposes, they divided paragraph 29 into five sections, with votes taken on each section. One vote in particular related to subsidiarity. On October 29, the bishops voted on whether the various episcopal conferences would need to secure the Holy See's permission before ordaining "permanent" deacons or if episcopal conferences enjoyed this competence themselves. They voted 1,523 to 702 that the conferences would need the Holy See's approval, probably because they also voted to open the diaconate to married men. (It is interesting that more than seven hundred bishops didn't see the need for such approval and were willing to decide on their own.) In 1968, when the United States bishops requested and received this authority, they delegated that authority to each diocesan bishop. In other words, even though the entire Conference now had the authority to ordain such deacons, the decision was not imposed on every diocesan bishop. Each bishop could decide for himself whether the ministry of permanent deacons would best serve his diocese. This has remained the practice in the United States for more than fifty years. To borrow Congar's terms, we can say that the diaconate's renewal appeared on the peripheries and moved to the center.

Element Four. Quinn's "Structures of Communion": Unity and Diversity in Governance

In his books, Archbishop Quinn wrote about particular topics and structures that relate directly to the exercise of the papacy. His second book refers specifically to the synodal systems of the Church as structures of communion. He writes,

> Communion in the Church is not simply a feeling or an abstraction. It is a manifestation of the mystery of the Most Holy Trinity revealed in Christ Jesus our Lord and accomplished through the Spirit of the Father and the Son. Yet as an earthly and visible reality, communion requires a structure. In this book, I deal with the fact that the Church from its inception thought of itself as a communion and then expand upon the development of the great historic structures of communion: synods, patriarchates, and councils. My point is that these collegial structures of communion have opened a path today for the Latin Church to remedy what Joseph Ratzinger once called "extreme centralization."[21]

As we evaluate structures, the foundational question is how well the system in question enhances *communio*. Building on Quinn's analysis of synods, patriarchates, and councils, we can add other structures: for example, the reinstitution of ancient deaconries, the development of deanery councils, and perhaps the creation of totally new systems. It is helpful to recall the archbishop's fundamental analysis that "in the exercise of the papacy two things, more than others, are the greatest problem for the Church and for Christian unity. The first is centralization, the other, the need for reform of the Roman Curia."[22] The critical point with diversity in governance is that one size need not fit all circumstances. In fact, not only does one size not fit all in cases of governance, the demands of a global Church require a diversity of approaches based on culture, geography, intersectionality, and many other factors. The Church is one, of course, but this unity in faith does not equate to uniformity of practice, including governance systems. One may point to the Eastern Catholic Churches, whose governance, discipline, and sacramental practice vary significantly from the Latin Church. There is no reason why such unity in diversity should not be explored in the Latin Church. As we saw only too well in the Synod for the Amazon, Christian life is experienced differently in different parts of the world, different parts of the same country, and sometimes even in different parts of the same city or town. Closely related to subsidiarity, this element tailors the structure to permit the most appropriate governance for carrying out the institution's mission.

For centuries, governance has been associated with—and exercised by—the clergy (bishops, deacons, and presbyters). Laypersons are said to "cooperate" in the exercise of governance.[23] In the canonical Tradition, only those who possessed the *potestas ordinis* could exercise the *potestas iurisdictionis*. This association needs to be analyzed in depth. Do the current and future needs of the Church still require this linkage between clergy and jurisdiction? It seems unlikely.

Element Five. Pastoral Experience

As mentioned above, Archbishop Quinn cites three interrelated concerns in addressing the pastoral challenge of welcoming Jewish converts into the earliest Christian communion: pastoral experience, appeal to Scripture, and synodal response. We will consider each in turn. Pastoral experience is evaluated in dialogue with doctrine. In this case, the doctrinal understanding was straightforward: to become a disciple of Christ demanded that a person do so through the doorway of Judaism. Therefore, "conversion" was a two-stage process: a person first became a Jew who then became a Christian. Paul and the leaders in Jerusalem all knew the doctrine well. But Paul's concrete pastoral experience (and later, Peter's) revealed that the Spirit was already active in these converts' lives and that becoming Jewish was unnecessary. Therefore, a blind application of the former practice was inadequate and insufficient to solve the problem.

> It was through and in the pastoral experience of the exemplary Christian life of the Gentiles whom Paul baptized without the requirement of circumcision, and of the outpouring of the Spirit on Cornelius and his Gentile friends as soon as Peter had preached the Gospel to them (Acts 10), that a singularly important doctrinal development took place in the Church....In this New Testament concern, the plan of God for the Church was discerned only after long, arduous search and controversy.[24]

We must face the future with the same willingness to engage in a similar "long, arduous search and controversy." An appeal to doctrine in isolation from pastoral experience is both facile and sterile. Just as those early Christians, we today must engage in the sometimes-messy business of discernment and "humble listening for the voice of God."[25]

Element Six. Appeal to Scripture

In a now-classic text, the bishops of Vatican II remind us that the Church has the single goal of extending the mission of Christ. "And Christ entered this world to give witness to the truth, to rescue and not to sit in judgment, to serve and not to be served....To carry out such a task, the Church has always had the duty of scrutinizing the signs of the times and of interpreting them in the light of the Gospel" (*GS* 3–4). We must exercise caution not simply to adapt to contemporary crises alone, but to do so always "in the light of the

Gospel." In the example of the Jerusalem gathering, James does precisely that within the assembly (Acts 15:12–21, citing Amos 9:11–12). After they had listened to Peter and Paul, James connects what they had just heard with the prophet Amos, noting that their pastoral experience and witness "agreed with the prophets." It is only then, and because of this interplay between experience and Scripture that James goes on to say, "Therefore I have reached the decision that we should not trouble those Gentiles who are turning to God" (Acts 15:19).

As Archbishop Quinn wrote, "The pastoral experience of Peter and Paul was not an independent factor. They were conscious of the normative character of the Scriptures. Consequently, it was the painstaking discernment of the pastoral experience in light of the Scriptures and discernment of the Scriptures in light of the pastoral experience, which led to clarity about the place of the Mosaic Law and the absolute centrality of Christ."[26]

Element Seven. Synodal Response

The next element identified by Archbishop Quinn is the synodal response undertaken by the Jerusalem leadership to decide the question. There was no appeal to a single authority, such as Simon Peter or James; instead, the question was placed before a group of leaders. I have always been struck by some of the similarities between this account and the notion of the Jewish *minyan* (מִנְיָן). The minyan is an assembly of adult Jewish men (some congregations today include women) for certain acts of worship or other proceedings. This is often a group of ten people, although a community might determine different numbers as the situation demands. In rabbinical literature, there is also the idea that God is present within the assembly when a minyan assembles. In this light, consider the phrasing of the letter sent from Jerusalem to Paul's converts. The decision made by the leadership was not reached through human deliberation alone: "For it has seemed good to the Holy Spirit and to us to impose on you no further burden than these essentials" (Acts 15:28). And, of course, as Jewish Christians, they would also still be thinking of Christ's words, "Again, truly I tell you, if two of you agree on earth about anything you ask, it will be done for you by my Father in heaven. For where two or three are gathered in my name, I am there among them" (Matt 18:19–20). It seems reasonable to suggest that the first leaders of the Church, Jewish men, naturally fell back on their familiarity with the minyan to resolve specific issues. Indeed, Acts describes a gathering in which Paul, Peter, James, and the others are supremely confident that the best way to find a solution was to use this synodal approach.

Archbishop Quinn observes, "[Pastoral questions] were not to be settled by one apostle alone or by one independent church community. The questions were to be resolved in communion with the whole Church."[27] Notice Paul's humility in submitting the question to the whole Church. Certainly, he had his opinion on the matter! However, he knew that the communion of the Church demanded that he place the question to the entire assembly. This realization that God is present in the *communio* of the whole Church and that it is within this *communio* that deliberations should take place and decisions be made has influenced the Church ever since. Regional synods, general councils of the Church, and even the shared governance models of monastic life and counsels of canons all reflect this approach. Today we might include diocesan, deanery, and parish pastoral councils, all of which reflect this fundamental conciliar model. As is well known, current policy is that these contemporary structures are consultative in nature, not determinative. It is necessary to evaluate these and similar structures with a view to sharing decision-making in a model more reflective of the original synods and councils.

This brings us to the contemporary Synod of Bishops and Pope Francis.

Synods, Synodality, and Pope Francis

Pope Francis has made synodality a cornerstone of his ecclesiology. As we will see shortly, he has declared synodality to be a "constitutive element of the Church." In other words, we cannot be Church without synodality. Where did this idea come from? Not only does the history of the Church show the necessity of regional, provincial, and general councils, the current Synod of Bishops is a direct result of the work of the world's bishops at the Second Vatican Council.

As the bishops came to the end of the Council, they realized that their four years of deliberation and collegial decision-making was something they did not want to surrender. Obviously, they could not assemble in full, general Council every year! Therefore, they recommended to Pope Paul VI that he establish a permanent office in the Vatican to coordinate and support regular synods of bishops.

St. Paul responded quickly. On September 14, 1965, as the bishops gathered for the beginning of the fourth session of the Council, he announced that, effective the next day, September 15, he was establishing the Synod of Bishops. A month later, the Council fathers referred to the new body in its decree on the ministry of bishops, *Christus Dominus* (October 28, 1965). They described its purpose: to "render more effective assistance to the supreme pastor of the Church in a deliberative body which will be called by the proper name of Synod of Bishops."

Popes have adapted the synod over the years, and it now appears within the legal structure of the Church, with norms provided in both the Code of Canon Law for the Latin Church and the Codes of Canons for the Eastern Catholic Churches. Popes Paul VI, John Paul II, Benedict, and now Francis have addressed the purposes and inner workings of the synod. His apostolic constitution *Episcopalis Communio* (September 15, 2018) echoed many of the themes we have discussed in this chapter. He teaches,

> Although structurally it [the Synod] is essentially configured as an episcopal body, this does not mean that the Synod exists separately from the rest of the faithful. On the contrary, it is a suitable instrument to give voice to the entire People of God, specifically via the Bishops, established by God as "authentic guardians, interpreters and witnesses of the faith of the whole Church," demonstrating, from one Assembly to another, that it is an eloquent expression of synodality as a "*constitutive element of the Church*" [emphasis added]. (no. 6)[28]

The first synod took place in 1967, and since then every pope (except John Paul I) has used the Synod of Bishops on a regular basis, assembling the synod in ordinary general assemblies, extraordinary assemblies, and special assemblies.

On October 9–10, 2021, Pope Francis opened a three-phased Synod of Bishops. This is the 16th Ordinary General Assembly of the Synod, and its focus is "for a synodal Church: communion, participation and mission." The first phase calls on every diocesan bishop to initiate his own diocesan synod on October 17, 2021, beginning the diocesan phase of the synodal process. The second phase is continental in scope beginning in 2022, and the third phase will be universal, with the formal ending being celebrated in October 2023. This multiyear "synod on synodality" will no doubt raise significant issues and—we dare to hope—substantive recommendations for the ongoing renewal of the living Church. If synodality is truly to be a constitutive element of the Church called for by Pope Francis, it is essential that all voices be heard, that the concerns of those voices be heard, and, finally, that concrete actions be taken as a result.

This is far more than a multiphase exercise in "pastoral planning," which will come to an end with the formal ceremonies of October 2023. Rather, synodality as a constitutive element of the Church must be part of the *novus habitus mentis* we have already discussed, a new way of being the true and proper *communio* that should be the Church. Shortly before he opened the synod, Pope Francis, the Bishop of Rome, addressed the faithful of his own diocese. He taught them that "the theme of synodality is not the chapter of a treatise on ecclesiology, much less a fashion, a slogan or the new term to be used or exploited in our meetings. No! Synodality expresses the nature of the Church, its form, its style, its mission."[29]

True synodality cannot be something that is done every few years by a relative handful of people (and certainly not just by the clergy), with its documented results filed away for further study by scholars. A constitutive synodal approach must be part and parcel of everyday ecclesial relationships and decision-making. For this to happen, all members of the Church—laity, religious, and clergy—must participate in the process, a process that is open and humble enough to listen and courageous enough to act.

Conclusion

Evangelization is entirely about the "Other." The message we proclaim is not ours; it is God's. We proclaim God's word to others. We proclaim God's word, not to hear the sound of our own voices, or out of our own need, but to introduce others to Christ—and then back out of the scene and get off the stage. "If I speak in the tongues of mortals and of angels but do not have love, I am a noisy gong or a clanging cymbal" (1 Cor 13:1). This demands humility and the acceptance of the fact that evangelization is never about us. It's about God and the Other. As my priest friend mentioned above, we should be invisible, the medium through which we facilitate the connection between God and the Other. Evangelization should be an act of humility by Christians who are themselves humble.

Our structures exist to help us with our mission of evangelization. Therefore, as extensions of ourselves, our institutions should be structured to operate with pastoral humility. They do not exist for their own good; they are not ends in themselves. Pope Francis has encouraged us to examine all our structures with a critical eye to ensure that they are still serving the needs of evangelization effectively. If they are not, they should be renewed or replaced. If there are needs not being met, new structures might be established to meet those needs. For example, in one diocese in Germany, deacon candidates are asked to identify a pastoral need not being met in their hometowns. They are directed to do whatever they can to meet that need. In one case, a candidate realized there was no facility offering day care for the children of working single parents. He set up various teams to assess the issues related to setting up such a facility, and within a short time, those teams created a self-sustaining day-care center. This facility is open to all who need its services, although its leadership is primarily Catholic. In the opinion of local religious leaders, this facility is a powerful tool of evangelization because the faith is expressed in concrete pastoral care.

The Council and Pope Paul VI renewed the diaconate to exercise just such creative pastoral responses. While there are traditional roles for the deacon to carry out, the Council recognized that the needs of the contemporary world demanded new approaches. John Paul II, recalling his time as a Council father, observed, "A deeply felt need in the decision to re-establish the permanent diaconate was and is that of a greater and more direct presence of Church ministers in the various spheres of the family, work, school, etc., in addition to existing pastoral structures."[30] The key to this brief passage lies in the papal et cetera! As the "eyes and ears" of the bishop on behalf of the whole Church, deacons are expected to see needs that others miss or ignore, and have the skills to encourage, inspire, and support creative ways to meet those needs.

I have already cited John Paul II's *Pastores Dabo Vobis*. Again, in words directed at priestly formation, he describes behavior that applies to all disciples: "It is necessary that following the example of Jesus who 'knew what was in humanity' (Jn. 2:25; cf. 8:3–11), the priest should be able to know the depths of the human heart, to perceive difficulties and problems, to make meeting and dialogue easy, to create trust and cooperation, to express serene and objective judgments" (*PDV* 43). Our structures should facilitate those behaviors, and our exercise of leadership should itself be kenotic and unlike the way secular authority is sometimes exercised. Rather, "the greatest among you must become like the youngest, and the leader like one who serves. For who is greater, the one who is at the table or the one who serves? Is it not the one at the table? But I am among you as one who serves" (Luke 22:26–27).[31]

Human life means change. The institutions we create change, even our Church institutions. Of course, there are differences between our secular and religious structures. Making changes to our systems is more than a corporate restructuring, such as one might find at a bank or other secular corporation. For believers, believing as we do that God is with us, God's will is the foundation, inspiration, and end of our human strivings. Some years ago, during the homily at a diocesan Chrism Mass, the bishop addressed his priests, challenging them to confront the demands of today's Church. "The parish you are in today is not the same parish it was fifty years ago; the parish you lead today is not the same parish you grew up in; the parish of today is not the church of tomorrow." In humility, we embrace change as part of constant conversion, creating, adapting, and renewing ourselves and our structures to carry out our mission of evangelization. In the words of Vatican II, we serve "as a leaven and as a kind of soul for human society as it is to be renewed in Christ and transformed into God's family."

CHAPTER FOUR

STRENGTHENED BY SACRAMENTAL GRACE

The Sacramentality of the Diaconate

Introduction

Deacons should be icons of the Church's humility. How the Church faces the world in the future will determine its effectiveness in evangelization, and that face should be one of humility. While the virtue of humility is not coterminal with the concept of *diakonia*, it is a vital component. You cannot have true *diakonia* without humility. Deacons should be a "sign and instrument" of humility, or as Sts. Paul VI and John Paul II wrote, the "animators of the Church's *diakonia*"[1] and "the Church's service sacramentalized."[2] In short, the sacrament of the diaconate is, among other things, a sacrament of humility. In the words of *Lumen Gentium* 29, deacons serve *gratia etenim sacramentali roborati*: strengthened by sacramental grace. But the questions remain: Why does the Church ordain deacons? Specifically, why do we sacramentalize *diakonia* through sacred ordination? Why should the Church sacramentalize the *diakonia* that we all already owe to each other as creatures of a loving God whether or not we are ordained? This chapter will explore several essential elements responding to those questions. The bottom line is that this is a matter of grace.

Like most deacons, I spent many years serving in various lay ministries before ordination. This included serving three years as a lay parish life coordinator, assigned by the bishop under c. 517 §2. I even wrote a couple of books on lay ministry.[3] I was ordained a deacon over thirty years ago while still on active duty in the U.S. Navy. Immediately after ordination, I was sent to Okinawa by the Navy, and it was several years before we returned to the United States.

Upon our return, I reconnected with a good friend and former teacher, a woman religious I had not seen in many years. In catching up on each other's lives, we talked about our families and our professional and ministerial experiences. Finally, I mentioned that I was now a deacon, and suddenly she became very quiet. She said, in a low, sad voice, "Why did you do that?" I was surprised by her question and her evident distress. She reminded me of that past lay ministry. Why in the world, she asked, did I pursue ordination? "You don't need ordination to serve." Decades later, I participated in a panel discussion on the diaconate in Chicago. A member of the audience stood and asked, "Why does the Church need to ordain anyone anymore, especially deacons?" In her question, I heard an echo of my friend's question from all those years before.

This chapter will examine several aspects of the sacramental nature of the diaconate as a way of answering that question.

The Ancient Diaconate: Christ and the Bishop

The Church has always understood the diaconate to be a major order of ministry, from the earliest references to Scripture and the Tradition, throughout history, and in the contemporary magisterium. From the beginning, the diaconate (not unlike other ministries) has been a matter of the Holy Spirit and grace. In the biblical passage most frequently associated with the diaconate, the Twelve tell the Hellenists in Acts 6 to select "seven men of good standing, full of the Spirit and of wisdom, whom we may appoint to this task" (v. 3). One of the Seven chosen, Stephen, is described as "a man full of faith and the Holy Spirit." The apostles "prayed and laid their hands" on them, and there we have the first scriptural account of an ordering of ministry. However, contemporary biblical analysis challenges the traditional view that Acts 6 is about the diaconate itself. None of the Seven are explicitly referred to as office holders called "deacons," and the service they are to provide is not called *diakonia*. As crucial as this passage is concerning ordered ministry in the ancient Church, it is the later Tradition of the Church that will make the direct association of the Seven with the diaconate.

Grace is the sacramental foundation of the diaconate. *Lumen Gentium* 29 unequivocally refers to the deacon's ordination giving the ordinand the strength to carry out his functions, which the bishops characterize as "supremely necessary for the life of the Church." Historically, the Church has consistently recognized deacons as a major order of ministry, one in which the deacon is "in the ministry of Jesus Christ" and the closest collaborator with the bishop, who is "in the ministry of God the Father." The following highlights summarize several key patristic sources.[4]

Perhaps the most singular feature of the ordination of a deacon is found in what does *not* happen. At a bishop's ordination, all the bishops present lay hands on the new bishop; at the ordination of a presbyter, all the presbyters present lay hands on the new presbyter. At the ordination of a deacon, *only* the ordaining prelate lays hands on him. This unique act is explained in two principle sources in our Tradition: the *Apostolic Tradition* of circa AD 215, often associated with St. Hippolytus, and the much later *Statuta Ecclesiae Antiquae* of circa 450.

The *Apostolic Tradition* of the early third century is the only surviving order of the Western Church.[5] In its section on the ordination of a deacon, we find the following instruction:

> When the deacon is ordained, this is the reason why the bishop alone shall lay his hands upon him: he is not ordained to the priesthood but into the service of the bishop [*non ad sacerdotium sed in ministerio episcopi*] and to carry out the bishop's commands.[6]

The "service" the deacon is to provide is clearly laid out, without any confusion or speculation: the deacon is explicitly ordained to serve the bishop and to carry out his commands. The ancient diaconate was a powerful ministry that worked intimately with the bishops in diverse ways. They served in the bishop's liturgy and as catechists, as advisors to the bishops, as leaders in serving the community's needs, as legates from one bishop to another, and sometimes as the representative of the bishop at councils. The Syrian *Didascalia Apostolorum* gives us the familiar description of the deacon as the bishop's hearing, mouth, heart, and soul. It also offers a remarkable picture of the deacon and his bishop as "one soul in two bodies."[7] This multifaceted service was so intimately connected to the bishop that it was most frequently the deacon who would become the bishop's successor upon his death.

Even more striking is the association of the ministry of the deacon with the ministry of Christ. St. Ignatius of Antioch wrote that deacons "represent Jesus Christ, just as the bishop has the role of the Father....Let the deacons (my special favorites) be entrusted with the ministry of Jesus Christ who was with the Father from eternity and appeared at the end of the world."[8] The *Didascalia Apostolorum* instructs deacons to act like Christ: "Accordingly you deacons also should behave in such a way that, if your ministry obliges you to lay down your lives for a brother, you should do so....If the Lord of heaven and earth served us and suffered and sustained everything on our behalf, should not this be done for our brothers all the more by us, since we are imitators of him and have been given the place of Christ?"[9]

As church structures continued to evolve, so too did the roles of bishop and presbyter. Increasingly presbyters were placed in charge of local communities while bishops focused increasingly on "central administration." If a bishop assigned a deacon to one of these local parishes, an issue emerged. Was the deacon still serving the bishop or the presbyter? For this reason, the ancient teaching was adapted, unintentionally adding more confusion. In the *Statuta Ecclesiae Antiquae* and its derivatives, written some 250 years after the *Apostolic Tradition*, we find the edited instruction that "deacons are ordained, not to the priesthood but to service" (*non ad sacerdotium sed ad ministerium*). Unfortunately, this *ministerium* remains undefined and open ended. Now the deacon could be expected to act for the bishop, for the presbyter, for just about anyone! His unique connection to the bishop is now almost broken; the word *ministerium* was now devoid of any specific content, whereas before, it was highly focused on the bishop.

The diaconate gradually became part of the *cursus honorum*, the penultimate stage before ordination to the presbyterate. The long-standing practice of conferring the stole to ordinands to the three orders of deacon, presbyter, and bishop reflects each order's sacramental character. It is clear that from the beginning, the diaconate has always been understood as a sacred order. However, beginning at least by the twelfth century and especially following the Council of Trent, the priesthood became the primary model of ordained ministry and the goal of all subordinate ordinations. In the words of James Barnett, an "omnivorous priesthood" emerged, and the diaconate ceased being "a full and equal order."[10]

Even as the deacon gradually and increasingly became associated with and subordinate to the presbyter, the connection with the bishop never entirely disappeared. It is still the bishop alone who ordains the deacon, and it is on behalf of the bishop and under his authority that the deacon acts. On a popular level, however, that unique relationship is tenuous at best. For example, I was once in the sacristy vesting for Mass along with a newly ordained young priest. As we chatted, for some unknown reason, Father mentioned, with emphasis, that *his* faculties came from the bishop. His tone caught my attention, and I asked him where he thought *my* faculties came from. Father responded with assurance that deacons' faculties came from the pastor, and that only priests' faculties came from the bishop. I corrected him gently, but clearly: clerical faculties come from either the law itself or from the diocesan bishop (or religious superior). Father (and I am sure, others) had mistaken ideas about faculties, but even more important, about the bishop's relationship to the deacon.

Until the Second Vatican Council, for well over a millennium, deacons exercised their ministry rarely, if at all, and when they did, it was usually restricted to the liturgy. By the twentieth century, under the 1917 Pio-Benedictine Code of Canon Law, deacons exercised functions such as distributing holy communion, witnessing marriages, performing baptisms, but only as extraordinary ministers.

The law intended to provide a kind of on-the-job training for these young deacons about to be ordained to the presbyterate. The diaconate was a preparation for the priesthood; in fact, until relatively recently, the term *ministerial priesthood* applied—at least in a nontechnical way—to all three of the former major orders, especially the diaconate and the presbyterate, with subdiaconate and diaconate seen as lesser and partial participations in the one ministerial priesthood.[11]

For example, in the late 1970s, I was invited to attend a meeting of a diocesan presbyterate in the Midwest. The bishop spoke to his priests about the imminent ordination of their first class of permanent deacons, all of whom were married men. After the bishop's presentation, he opened up the meeting for questions. One of the senior pastors rose to ask, "After this weekend's ordination, Bishop, are we opening the door to a married priesthood in our diocese?" The bishop responded, "You already know the answer to that, Bob. That's exactly what this ordination means. After this weekend, we will have a married priesthood here." This terminology was not unusual in those days. For many people, priesthood ordination was the only "real" ordination, the only one that mattered sacramentally, and that attitude persists in some circles even today. The Pio-Benedictine Code of Canon Law (c. 817) directed that bishops only ordain men "who intend to ascend to the priesthood, and of whom one can reasonably expect that they will be worthy priests." Deacons were no longer understood by their relationships with Christ and with their bishops, but as an abridged and preparatory phase of the priesthood. This was the situation well into the twentieth century. For more than a millennium, theologians did not develop a fulsome theology of the diaconate because the Church did not need one. Any kind of theology of the diaconate was simply an abridged theology of the priesthood.

Recovering a Theology of Diaconate

However, theological discourse on the nature of the presbyterate has been developing steadily over two millennia, especially since the twelfth century. As we have seen, the diaconate has a different history. Because of the diminution of the diaconate in the Middle Ages, we must leapfrog over the period of its existence as a transitory order and return to its "golden age" as a permanent order of ministry. As we have seen, the deacon as described in the patristic literature is never dependent upon the presbyterate, nor is he ever described as a priest-in-training. Through his ordination by his bishop, the deacon participates in the kenotic ministry of Christ under the pastoral leadership of the bishop. This is the logical starting point for a contemporary sacramental understanding of the deacon.

One theologian who pondered a renewed and permanent diaconate was the Belgian Benedictine Augustinus Kerkvoorde. In 1962, on the eve of the Council, he wrote that a theology of the diaconate had not been needed before, since the diaconate for more than a millennium had been more of a "theoretical" function on the road to the priesthood and, as such, didn't "arouse a demand for a thoroughly elaborated dogma about the diaconate."[12] All of that changed with Vatican II and St. Paul VI.

Kerkvoorde predicted that if the Council restored the diaconate as a stable and permanent order, all that would change. Theologies of the diaconate "will undoubtedly spring up like mushrooms….There will be plenty of authors and publishers who will routinely pounce on this unexpected inheritance."[13] One can argue that a body of research on the diaconate has developed since its renewal, although no one would describe it as springing up like mushrooms! Even more disappointing is that little work has been done to integrate this research into a systematic treatment of ministry in general and the sacrament of holy orders in particular. Contemporary theologies of ministry, for example, often ignore the topic of the diaconate altogether or treat it as some kind of aberration. It's long past time to add the "mushrooms" to the stew.

The renewed diaconate offers a complementary expression of ordained ministry. The diaconate is not a lesser form of priesthood, not an elevated form of lay ministry, and not a part-time "auxiliary" to the sacerdotal orders. While connected to the sacerdotal orders, the diaconate's nature and ends have their own unique features. This section reviews several texts that trace these features: distinguishing power to act from strength to serve, the configuration to Christ the

Servant, and the deacon's unique and sacramental relationship to the bishop and the bishop's ministry of *diakonia*. All of this flows from the sacramental grace of the deacon's ordination.

Pope Pius XII opened the door to a contemporary discussion of the sacramentality of the diaconate in 1947. For quite some time, theologians and Church officials had questioned the essential components for the validity of ordination. Specifically, was the handing of the instruments of office to the ordinand necessary for sacramental validity? Since at least the thirteenth century, the *traditio instrumentorum* had been an important part of the Latin rite of ordination. However, the Eastern Catholic Churches did not include a similar ceremony. In the apostolic constitution *Sacramentum Ordinis*, Pius decided the question. He explained, "Over time, according to varying local and temporal conditions, various rites have been added in its conferring; this was surely the reason why theologians began to inquire which of the rites used in conferring the Sacrament of Order belong to its essence, and which do not" (no. 2).[14]

For our purposes, it is significant that the pope included the diaconate unequivocally as a sacred order of ministry; there is no question about it being something less than a completely sacramental order. The details also provide an insight into why this is so. Pius decreed that "the matter, and the only matter, of the Sacred Orders of the Diaconate, the Priesthood, and the Episcopacy is the imposition of hands" (*SO* 4). While the matter is identical for each order, there is a distinct form for each. The prayer of consecration for a deacon included the sentence "Receive the Holy Spirit for strength [*ad robur*], and to resist the devil and his temptations, in the name of the Lord." Then come the words decreed by the pope to be the form of the sacrament: "Send forth upon him, O Lord, we pray, the Holy Spirit, by whom he may be strengthened by the gift of your sevenfold grace in the faithful carrying out of the work of service" (*SO* 5).[15] Pius continues that the words of the form "determine the application of this matter, [and] which univocally signify the sacramental effects—namely the power of Order and the grace of the Holy Spirit" (*SO* 5).

The emphasis for the diaconate is the strength that is conferred upon the ordinand. This sacramental "strength" is distinct from the "power" conferred on presbyters and bishops. Before the liturgical reforms following Vatican II, ordinations to the presbyterate and episcopate spoke of the power to act: the power to preside at the Eucharist, for example, or the power to hear confessions. The ordination to the episcopate included the power to ordain. This has never been the case with the deacon, who is ordained "not to the priesthood but to the service of the bishop." Reflecting on his own diaconate ordination in March 1949, Thomas Merton pondered ordination *ad robur*, writing, "The first thing about the diaconate is that it is *big*. The more I think about it, the more I realize that it is a *major* Order. You are supposed to be the strength of the Church. You receive the Holy Spirit *ad robur*, not only for yourself but to support the whole Church."[16] In the same diary passage, Merton observes that the Holy Spirit given *ad robur* at the deacon's ordination is the Spirit of the martyrs. The strength of ordination is to help the deacon lay it all on the line as a public witness to—and in imitation of—the kenotic Christ.

Understood in this way, we return to the christological insights of the patristic writers regarding the diaconate. To say, with Bishop Ignatius, that deacons "represent Jesus Christ…[and] are entrusted with the ministry of Jesus Christ" takes on a deeper meaning. The *Didascalia Apostolorum* is even more explicit in addressing the ministry and life of deacons: "If your ministry obliges you to lay down your lives for a brother, you should do so….If the Lord of heaven and earth served us and suffered and sustained everything on our behalf, should not this be done for our brothers all the more by us, since we are imitators of him and have been given the place of Christ?"

Vatican II and the Diaconate: A Matter of Grace

The question of a renewed diaconate had been the topic of research in Western Europe beginning in the nineteenth century and, in a more intentional manner, following the Second World War. The complex history behind the renewal of the diaconate at the Council is well documented.[17] A popular preconciliar catechism in the United States defined a sacrament as "an outward sign, instituted by Christ, to give grace." Ordination, as a sacrament, is a public act grounded in the priesthood and diaconate of Christ, which gives God's strength and support, both to the ordinand and to the whole Church. In the Dogmatic Constitution on the Church (*Lumen Gentium*), the bishops of the Second Vatican Council opened their treatment of the diaconate with the words,

> At a lower level of the hierarchy are deacons, upon whom hands are imposed "not unto the priesthood, but unto a ministry of service." For strengthened by sacramental grace, in communion with the bishop and his group of priests, they serve in a diaconate of the liturgy, of the Word, and charity to the people of God. (*LG* 29)

Grace is the free and undeserved help of God, help to live out our vocation to be children of God and partakers of the divine nature and eternal life. It is a participation in the very life of God. God acts through all of the Church's sacraments, imparting graces specific to each sacrament, divine gifts from the Holy Spirit that empower us to work for others' salvation and build up the Body of Christ, the Church. There are sacramental graces, gifts proper to the various sacraments. In the Tradition, the sacramental grace associated with ordination has often been associated with a "transfer of power" from the ordaining bishop to the ordinand. This led to the development of concepts such as *potestas ordinis* and *potestas iurisdictionis*, the powers of order and jurisdiction. For example, in earlier editions of the pontifical, the ordination of a priest contained a prayer that referred to receiving the power (*potestas ordinis*) to offer the sacrifice; possessing this power made him capable (*capax*) to exercise the ministry of governance (*potestas iurisdictionis*).

The bishops of Vatican II moved the Church in a different direction. In the revised pontifical, for example, ordinations are less about a "transfer of power" and more about establishing new relationships in the power of the Holy Spirit. Some people still struggle with this paradigm shift. When looking at the presbyterate and episcopate, one can discern areas of empowerment through which the presbyter or bishop can act in ways he could not before ordination. The deacon who could not preside at the Eucharist the day before his priestly ordination can now, as a presbyter, do so. The priest who, the day before his episcopal ordination, could not ordain, is now, as a bishop, able to do so. There is no analogous "power" associated with the sacramental grace of diaconal ordination. This perceived "lack" often leads some to question the need for deacons to be ordained in the first place. And yet, as we shall see, the Council fathers saw a necessary connection between the diaconate and the sacramental grace of holy orders.

I have written elsewhere and more extensively about the development of the various proposals considered by the Council and the conciliar discussions and debates leading to the decision to renew the diaconate.[18] Here, I want to spend some time with the Council's view of the diaconate itself. How did the bishops envision a renewed diaconate? After all, with rare but significant exceptions in the nineteenth century, there had been no "permanent deacons" for centuries; none of the bishops at the Council had any direct experience with a permanent diaconate that could inform their deliberations.

During the antepreparatory period, the world's bishops submitted nearly nine thousand proposed topics for the Council's agenda. One hundred and one proposals addressed a renewal of a diaconate permanently exercised. Ninety *vota* favored it; eleven were against it. Seventy-one bishops listed functions that such deacons would exercise.[19] In addition to sacramental and liturgical functions, some interesting details include the desire that deacons might serve as ministers of extreme unction (the sacrament of the sick) and that they could "bring solace to the faithful in extreme situations." Administration of the Church's temporal goods, long associated with the diaconate, is prominent on the proposed lists of functions. Still, the single most essential functions listed are those of official preaching and teaching. Of significance is the lack of any reference to ministries of charity, so often identified with deacons. This suggests that the conciliar bishops had a much broader understanding of *diakonia* than many other people, even in our own day.

During the Council, the bishops discussed and debated the diaconate from October 4 to 16, 1963. Two bishops, in particular, offer critical insights for our topic: Cardinal Julius Döpfner of Munich-Freising[20] and Cardinal Leo-Josef Suenens of Malines-Brussels.[21] Döpfner was the first speaker in favor of a renewed diaconate. He was only forty-nine when the Council began in 1962, but he had extensive pastoral experience. Ordained a priest for the Diocese of Würzburg, by the age of thirty-five, he was the bishop of his diocese. He then served as bishop of Berlin before becoming the archbishop of Munich-Freising in 1961. Döpfner strongly urged acceptance of the proposals to renew the diaconate. He offered several crucial points.

Some bishops had objected to the inclusion of the topic of the diaconate in a dogmatic document, considering it merely a disciplinary matter. Döpfner, however, supported its inclusion because the sacrament of orders is a dogmatic issue, a part of the divine law, and therefore an essential part of the nature of the Church. He pointed out that the diaconate, ever since Trent, had been understood as part of the sacramental priesthood. Döpfner pointed out that many persons, many of them married, were already serving the Church in diaconal roles. In his intervention, he asked, "Why should these people be denied the grace of the sacrament?"[22] He affirmed the value of clerical celibacy, but he also declared that celibacy should not be an obstacle to the evolution of beneficial ways to serve that may be necessary. In his view, the fundamental reason for ordination was the grace associated with the sacrament. The sacramental grace of ordination will support, nurture, and strengthen the ordinand to carry out the various diaconal roles assigned. If persons are acting in diaconal ways in the name of the Church, they are entitled to the divine grace of the sacrament.

Such a view seems to answer those who say, "You do not need to be ordained to serve." This statement is, of course, accurate and valid. One does not need to be ordained to serve since we are all called to serve in virtue of baptism. However, Vatican II spoke of the ordained (especially with regard to the sacerdotal orders) acting both *in persona Christi* and *in nomine Ecclesiae*, in the person of Christ and in the Church's name. These terms should not be limited to the priesthood. As a sacred order, the diaconate also shares in the bishop's responsibility—what Vatican II refers to as the bishop's *diakonia*—for the people of God. For this reason, the Council reiterates the right for the deacon to be "strengthened by sacramental grace" (*LG* 29; *Ad Gentes* 16).[23] What's more, the Church deserves the grace of the sacrament being poured out on the entire Church through ordination, a point made explicitly by Cardinal Leo-Josef Suenens of Malines-Brussels.

Cardinal Suenens gave the most comprehensive intervention on the diaconate during the discussions. Another brilliant and pastorally experienced leader, Suenens became a priest for the Archdiocese of Malines-Brussels at twenty-three. In 1940, serving as the vice-rector of the University of Louvain, he became acting rector when the Nazis arrested and killed the incumbent for refusing to provide them with student and faculty information. He also refused to collaborate, and the Nazis scheduled his execution. Fortunately, the allies liberated Belgium the week before his execution could be carried out. After the war, he became a bishop and eventually a cardinal shortly before the Council opened. A close friend and trusted collaborator of both St. Pope John XXIII and St. Pope Paul VI, Suenens was an important influence on the Council and its work.

Before the Council began, he had already included a renewed diaconate as part of his hopes for the Council. During the antepreparatory phase, Suenens had indicated his support in a letter of November 10, 1959. First alluding to the 1957 address by Pius XII in which the pope had observed that the question of restoring the diaconate was not yet ripe but was worthy of continued attention, Suenens wrote that the Council would provide a most appropriate opportunity to highlight the question. He noted that a diaconate distinct and separate from the priesthood, a state in which married men might participate, would be part of a movement of overall renewal in the Church. He pointed out that the diaconate was one of several ministries consistently and traditionally recognized in the life of the Church.

Suenens wrote that the Church has a command from the Lord to proclaim the gospel to all peoples and baptize all nations. This mission is impossible without the participation of all the faithful, and he highlighted the deacon as a minister of this evangelization. The deacon could serve in a variety of ways as pastoral needs dictate. He would write later, "Undoubtedly, this decision [to renew the permanent diaconate] was made for pastoral reasons, but these were not the only factors operative. The restoration of a Permanent Diaconate would find its fundamental clarification and justification in the sacramental character of the diaconate itself."[24] During the conciliar debate, Suenens articulated this "sacramental character of the diaconate."

He began by outlining the theological principles grounding the diaconate. Citing Scripture, the patristics, Tradition, and the liturgical books of East and West, he spoke of the many charisms evident throughout the Church. Many of these charisms are distinct from priesthood, he said, established to provide direct assistance to the bishop in the care of the poor and the nurturing of the community. To return the diaconate to its permanent exercise would restore the patristic enumeration of the three major orders of ministry: bishops, their deacons, and the presbyters, such as found in St. Ignatius of Antioch. Bishops should give diaconal tasks only to persons (ordained or not) who have the necessary graces. Furthermore, the Church has the right to the benefit of all the graces given to it by God, including the graces of the diaconate.

Suenens's presentation on sacramental grace and the diaconate is even broader than Döpfner's. Here the emphasis is not merely God's grace to the ordinand, but to the entire Church. I recall a conversation with a religious sister on the staff of the same parish I was assigned to as deacon. Sister worked tirelessly across an entire spectrum of ministry: catechesis, care of the poor, administration, and more. One evening, a parishioner commented to Sister that it was too bad that she could not be ordained a deacon. Her response was to dismiss the idea, saying, "Oh, I don't need ordination to do what I'm doing." However, another parishioner said, "That's not the point, Sister. The Church would benefit by seeing what you do in our name as diaconal." Our parishioners were expressing intuitively and wisely the same sense of sacramental grace as Cardinal Suenens.

The conciliar debates led to a final vote in overwhelming support of a renewed diaconate. It is addressed in *Lumen Gentium* 29; *Orientalium Ecclesiarum* 17; *Sacrosanctum Concilium* 35; and *Dei Verbum* 25. Particularly interesting is the insight of the decree *Ad Gentes*, echoing both Döpfner and Suenens:

> Where episcopal conferences deem it opportune, the order of the diaconate should be restored as a permanent state of life according to the norms of the Constitution "*De Ecclesia*." For there are men who actually carry out the functions of the deacon's office, either preaching the Word of God as catechists, or presiding over scattered Christian communities in the name of the pastor and the bishop, or practicing charity in social or relief work. It is only right to strengthen them by the imposition of hands which has come down from the Apostles, and to bind them more closely to the altar, that they may carry out their ministry more effectively because of the sacramental grace of the diaconate. (*AG* 16)

The Council's teaching about the diaconate is grounded in the Church's understanding of grace. Cardinals Döpfner and Suenens point the way to that insight. Why do we need a sacrament of the diaconate? Grace: the Holy Spirit's great gift to the entire people of God, including those who serve in the name of the Church. "It is only right to strengthen them...to bind them more closely to the altar...so they may carry out their ministry more effectively."

Implementing the Renewal

To implement the Council's decision to renew the diaconate, St. Paul VI issued *motu proprio* the apostolic letter *Sacrum Diaconatus Ordinem* (*SDO*) on June 18, 1967. Offering the legal and administrative norms to be followed, the document does not raise issues of the sacramentality of the diaconate itself. With *SDO*, the renewed diaconate was up and running, and the first postconciliar "permanent" deacons were ordained in Germany the following year. Five years later, on August 15, 1972, Paul completed his realignment of the sacrament of orders. He issued two apostolic letters on that date: *Ministeria Quaedam* and *Ad Pascendum*. The Council had recommended that the Holy Father streamline the sacrament of orders to better align with contemporary pastoral needs. *Ministeria Quaedam* suppressed tonsure, the minor orders, and the major order of the subdiaconate in the Latin Church. It also established two of the former minor orders (lector and acolyte) as lay ministries to be conferred, not by ordination, but by a simple installation by the bishop. Admission to the clerical state, associated with tonsure, was now attached to diaconate ordination. *Ad Pascendum* addressed additional norms on the diaconate, with an extended introduction citing the various scriptural and patristic referents on the diaconate, as we have already seen, stressing the unique relationship of the deacon to the bishop, and that the deacon is "in the ministry of Christ."

Other developments followed. In 1992, the first edition of the *Catechism of the Catholic Church* was released in French. It contained this text at paragraph 875: "From Christ, they [referring to all three orders of bishops, presbyters, and deacons] receive the mission and faculty (*sacra potestas*) to act in the person of Christ the Head." But in the subsequent Latin *editio typica* promulgated in 1997, an important distinction is introduced without commentary or explanation: "From Christ, *bishops and priests* receive the mission and faculty [*sacra potestas*] to act in the person of Christ the Head, while *deacons* receive the strength to serve the People of God through the ministry of Worship, Word and Charity in communion with the bishop and his presbyterate" (emphasis added). "Sacred power" applies only to bishops and presbyters, while deacons receive an unspecified "strength" to serve.

In 1995, the Congregation for the Clergy and the Congregation for Catholic Education began preparing two documents on the diaconate, which would be released jointly in February 1998. The cardinal members met in a joint plenary session with St. Pope John Paul II as part of that process. In his address, the pope offered the following comments:

> Catholic doctrine teaches that the degrees of priestly participation (episcopate and presbyterate) and the degree of service (diaconate) are all three conferred through a sacramental act called "ordination," that is, by the sacrament of Holy Orders. Through the imposition of the Bishop's hands and the specific prayer of consecration, the deacon

> receives a particular configuration to Christ, Head and Shepherd of the Church [*una peculiare configurazione a Cristo, Capo e Pastore della Chiesa*] who, for love of the Father, made himself the last and servant of all. Sacramental grace gives deacons the necessary strength to serve the people of God in the "diakonia" of the Liturgy, the Word, and charity, in communion with the Bishop and his presbyterate. By virtue of the sacrament received, an indelible spiritual character is imprinted, which marks the deacon permanently and precisely as a minister of Christ.[25]

It is noteworthy that John Paul spoke of the deacon's configuration to Christ, the Head and Shepherd of the Church, since that language was already being questioned in other documents. The pope continued by repeating the Council's teaching that sacramental grace gives the deacon strength to serve the people of God in an integrated *diakonia* of Liturgy, Word, and Charity. Another essential element is that the sacramental effect of ordination is permanent. The diaconate is not a temporary or a part-time ministry; like bishops and presbyters, we're in it for keeps. As I tell candidates in formation for the diaconate, they will never again, after ordination, be private persons in the Church; the effects of the deacon's ordination are *public* and *permanent.*

The growing distinction between the sacerdotal orders and the diaconal order continued to be reflected in ecclesial documents. For example, in the joint documents promulgated by the Congregations for Clergy and Religious Education in 1998, the *Basic Norms for the Formation of Permanent Deacons* refers to the special strength (*vigor specialis*) associated with the sacramental grace of the diaconate. Notice that the Congregations do not use the language John Paul had used in their earlier *plenarium.* He spoke of the deacon being configured to Christ, "the Head and Shepherd." Now, the language has shifted to teach that the deacon is configured to Christ the Deacon and Servant.

The diaconate imprints a character and communicates a specific sacramental grace. The diaconal character is the configurative and distinguishing sign indelibly impressed in the soul, which configures the one ordained to Christ, who made himself the deacon or servant of all. It brings with it a specific sacramental grace, which is strength, *vigor specialis*, a gift for living the new reality wrought by the sacrament.[26]

Finally, on October 26, 2009, Pope Benedict XVI adapted the Code of Canon Law, cc. 1008 and 1009, to codify the language found in the *editio typica* of the *Catechism*. Specifically, c. 1009 now has a new text for its third paragraph, which reads, "Those who are constituted in the order of the episcopate or the presbyterate receive the mission and capacity to act in the person of Christ the Head, whereas deacons are empowered to serve the People of God in the ministries of the liturgy, the word, and charity."[27]

Conclusion: Deacons as Icons of Humility

"Why ordain?" Why do we ordain some among us and not others? We are called in Scripture a priestly people, and yet we ordain some to serve us as priests: priests within a priestly people. St. Paul VI reminded us that we are a servant Church: we are a Church of servants, and yet we ordain some to serve as deacons: deacons within a diaconal Church. The answer to the question, "why ordain?" depends on one's understanding of what ordination is and what it means.

Ordinatio involves the integration of a person into an *ordo*, a body of believers with particular responsibilities: the *ordo* of the baptized, the *ordo* of catechumens, the *ordo* of virgins, the *ordo* of spouses, the *ordo* of widows, and the *ordines* of bishops, deacons, and presbyters (cf. *CCC* 1537–38). I have often been struck by Mark's description of the people assembling to hear Jesus and to be fed by him. "Then he ordered them to get all the people to sit down in groups on the green grass. So they sat down in groups of hundreds and of fifties" (Mark 6:39–40). Everyone has a place in the Lord's community and at the Lord's table.

What's more, no one operates alone. Ordination brings an ordinand into the *communio* of the *ordo* through the power of the Holy Spirit. In short, ordination is not an act undertaken simply for the good of the individual ordinand; it is an act of, by, and for, the common good of the entire Church.

As we have seen, the contemporary Church distinguishes between the sacerdotal orders and the diaconal order, echoing the ancient maxim that a deacon is ordained "not unto the priesthood but into the service of the bishop." From the most ancient days of the Tradition, the Church has consistently taught that even though the deacon is not a priest, he is nonetheless ordained. The ordination of a deacon is sacramental but not sacerdotal. Today's confusion over the sacramentality of the deacon seems to rest in a presumption that the only genuinely sacramental ordination is that of the priesthood. Closely associated with sacerdotal ordinations of bishops and presbyters are the notions of *sacra potestas* and *potestas ordinis*. In the revisions made to the *editio typica* of the *Catechism* and the Code of Canon Law, the distinction is made between the sacerdotal orders that receive "sacred power" and the diaconal order, which does not. Instead, the traditional use of the language of "strengthening" is applied to the diaconate.

It is precisely at this point that an opportunity can be missed. Instead of (mis-) understanding this distinction between the sacerdotal and the diaconal orders as a kind of "lessening" of the sacramentality of the diaconate (the "mini-priest" or "priest-in-training" approach), we can instead see the deacon's ordination as its own paradigm. The diaconate offers a different, substantive, and complementary model of ordained ministry. When priest prisoners at Dachau began discussing the possibility of renewing a diaconate to be exercised permanently, they were not doing so because of a shortage of presbyters. Instead, their vision was of a different form of ordained ministry: a ministry that would serve in tandem with the presbyterate and present to the world a richer image of the Christ as both King and Servant.[28]

What is sacramentalized in the deacon's ordination? St. Paul VI referred to the diaconate as "the driving force" (*instimulator*) for the Church's *diakonia*. St. John Paul II, after first repeating Paul's comment, continued that "the service of the deacon is the Church's service sacramentalized...[deacons] are meant to be living signs of the servanthood of Christ's Church.[29] Then, in *Deus Caritas Est*, Benedict XVI wrote,

> A decisive step in the difficult search for ways of putting this fundamental ecclesial principle into practice is illustrated in the choice of the seven, which marked the origin of the diaconal office (cf. *Acts* 6:5–6)....The social service which they were meant to provide was absolutely concrete, yet at the same time it was also a spiritual service; theirs was a truly spiritual office which carried out an essential responsibility of the Church, namely a well-ordered love of neighbor. With the formation of this group of seven, "*diaconia*"—the ministry of charity exercised in a communitarian, orderly way—became part of the fundamental structure of the Church. (no. 21)[30]

Therefore, the nature of the diaconate is not merely something one does in or for the Church: *diakonia* is part of the very foundation of the Church, an essential part of the Church's identity. The "Church's *diakonia*" has several critical components. First, *diakonia* is grounded in Christ, "who came not to be served, but to serve." *Diakonia* is ultimately about Christ and the kenosis of God, "a grand and mysterious truth for the human mind, which finds it inconceivable that suffering and death can express a love which gives itself and seeks nothing in return" (*Fides et Ratio* 93). We have already seen how Paul VI characterized the work of the Second Vatican Council by saying that "the Church has declared herself the servant of humanity" and that "the exercise of service is its principal purpose."[31] Therefore, in this understanding, everything the Church does is to serve, and traditionally the Church has characterized this singular *diakonia* through the elements of Word, Sacrament, and Charity. Every member of the Church has, each in their own way, responsibility for this *diakonia*. The deacon's ordination designates some disciples to a ministry of leadership-in-service. Deacons are to lead, inspire, encourage, empower, and assist others in their servant responsibilities. What is even more profound is that the deacon's ordination marks the order of deacons as servant leaders who follow the kenotic path of Christ, who "having loved his own who were in the world, he loved them to the end" (John 13:1).

In a recent address to the deacons of the Diocese of Rome, Pope Francis offered some enlightening comments about the role of the deacon.[32] He observed that only by being involved with the poor can deacons avoid being thought of as "'half-priests' or second-rate priests, nor with [*sic*] they be 'special altar boys.'" He summarized the deacon's spirituality of service as consisting of "willingness on the inside and openness on the outside":

> Willingness on the inside, from the heart, ready to say yes, docile, without making life revolve around one's own agenda; and open on the outside, looking at everyone, especially those who are left out, those who feel excluded....I entrust this to you.

The Holy Father challenged not only his own deacons of Rome, but all deacons to cultivate three "dimensions":

> Firstly, I expect you to be humble. It is sad to see a bishop and a priest showing off, but it is even sadder to see a deacon wanting to put himself at the center of the world, or at the center of the liturgy, or at the center of the Church. Be humble. Let all the good you do be a secret between you and God. And so it will bear fruit.
>
> Secondly, I expect you to be good spouses and good fathers. And good grandparents. This will give hope and consolation to couples who are going through difficult times and who will find in your genuine simplicity an outstretched hand. They will be able to think: "Look at our deacon! He is happy to be with the poor, but also with the parish priest and even with his children and his wife!" Even with his mother-in-law, that's very important! Doing everything with joy, without complaining: it is a testimony that is worth more than many sermons. And out with the complaints. Without complaining. "I had so much work, so much...". Nothing. Send these things away. Away.

> Thirdly, I expect you to be sentinels: not only to know how to spot the poor and the distant—this is not so difficult—but to help the Christian community to recognise Jesus in the poor and the distant, as He knocks on our doors through them. It is also a catechetical and prophetic dimension of the sentinel-prophet-catechist who knows how to see beyond and help others to see beyond, and to see the poor who are far away.

I have included these lengthy citations to capture Pope Francis's unique style of heartfelt and joyful expression. The image of the deacons as "sentinel—prophet—catechist" is particularly powerful. To be a courageous and humble sentinel, a watchman, a guardian lies at the heart of the diaconate.

It has become traditional to associate the celebration of the Last Supper with the establishment of the Eucharist and, therefore, the priesthood, who "do this in memory of me." As discussed above, it is also traditional to associate the selection and ordination of the Seven in Acts 6 with the establishment of the diaconate. However, from a theological perspective based on contemporary biblical scholarship, this association is not sustainable. This conclusion is not particularly novel; the Council of Trullo in 692, for example, reached the same one.[33] From a sacramental perspective, it seems far more appropriate to suggest that the biblical foundation of the diaconate is Christ's washing of the disciples' feet during the Last Supper and the institution of the Eucharist. Several points should be considered.

First, only John's Gospel recounts the foot washing. It occurs within the context of the Last Supper, and there is no account of the institution of the Eucharist. The language used by Christ to describe the meaning of his actions includes the Greek word *upodeigma* for "model" or "example." "For I have set you an example, that you also should do as I have done to you. Very truly, I tell you, servants are not greater than their master, nor are messengers greater than the one who sent them" (John 13:15–16). The term *upodeigma* is no superficial term; it conveys the sense of sacrificial death: an example of how to spend one's life totally in service to another.

Second, much like the command of Christ during the institution of the Eucharist recounted in the Synoptic Gospels and St. Paul to "do this in memory of me," this account also includes a command from Christ to "do as I have done to you." Scripture affirms a dual obligation laid upon the early Church by Christ.

Third, the connection to the Eucharist is meaningful and significant. When considering the totality of all accounts of the Last Supper, the conclusion is clear that the institution of the Eucharist and the washing of the feet are like two sides of the same coin: Christ is establishing his lasting sacramental presence through his sacrificial actions in both accounts. One focus is on wine and bread, blessed, broken, and shared, and the other focus is on the self-sacrificial *upodeigma* of washing of feet. Both will culminate in his sacrificial death on the cross. There is one sacrament of holy orders, in which bishops, deacons, and presbyters participate, each in their unique ways. At the Last Supper, we see the beginnings of the apostolic ministry as the apostles receive Christ's commands. In a sense, we can say that we are witnessing the origins of both the episcopate and the diaconate.[34] Later, presbyters will be admitted into a particular and vital share of the episcopal responsibility.

Fourth, we return to the traditional and ancient relationship of the deacon to the bishop. The deacon is ordained to assist and to extend the mission of the bishop himself. *Diakonia* is not the province of the deacon alone but of the bishop and the entire Church; deacons are simply privileged to participate in it in a particular way. The deacon serves, not on his own authority, but as a representative, a "legate" of the bishop serving in various ministries the bishop deems necessary. He does this in a particularly "diaconal" way, imaging Christ the Servant, in partnership with the presbyters who are imaging Christ the Priest. In virtue of ordination, the deacon serves to link the bishop with the community and extend the bishop's pastoral care into areas the bishop may be unable to reach.

Fifth. *diakonia* is singular. There is *one* "service," which is "part of the fundamental structure of the Church." *Diakonia* is not a set of things we Christians do; it is part of who we are. "Christ the Lord promised the Holy Spirit to the Apostles, and on Pentecost day sent the Spirit from heaven, by whose power they would be witnesses to Him before the nations and peoples and kings even to the ends of the earth. And that duty, which the Lord committed to the shepherds of His people, is a true service, which in sacred literature is significantly called 'diakonia' or ministry" (*LG* 24). Traditionally, this one *diakonia* has been expressed through the three "functions" of Word, Sacrament, and Charity.

Sixth, the Church has consistently taught of the unity of functions within the Church's one *diakonia*. The bishops of the United States, for example, have stressed this point from the beginning of the renewed diaconate in our country: "By ordination, the deacon, who sacramentalizes the Church's service, is to exercise the Church's *diakonia*. Therefore, 'the diaconal ministries, distinguished above, are not to be separated; the deacon is ordained for them all, and no one should be ordained who is not prepared to undertake each in some way.'"[35]

A proper understanding of *diakonia* must avoid reducing this rich biblical concept to just one type of servanthood. The invaluable work of John Collins has, since his magisterial text *Diaconia: Reinterpreting the Ancient Sources* appeared in 1990, emphasized that we must never limit this term to tasks of menial service. The Church and its deacons should take the ministry of Word, Sacrament, and Charity as a whole reality, demonstrating through our lives just how Word leads to Sacrament, and Sacrament leads to Charity. Furthermore, as Collins reminds us, *diakonia* involves serving as one who bridges: the image of the deacon as a waiter is important, not because "waiting on tables" is a menial task, but because the waiter "connects" the kitchen with the customer. The ancient practice of deacons serving as legates and representatives of their bishops confirms and emphasizes this point. We shall return to Collins's work in chapter 8.

Seventh, the deacon is ordained precisely because he connects and integrates the full range of biblical *diakonia*: Word, Sacrament, and Charity. *Diakonia*, then, is a profoundly rich concept that transcends facile associations of the term with notions of menial service alone. It is not adequate to say that deacons exercise all three areas of ministry, like some kind of grocery list: "First I will do this, then I will do that, and then I will do the other." Not only are there three areas of ministry, but there is also a fundamental interpenetration of each of them with the other. When preaching or teaching, how are we led to a more profound celebration of sacrament and worship and a more active presence in caring for those at the margins of society or in any kind of need? How does our celebration of sacrament flow from our breaking open the word of God, and how well does that help us go forth to serve others? How do we bring back our experiences from service "in the streets" to our growing understanding of God's word and again lead us to celebrate an even richer sacramental life? In a very real, perichoretic sense, we cannot have one function without the others because each addresses, informs, and penetrates the others. Addressing the deacons of the United States in 1987, John Paul II said, "Yours is not just one ministry among others, but it is truly meant to be, as Paul VI described it, a 'driving force' for the Church's *diakonia*. You are meant to be living signs of the servanthood of Christ's Church."[36]

In conclusion, we ordain deacons for the "special strength" they need to serve, animate, and inspire the Church's own diaconal identity. They are not priests, who offer the sacrifice. They are servants, who offer themselves entirely to God in service to their bishops and their communities. *Diakonia*, and the deacon's participation in it, is understood as part of the ministerial identity of the entire Church even while returning to the ancient language that "the deacon is not ordained to the priesthood, but into the service of the Bishop." In the future, emphasis needs to be placed on constantly nurturing this special relationship the deacon enjoys with his bishop.

I was ordained a deacon while still serving on active duty in the U.S. Navy. A few months before the scheduled ordination of our class, I received urgent orders to return overseas. Our archbishop, Cardinal James Hickey, the archbishop of Washington, DC, graciously agreed to ordain me ahead of schedule so I could carry out those orders. As a result, I was ordained alone, and I received the cardinal's full attention! Two things happened during the ordination that were not expected and will stay with me forever. I received communion from the cardinal and prepared to take one of the cups with the precious blood to serve as a minister of communion. This is what the master of ceremonies had instructed me to do when we had the rehearsal for the ordination the day before. Instead, the cardinal approached me again with the ciborium, handed it to me, leaned forward, and whispered, "Bill, you are my deacon now; minister in my place," which I did (the master of ceremonies was as surprised as I was).

Then, after the Prayer after Communion, the cardinal asked us all to be seated for a moment. He thanked all of those who had made the celebration possible, and then he addressed the assembly. He explained that many people might not realize just how close the deacon was to his bishop. He then lifted his chasuble slightly with one hand. He said, "On days of great joy, like a day of ordination, the Church asks her bishops to wear, under the chasuble of the priest, the dalmatic of the deacon." He then lifted the edge of his own dalmatic with his other hand. Now standing with his chasuble in one hand and his dalmatic in the other, he concluded, "This is how close Bill and I are now." It was a powerful moment and a brilliant demonstration of the significance of this relationship, one based on a shared and humble *diakonia*.

CHAPTER FIVE

THE CODE OF CANON LAW, A SERVANT CHURCH, AND DIACONATE

A Proposal in Honor of James Provost

Introduction: Law and the Church

Father James Coriden reminds us that canon law is first and foremost a ministry in, of, and for the Church. He writes, "The practice of the ministry strives to achieve two main goals for its communities: genuine Christian freedom and good order. These twin goals and overarching purposes give focus to the canonical ministry."[1] Few scholars worked harder at the nexus between ecclesiology and canon law than the late Father James H. Provost. A native of Montana and a priest of the Diocese of Helena, he served in parish and diocesan ministry before joining the faculty of the Catholic University of America in Washington, DC, in 1979. From 1980 until his death in 2000, Jim also served as the managing editor of *The Jurist* and in various leadership capacities in the Canon Law Society of America (CLSA) for over thirty years. In 1991, the CLSA awarded him its highest honor, the Role of Law Award, for his contribution to the reform of Church law. In the words of his friend and fellow canonist, Father John Beal, "Provost saw the great task of canon law in the last four decades of the twentieth century to be translating the ecclesiological vision of the Second Vatican Council, whose sessions he had observed while a student in Rome, into concrete reality. As a result, he approached canon law as an instrument not to exert control over the faithful, but to facilitate the actualization of the Church's self-understanding expressed in its theology."[2]

Father Provost offers the starting point for this chapter. He once wrote that in the 1983 Code of Canon Law, "there is still no coherent treatment of permanent deacons as a 'proper and permanent rank of the hierarchy' comparable to the treatment given presbyters and bishops in the code; rather, they are treated as exceptions to the norms for presbyters."[3] In subsequent conversations over the years, he often expressed hope that future revisions to the Code would correct this shortcoming. In the years since his death, the need for such a "coherent treatment" is more apparent than ever. It is my hope that canonists will find the modest proposals made here helpful in developing future revisions to the Code.

Pope John Paul II, in promulgating the 1983 Code of Canon Law, wrote that the Code "fully corresponds to the nature of the Church, especially as it is proposed by the teaching of the Second Vatican Council in general and in a particular way by its ecclesiological teaching."

> Indeed, in a certain sense this new *Code* could be understood as a great effort to translate this same conciliar doctrine and ecclesiology into canonical language. If, however, it is impossible to translate perfectly into canonical language the conciliar language the conciliar image of the Church, nevertheless the *Code* must always be referred to this image as the primary pattern whose outline the *Code* ought to express insofar as it can by its very nature.[4]

The pope extended this hermeneutical principle in a subsequent address to the Roman rota: "Even when the new *Code* takes over verbatim canons from the old *Code*, canons for which there is a noble and extensive tradition of interpretation, it is still necessary to consider them anew in light of the teaching of the Second Vatican Council."[5]

In that light, our specific concern in this chapter is how post-conciliar law reflects the ecclesial vision of the diaconate found in the various documents of the Council. For example, *LG* 29 shifted the paradigm vis-à-vis the diaconate. First, it grounds the contemporary diaconate in the biblical and patristic sources, before the diaconate began its transition into a partial participation in the ministerial priesthood. Second, the Council fathers refer to the diaconate and its functions as "extremely necessary" for the life of the Church and note that these functions are "difficult to fulfill" today because of the current laws and customs of the Latin Church. Therefore, they determined that the diaconate could be restored "as a proper and permanent rank of the hierarchy." While the diaconate functions in communion with the presbyterate, it has a "proper" identity unique in itself. Therefore, since the diaconate is an ordained ministry in its own right, theological language unique to the order as well as the legal expressions flowing from that language must continue to develop. Finally, in keeping with the overall theme of this book, we will bear in mind how the canonical treatment of the diaconate might better reflect the humility that should characterize the Church and its ordained ministers.

This chapter is divided into two major sections. The first examines the ecclesio-canonical vision of the Church and diaconate in the current Code of Canon Law. The second part will propose practical proposals for a potential future revision to the Code. A significant resource for this examination is the 1990 *Code of Canons of the Eastern Churches* (*CCEO*).[6] Anecdotally, some commentators have remarked that this should not be done in order to preserve the authentic traditions of each Church *sui iuris*. While preserving the unique features of the various ritual Churches is important, this should not preclude opportunities for mutual growth and enrichment within the Church as a whole. In today's global realities, it is essential to learn and grow from each other. Chorbishop John D. Faris wrote, "In light of c. 17,[7] the parallel passages of the Eastern code can contribute to the interpretation of ambiguous passages in the Latin code. Further, the Eastern code can serve as a supplementary source of law for the Latin Church."[8] With regard to the renewed diaconate itself, the Eastern Code is indeed a rich source. First, the Eastern traditions have a long history of married clergy, and these insights are reflected in the Eastern canons. Since most deacons, East and West, are married, it is invaluable to learn from Churches with greater experience in this regard. Second, the postconciliar papal magisterium has strongly encouraged the Church to "breathe with both lungs" of East and West, and this proposal gives a concrete opportunity to do just that, with mutual appreciation of the fullness of the Tradition.

Part One: Ecclesio-Canonical Foundations

The development of current canon law flows from the Second Vatican Council and its teaching on the Church. The Council's ecclesiology is readily apparent through a variety of canons and in the very structure of the Code itself. Consider the following table comparing the 1983 Code with its 1917 predecessor.

1917 Code of Canon Law	1983 Code of Canon Law
Book I. General Norms	Book I. General Norms
Book II. Persons First Part—Clerics Second Part—Religious Third Part—Laity	Book II. The People of God First Part—The Christian Faithful Second Part—Hierarchy Third Part—Religious
Book III. Things First Part—Sacraments Second Part—Sacred Places/ Times Third Part—On Divine Cult Fourth Part—Ecclesiastical Magisterium Fifth Part—Benefices Sixth Part—Temporal Goods	Book III. The Teaching Function of the Church
Book IV. Procedures	Book IV. The Sanctifying Office of the Church
Book V. Delicts and Penalties	Book V. The Temporal Goods of the Church
	Book VI. Sanctions in the Church
	Book VII. Processes

The 1917 structure consisted of five "books": General Norms, Persons, Things, Procedures, and Delicts and Penalties. Notice that book II, *De Personis*, began by addressing first, clerics; then, religious, then, the laity. However, book II of the 1983 Code reflects Vatican II in several distinctive ways. First, the title of the book itself does not use the traditional decretal language of *de personis* but the conciliar *de populo Dei*: the people of God. Second, the content of the book reflects the significant inversion of the subjects of the law. When the Council began, the first draft of what would become the Dogmatic Constitution on the Church (*Lumen Gentium*) reflected the same structure of clergy–religious–laity found in the 1917 Code. However, the bishops rejected this ordering, beginning instead with all the Christian faithful (*Christifideles*), then the clergy, and finally, the religious. This reordering is reflected in the internal structure of book II.

The Council's structural influence is found in the subsequent books as well. Bertram F. Griffin, among others, has demonstrated the centrality of the ministries of Christ within the documents of Vatican II.[9] "The doctrine of the three-fold *munera* [*munus docendi, munus sanctificandi, munus regendi*], originally a Christology, was translated into an ecclesiology by the Second Vatican Council, and many of the documents of the Council are structured in terms of these three offices or ministries."[10] This explains the inclusion of book III on the *munus docendi* and book IV on the *munus sanctificandi*. This structure has no parallel in the 1917 Code. While there is no comparable book on the *munus regendi*, Griffin's observations are helpful on this point:

> Even the Vatican Council was ambiguous regarding the significance of the *munus regendi*....Because of this ambiguity, several reasons are given for neglecting a book on the *munus regendi*.
>
> 1. Since the *munus regendi* includes the ministry of governance, the entire *Code* deals with the function or ministry.
> 2. From the standpoint of the lay apostolate and the transformation of social order, the *munus regendi*

must be left to the particular church by reason of the doctrine of subsidiarity. It is only the particular church that can make adequate decisions regarding this aspect of the *munus regendi.*

3. Even interpreting the *munus regendi* as pastoral care suggests that much legislation needs to be left to the particular church, although one could say that the *munus regendi* is dealt with in many sections of Book Two on the People of God.
4. Finally, the *munus regendi* includes the administration of temporalities for the sake of worship, ministry and the care of the poor, and from this point of view, Book Five on Church Property deals with some of the issues of this *munus regendi.*[11]

Turning specifically to the diaconate, we begin with several of the introductory canons of book II. According to Robert Kaslyn, these canons "introduce the contents of Book II; from a broader perspective, they present ecclesiological principles foundational to the entire code....[they] exercise a determinative role for the interpretation not only of the remaining canons in Book II but of the entire code."[12]

Here then are the full texts of cc. 204, 205, and 207 with a brief commentary highlighting several points that apply to the diaconate and the proposed revisions that follow.

> **Canon 204 §1** The Christian faithful are those who, inasmuch as they have been incorporated in Christ through baptism, have been constituted as the people of God. For this reason, made sharers in their own way in Christ's priestly, prophetic, and royal function, they are called to exercise the mission which God has entrusted to the Church to fulfill in the world, in accord with the condition proper to each.
>
> **§2** This Church, constituted and organized in this world as a society, subsists in the Catholic Church governed by the successor of Peter and the bishops in communion with him.

> **Canon 205** Those baptized are fully in the communion of the Catholic Church on this earth who are joined with Christ in its visible structure by the bonds of the profession of faith, the sacraments, and ecclesiastical governance.
>
> **Canon 207 §1** By divine institution, there are among the Christian faithful in the Church sacred ministers who in law are also called clerics; the other members of the Christian faithful are called lay persons.
>
> **§2** There are members of the Christian faithful from both these groups who, through the profession of the evangelical counsels by means of vows or other sacred bonds recognized and sanctioned by the Church, are consecrated to God in their own special way and contribute to the salvific mission of the Church; although their state does not belong to the hierarchical structure of the Church, it nevertheless belongs to its life and holiness.

Orthodox theologian John D. Zizioulas has written that the theological significance of the link between the Eucharist and baptism/confirmation lies in the fact that "it reveals the nature of baptism and confirmation as being essentially an ordination, while it helps us understand better what ordination itself means."[13] He goes on to point out that "the immediate and inevitable result of baptism and confirmation was that the newly baptized would take his particular "place" in the eucharistic assembly, i.e., that he would become a layman."[14] It is from the *ordo* of the *christifideles* that certain members are called to become members of other *ordines* (such as the *ordo diaconorum*) in the eucharistic assembly.

These canons address the identity, mission, and uniqueness of being a member of the "Christian faithful." Christian identity is both individual and communal. As an individual and by name, a person approaches the waters of baptism. Baptism into the life of Trinity incorporates individual believers into a new identity as part of the *communio* of love that is God. Baptism is the decisive moment when the newly baptized is changed forever, called to participate in Christ's own mission as priest, prophet, and king.

The Church is not an ethereal, incorporeal reality: it exists in the world, as a type of human society within the world. It has institutional structures to carry out its mission. Repeating the classic text from *LG* 8, the law speaks of the Church "subsisting in" the Catholic Church under the authority of the pope as the successor of Peter and college of bishops in communion with him. Within this *communio*, the law identifies a subgroup known as "sacred ministers," known by the legal term *clerics*. Specifically, these clerics are "by divine institution" (see *LG* 18). This canon emphasizes that clergy come from *among* the faithful and are not (as in the 1917 Code) *distinct* from them. Sacramental initiation is the "common denominator" for all the faithful.

Two points suggest themselves. First is the distinction between the terms *sacred ministers* and *clerics*. This seems to emphasize that the foundation of ordained ministry is found in service to the people of God, limiting the term *cleric* to the law itself. Second, this distinction recalls *LG* 10, describing the ministerial priesthood within the common priesthood of all the faithful. "Though they differ from one another in essence and not only in degree, the common priesthood of the faithful and the ministerial or hierarchical priesthood are nonetheless ordered to each other: each of them in its own distinct way is a participation in the one priesthood of Christ." This becomes a significant question when considering the canonical treatment of the diaconate. On the one hand, deacons are clearly ordained into "sacred ministry" and fall into the canonical category of "clerics." However, left unaddressed is the "no-man's-land" *LG* 10 unintentionally creates for the deacon. As we have already encountered in chapter 4, deacons are ordained but they are not part of the "ministerial priesthood." Given the binary approach of *LG* 10 between the ministerial priesthood on the one hand and the common priesthood on the other, where does the deacon fit?

The comparable *CCEO* canons 323 and 324 provide an interesting contrast. Canon 323 §1 states, "Clerics, who are also called sacred ministers, are Christian faithful who, chosen by the competent ecclesiastical authority, are deputed through a gift of the Holy Spirit received in sacred ordination to be ministers of the Church participating in the mission and power of Christ, the Pastor." As in the Latin Code, clerics are identified first as *christifideles* who assume an additional responsibility through ordination, and, significantly for this study, they are described as "participating in the mission and power of Christ the Pastor." The underlying assumption in this text is that all clerics, regardless of order, have a role in governance, a fact made explicit in the 1917 Code (*CIC*): "Those who have received sacred orders are qualified, according to the norm of the prescripts of the law, for the power of governance, which exists in the Church by divine institution and is also called the power of jurisdiction" (129 §1); "Only clerics can obtain offices for whose exercise the power of orders or the power of ecclesiastical governance is required" (274). *CCEO* 743 describes this effect in this way: "Through sacramental ordination celebrated by a bishop in virtue of the working of the Holy Spirit, sacred ministers are constituted, who are endowed with the function and power the Lord granted to his apostles, and in varying degrees share in the proclamation of the gospel, shepherding and sanctifying the people of God."

To summarize:

1. The *communio* that is the Church is formed through God's initiative.
2. Through sacramental initiation, each member of the Church participates in various ways in the threefold ministry of Christ.
3. The Church of Christ finds its fullest expression in the communion of Creed, sacraments, and the bond of unity with the vicar of Peter. Even those who are not in "full communion" are still related to God and to others in various ways, including catechumens, and elements of God's salvation exist outside the formal parameters of the Catholic Church.
4. Within the *communio*, some people are constituted as sacred ministers.
5. The relationships within and among these sacred ministers should be reflected in the law. The history and theology of the Church has long recognized the

unique relationship between a bishop and his deacons, his "eyes, ears, heart and hands." The law should reflect that relationship as well.

Part Two: Proposed Revisions to the Code of Canon Law

Canons concerning clergy are found in widely disparate sections of the Code. Our review will proceed by first examining the canons related to the nature of the diaconate itself. From there we shall proceed to the deacon's participation in the triple *munera*: *docendi, sanctificandi, regendi*. The following chart summarizes the canons (and issues) under review.

Topic	**Canons (*CIC* and *CCEO*)**
1. The Diaconate: Nature and Formation	c. 266 (*CCEO* 358 and 428); cc. 1008, 1009; c. 236 (*CCEO* 354); cc. 274–77 (*CCEO* 373–75) 284–89; c. 129
2. *Munus Docendi* (book III)	cc. 757; 762; 764 (*CCEO* 610.2/610.3); 767 (*CCEO* 614)
3. *Munus Sanctificandi* (book IV)	cc. 835; 861 (*CCEO* 677); 910 (*CCEO* 709); 930; 1031 (*CCEO* 758, 759); 1108 (*CCEO* 828); 1111 (*CCEO* 830); 1169.
4. *Munus Regendi*	c. 129; c. 517.2

It is beyond the scope of the current project to review every canon that touches upon the deacon. The goal at this point is to highlight critical issues related to the nature and functions of the deacon in the law that are particularly significant, problematic, or require additional clarification.

We have already seen the importance of the Eastern Code of Canons to this task. To repeat, the Eastern Code reflects the long-standing experience of a "stable and permanent" diaconate within many of *sui iuris* Catholic Churches, as well as their experience with a married clergy. These realities are still a relative novelty in the Latin Church, while they are venerable traditions in the Eastern Churches.

The Latin canonical Tradition is, of course, respected and venerable in its own right. Father Joseph Pokusa traced the canonical history of the diaconate of the first eight centuries of the Church,[15] revealing a highly complex and varied pastoral and canonical reality. Unfortunately for our purposes, canonical jurisprudence emerges in full flower only in the twelfth century. By then, the diaconate had already become a transitory and largely invisible adjunct to a rapidly growing and increasingly powerful priesthood. The emerging law naturally reflected that reality, and the twentieth-century codes have built on those realities, struggling—as Father Provost has suggested—to reflect the once and future realities of the laity, diaconate, and other forms of ecclesial ministry and life.

Father Provost wrote of the need for a coherent treatment of the diaconate; I believe that this can be found already at hand in the Eastern Code. This proposal consists of incorporating and adapting Eastern canons for their Latin Code counterparts (where they exist) and replacing or eliminating certain existing canons of the Latin Code. The desired result would be a much more streamlined and, indeed, coherent treatment.

I. The Diaconate: Nature and Formation

A. The Deacon as Cleric

One immediate contrast between the two codes is apparent from the outset. Both codes have sections *de clericis*: on the clergy. The Eastern Code immediately establishes the sacramental and canonical identity of the clergy. The Latin Code, however, begins this section with the formation of clerics without first establishing who clerics are in the first place. Some of the parallel canons on the identity of clerics are actually placed at the end of the second section on the *munus sanctificandi*. To provide consistency and to begin the discussion on the clergy in a logical way, I propose the following recommendation: to create four new canons adapted from the Eastern Code and insert them at the beginning of the section *de clericis*. The existing canons would remain, but simply be renumbered to follow the new canons.

Recommendation #1:
Insert four new canons after c. 231; adapted from *CCEO* 323–26:

NEW canon 232 §1 Sacred ministers, who are also called clerics, are Christian faithful who, chosen by the competent ecclesiastical authority, are constituted through a gift of the Holy Spirit received in sacred ordination to be ministers of the Church participating in the mission and power of Christ, Servant and Pastor.

§2 In virtue of sacred ordination clerics are distinguished from the other Christian faithful by divine institution.

NEW canon 233 Clerics joined among themselves by hierarchical communion and constituted in various degrees participate in diverse ways in the one ecclesiastical ministry of divine origin.

NEW canon 234 In virtue of sacred ordination, clerics are distinguished as bishops, presbyters, and deacons.

NEW canon 235 Clerics are constituted into the degrees of orders by sacred ordination itself, but they cannot exercise that power except according to the norm of law.

Note: These are new canons being inserted at the beginning of the section on "Sacred Ministers or Clerics." The existing cc. 232–36 are retained and renumbered cc. 236–40.

These new canons, adapted from the Eastern Code, also address issues related to cc. 1008 and 1009. These canons have come under significant scrutiny since the publication of the *Catechism of the Catholic Church* in 1992. In certain key paragraphs, statements were made about the clergy that would be changed in subsequent revisions. In the original French text, it was said in general of all the ordained that from Christ "they receive the mission and faculty ('sacred power') to act in the person of Christ the Head."[16] But in the subsequent Latin *editio typica*, a distinction is introduced as a revision to this paragraph:

> From Him [Christ], bishops and priests receive the mission and faculty ("sacred power") to act in the person of Christ the Head, while deacons receive the strength to serve the People of God through the ministry of Worship, Word and Charity in communion with the bishop and his presbyterate.[17]

In this second edition, "sacred power" is communicated by the sacrament of orders only to bishops and presbyters, while deacons receive an unspecified "strength" to serve. No commentary or explanation was made for this change. It also created confusion because the text of c. 1008 contained language remarkably similar to the original phrasing of the *Catechism*.

In 2009, Pope Benedict XVI issued *motu proprio Omnium in Mentem*. Among other things, he addressed this discrepancy. "First, in c. 1008 and c. 1009 of the Code of Canon Law, on the sacrament of Holy Orders, the essential distinction between the common priesthood of the faithful and the ministerial priesthood is reaffirmed, while the difference between the episcopate, the presbyterate and the diaconate is made clear." The pope then directed that the changes already made by John Paul II to the *Catechism of the Catholic Church* be applied to canon law. The chart below contrasts the original and revised texts.

Original 1983 Text	*Omnium in Mentem*
Canon 1008: "By divine institution, the sacrament of orders establishes some among the Christian faithful as sacred ministers through an indelible character which marks them. They are consecrated and designated, each according to his grade, to nourish the people of God, fulfilling in the person of Christ the Head the functions of teaching, sanctifying, and governing."	Canon 1008: "By divine institution, some of the Christian faithful are marked with an indelible character and constituted as sacred ministers by the sacrament of holy orders. They are thus consecrated and deputed so that, each according to his own grade, they may serve the People of God by a new and specific title."
Canon 1009 §1: "The orders are the episcopate, the presbyterate, and the diaconate."	Canon 1009 §1: No change.
§2: "They are conferred by the imposition of hands and the consecratory prayer which the liturgical books prescribe for the individual grades."	§2: No change.
	§3: New Text: "Those who are constituted in the order of the episcopate or the presbyterate receive the mission and capacity to act in the person of Christ the Head, whereas deacons are empowered to serve the People of God in the ministries of the liturgy, the word and charity." (*Qui constituti sunt in ordine episcopatus aut presbyteratus missionem et facultatem agendi in persona Christi Capitis accipiunt, diaconi vero vim populo Dei serviendi in diaconia liturgiae, verbi et caritatis.*)

There has never been any specific rationale provided for the change, either to the *Catechism* or to the law. The intent of the change is clear, however: to distinguish the sacerdotal orders of presbyterate and episcopate on the one hand from the diaconal order, on the other. It also seems clear that there was a concern over including deacons as recipients of *sacra potestas* (sacred power) and that deacons might be understood as acting *in persona Christi Capitis* (in the person of Christ the Head of the Church). The changes to the *Catechism* and the Code explicate this distinction even further, and we have come to speak of two "modes of participation" in the one sacrament of order: the sacerdotal and the diaconal. In some texts, assertions about "the ordained" apply equally to both modes; in others, they apply only to one or the other. It remains to be seen how this new distinction will play out over time.

Before leaving this section, we must address a serious lacuna in the law regarding the uniqueness of the relationship between deacons and their bishop, a fact long established in the history and theology of the Church. The current law, under the responsibilities of a diocesan bishop, contains the following canon:

> **Canon 384** With special solicitude, a diocesan bishop is to attend to presbyters and listen to them as assistants and counselors. He is to protect their rights and take care that they correctly fulfill the obligations proper to their state and that the means and institutions which they need to foster spiritual and intellectual life are available to them. He also is to take care that provision is made for their decent support and social assistance, according to the norm of law.

This canon can be easily adapted, recognizing two factors. First, at the deacon's ordination, only the bishop lays hands on the ordinand, unlike the ordination of bishops and presbyters where all bishops lay hands on the new bishop and all presbyters lay hands on the new presbyter. Throughout the Tradition, this has been cited as marking the unique relationship of the bishop and the deacon. Second, the following adaptation recognizes the fact that many deacons and presbyters are serving within the sacramental context of matrimony. The *CCEO* (c. 192 §5) addresses the current lacuna and is added to the revised canon below.

Recommendation #2:
Revise c. 384 as follows:

> **NEW canon 384** With special solicitude, a diocesan bishop is to attend to his clergy and listen to them as assistants and counselors. He is to protect their rights and take care that they correctly fulfill the obligations proper to their state and that the means and institutions which they need to foster spiritual and intellectual life are available to them. He also is to take care that provision is made for their decent support and social assistance, according to the norm of law.
>
> **§1** Deacons, ordained "not to the priesthood but to the service of the bishop," enjoy a unique relationship to the diocesan bishop as his particular assistants and advisors in a *diakonia* of Word, Sacrament, and Charity. The diocesan bishop is to establish means to encourage and nurture this relationship so as to extend his own ministry to all.
>
> **§2** The diocesan bishop is to see that the families of his clerics, if they are married, be provided with adequate support, appropriate protection, and social security in addition to health insurance according to the norm of law.

If the new or revised canons above were incorporated in the Latin Code, the current cc. 1008–9 would be rendered redundant and inadequate; they could easily be deleted, unless, of course, there is a similar distinction to be described between presbyters and bishops. This would at least provide a more complete picture of the distinctiveness of each order, if that is deemed necessary in the law. But for now, my third recommendation is a simple, but significant deletion.

Recommendation #3:
Delete current cc. 1008–9.

B. The Formation of Deacons

Canon 236 introduces a problematic term into the canonical lexicon: the misleading and redundant expression of a "permanent" diaconate.

> **Canon 236** According to the prescripts of the conference of bishops, those aspiring to the permanent diaconate are to be formed to nourish a spiritual life and instructed to fulfill correctly the duties proper to that order:
>
> 1. young men are to live at least three years in some special house unless the diocesan bishop has established otherwise for grave reasons;
> 2. men of a more mature age, whether celibate or married, are to spend three years in a program defined by the conference of bishops.

The use of the expression "those aspiring to the permanent diaconate" is unfortunate. All ordinations are permanent in their sacramental and canonical effect; even those deacons who are later ordained to the presbyterate remain deacons. There is only one diaconate, not two. To speak of a "permanent diaconate" and a "transitional diaconate" adds significantly to the confusion surrounding the order. I have written elsewhere that one does not speak of a "transitional presbyter" to characterize a priest who is not later ordained a bishop. Speaking of a transitional priest versus a permanent priest is ridiculous; so too is speaking of a permanent or transitional deacon. And yet we still see liturgical worship aids and ordination invitations that speak of a person being ordained "a permanent deacon" as if there were any other kind. The adjectives are superfluous. While the rest of the canons of this section refer to seminary formation in some detail, this is the sole canon related to diaconate formation. Obviously, deacon candidates who are living and working in secular occupations are not able to be formed in residential seminaries. Still, it is interesting to see that "young men are to live at least three years in some special house." It is not clear why these "young men" could not go to a seminary, and why the law describes a separate house. This suggests an echo of part of the discussions at Vatican II at the beginning of the debate over renewing the diaconate.

Cardinal Spellman, with his intervention on October 4, 1963, the first day of the discussion on renewing the diaconate at the Council, was the first speaker to address the subject.[18] He spoke against the proposals to renew the diaconate, and one of the reasons he cited was that a bishop would not want to form candidates for the priesthood and candidates for diaconate in the same seminary. He argued that seminaries were already hard enough to maintain, and that distinct houses of formation would need to be established for deacons, since he believed it would be improper to train married men in the same institution as celibate men. Cardinal Spellman's objections were echoed by Cardinal Antonio Bacci (of the Secretariat of State) and Bishop Carlos Eduardo de Sabóia Bandeira Melo, OFM (bishop of Palmas, Brazil), both of whom thought the diaconate, especially if opened to married men, was not necessary and was perhaps even dangerous to priestly celibacy and priestly vocations. They agreed with Spellman that new seminaries would be needed for these deacons, for it would not be wise to train deacons who are to be dispensed from celibacy with those who are to remain celibate. Perhaps a similar concern was raised during the development of c. 236.

The parallel canon in the *CCEO* is c. 354:

> The formation of deacons not destined for the priesthood is to be appropriately adapted from the norms given above so that the curriculum of studies extends at least three years keeping in mind the traditions of their own Church *sui iuris* concerning the service of the liturgy, the word and charity.

The simplicity of this nuanced canon is attractive. Presumed is the involvement of the diocesan eparch or other authority of the particular Church *sui iuris* in the design of the formation process. The false distinction between a permanent and transitional deacon (all ordinations are permanent in their sacramental effects) is avoided by simply speaking of those deacons "not destined for the priesthood." Of course, in some Eastern Churches that same deacon, even if married, might at some future time be ordained to the priesthood. Finally, adaptability features prominently: flexibility in the overall design of the process, including the specific traditions of each Church *sui iuris*.

Therefore, I offer the following modification to c. 236.

Recommendation #4:

Rewrite (and renumber) current c. 236, adapting *CCEO* 354. Note: the current two subcanons (1° and 2°) are deleted.

REVISED canon 236 The formation of deacons not destined for the priesthood is to be appropriately adapted from the norms given above so that the curriculum of studies extends at least three years keeping in mind the traditions of the Latin Church concerning the service of the Word, Sacrament, and Charity, as determined and defined by the conference of bishops.

C. *The Deacon and the Care of Souls* (Cura Animarum)

Having identified the deacon as a member of the clergy and discussed deacon formation, we now turn to some of the obligations and rights that pertain to the deacon. It is in this section of the Code that we shall encounter some of the concerns raised by Father Provost.[19] We begin with the deacon's responsibility for the care of souls.

Canon 129 §1 Those who have received sacred orders are qualified, according to the norm of the prescripts of the law, for the power of governance, which exists in the Church by divine institution and is also called the power of jurisdiction.

§2 Lay members of the Christian faithful can cooperate in the exercise of this same power according to the norm of law.

Canon 274 §1 Only clerics can obtain offices for whose exercise the power of orders or the power of ecclesiastical governance is required.

The deacon's participation in the power of orders (*potestas ordinis*) and the power of governance (*potestas iurisdictionis*) is still the subject of considerable discussion and research. Several schools of thought emerged during and following the Code revision process about how the laity might exercise governance (or not), but there has been precious little written about how deacons might exercise governance. There is general agreement on the connection between bishops and presbyters and the power of jurisdiction, but great lacunae when dealing with deacons and with laypersons. Part of the problem goes back to the 1917 Code of Canon Law. Like the current c. 274, which specifies that "only clerics" obtain offices related to governance, the meaning was quite different. In 1917, "clerics" referred to those who had received tonsure. Tonsure was not an ordination, but it did make one a cleric. Since Vatican II, the clerical state is now linked to diaconate ordination. In other words, under the 1917 Code, one did not need to be ordained to exercise the power of jurisdiction. One became a cleric, not by ordination but by a liturgical rite and the law. The result is that today's canons are a bit more restrictive vis-à-vis governance than the 1917 Code.

While all of this is far too extensive to cover in detail here, we will review certain highlights as they related to the diaconate.[20] To begin, we return to Vatican II. The final text of *Lumen Gentium* 29 includes an extremely important phrase regarding governance. After declaring that the diaconate could in the future be restored as a "proper and permanent rank of the hierarchy," the bishops continued that it would be the responsibility of episcopal conferences, with the approval of the pope, "to decide whether and where it is opportune for such deacons to be established *for the care of souls* [*utrum et ubinam pro cura animarum huiusmodi diaconos institui opportunum sit*]." It is that phrase about "the care of souls" that is sometimes overlooked, and yet its significance cannot be ignored.[21] Canonist John Beal has noted that *cura animarum* is "a phrase with historic associations with the power of jurisdiction."[22] With this phrase, the bishops are specifying the very purpose of the restored diaconate: "The 'care of souls' refers to the pastoral activity of the Church to teach, sanctify, and govern the people of God....The 'care' of souls is the official activity whereby authorized persons provide ministry to people with a view to their salvation."[23] Simply put, the care of souls is a responsibility of the diocesan bishop, a responsibility that attaches to a particular office or ministry to ensure that it is carried out, a responsibility that involves all three areas of teaching, sanctifying, and ruling. We shall consider this further when we address the deacon's participation in the *munus regendi*.

Following Beal, and keeping the *cura animarum* in mind, we can now turn to the categories of the "power of orders" and the "power of jurisdiction" referred to in cc. 129 and 274. Thomas Aquinas speaks of a divine power associated with the sacrament of orders when he describes the character of order as a "spiritual power [*spiritualis potestas*]."[24] He distinguishes between the "characters" (and "spiritual power") of each order in these words:

> For some have said that a character is imprinted only in the Order of priesthood; but this is not true, since none but a deacon can exercise the act of the diaconate, and so it is clear that in the dispensation of the sacraments, he has a spiritual power which others have not. For this reason others have said that a character is impressed in the sacred [major], but not in the minor, Orders. But this again comes to nothing, since each Order sets a man above the people in some degree of authority directed to the dispensation of the sacraments. Wherefore since a character is a sign whereby one thing is distinguished from another, it follows that a character is imprinted in each Order.[25]

Aquinas, however, does not distinguish between a power of order and a power of jurisdiction. Neither will the Council of Trent, although the descriptions given us by that Council specify the "power" associated with the sacrament of orders as fundamentally sacerdotal. For example, in the decrees of session XXIII, we read,

> The sacred Scriptures show, and the tradition of the Catholic Church has always taught, that this priesthood was instituted by the same Lord our Savior, and that to the apostles, and their successors in the priesthood, was the power delivered of consecrating, offering, and administering His Body and Blood, as also of forgiving and of retaining sins.[26]

Clearly by the time of the Council of Trent in the sixteenth century, and after the radical shift in theological approaches to the sacrament of orders beginning in the twelfth century, the power associated with the sacrament of orders was conceived largely, if not exclusively, in sacerdotal terms. The diaconate had gradually diminished as a proper and permanent order of ministry. Vatican II and the revised Code moved beyond these strictly juridical terms in their own discussions about the various forms of ministry, but they remain terms of reference that need to be understood as precisely as possible.

"The power of governance is related to but distinct from the power of order and the *munus regendi*."[27] Commentators are agreed that the power of order is associated with the orders of episcopate and presbyterate; its association with the diaconate is less clear. This is a relationship that remains to be further developed. John Huels disagrees with Aquinas and concludes that "there is no power of a deacon, in virtue of his ordination alone, that the Church could not also delegate to a lay person, if it so wished....Deacons do not participate in the ministerial priesthood but in the common priesthood of the faithful."[28] However, I believe Aquinas has the proper sense of the matter; the "powers" associated with ordination are far more extensive than sacerdotal alone. In fact, Huels cites the diaconate as a prime example of the problem with such an exclusive association. Deacons clearly may exercise acts of governance and, since they are not ordained into the sacerdotal orders, the diaconate is unique within the ordained ministries. Without the power of order associated with the sacerdotal orders, and yet no longer laypersons under the law, deacons serve the Church in a particularly unique way. Nathan Mitchell makes the following observation: "Pope Paul VI's restoration of the diaconate was recognition, in principle, that ordained leadership in the church cannot be restricted to celibate priesthood."[29]

"The power of governance is a fundamental legal concept, so its proper juridical meaning must be understood and not be confused with separate though related concepts that are primarily theological, like the *munus regendi* and *sacra potestas*."[30] The power of governance has been defined as "the lawfully granted, public power necessary for validly performing a juridical act that is legislative, executive, or judicial."[31] In private correspondence with the author, Huels wrote, "Power of governance cannot be equated with sacred power. The first is a juridical concept; the other is theological, broader than power of governance and different from it. The notion of "sacred power" is not juridically precise, unlike power of governance, nor can it be reduced to canonical categories."[32] Furthermore, "all power of governance is not the same. Some powers of governance are exclusively episcopal, others are sacerdotal, and others can be exercised by deacons and lay persons."[33]

In summary, these distinct but related concepts of governance, powers of order and jurisdiction, and the *munus regendi* are all categories that demand further research to refine and apply these principles to the renewed diaconate. As we face the crises ahead, we need to be clear about what functions can be exercised, by whom, and for whom. Perhaps the following recommendations would be helpful; notice that we have no parallel canons from the *CCEO* to consult. In this approach, c. 129 expresses the longstanding Tradition that bishops possess fully the power of governance; in the bishop, the power of orders and the power of jurisdiction come together. For presbyters and deacons, ordination confers—according to their order—a lesser participation in both orders and jurisdiction. Finally, laity are no longer said to simply "cooperate" in the exercise of governance. Rather, they do so in virtue of their baptism and as authorized by the diocesan bishop. Obviously, the laity do not possess the power of order, but the current absolute link between ordination and jurisdiction (which, as we saw, was *not* the case in the 1917 Code) is removed and gives the diocesan bishop the authority to authorize and direct such exercise by laypersons. The skills and competencies for governance needed by the Church today are not guaranteed by sacred ordination alone. The following revisions give the diocesan bishop the authority to call upon the God-given skills, gifts, and experience of ordained and lay members of the *christifideles*.

Recommendation #5:

Rewrite current c. 129 and c. 274 as follows:

> **Canon 129 §1** Through episcopal ordination, bishops exercise fully the power of governance, which exists in the Church by divine institution and is also called the power of jurisdiction. Through ordination, presbyters and deacons are qualified, according to the norm of the prescripts of the law, for the power of governance as determined by the diocesan bishop.
>
> **§2** Lay members of the Christian faithful also exercise this same power as authorized and determined by the diocesan bishop.
>
> **Canon 274 §1** Clerics exercise the power of orders as determined by their order; they may obtain offices for whose exercise the power of ecclesiastical governance is required.

D. Deacons and the Liturgy of the Hours

The current c. 276 includes the obligation for clerics to pray the Liturgy of the Hours daily, but again refers to a distinction between "deacons aspiring to the presbyterate" and "permanent deacons": "priests and deacons aspiring to the presbyterate are obliged to carry out the liturgy of the hours daily according to the proper and approved liturgical books; permanent deacons, however, are to carry out the same to the extent defined by the conference of bishops." While no reason is given in the canon, it may be assumed that "permanent" deacons would be too busy with family and work obligations to be responsible for the entire Liturgy of the Hours. The following modification simplifies the matter.

Recommendation #6:
Adapt c. 276 §2.3 from *CCEO* 377:

> **REVISED canon 276 §2.3** All clerics must celebrate the Liturgy of the Hours according to the particular law of the regional episcopal conference or the diocesan bishop.

E. Deacons: Matrimony, Celibacy, and Clerical Continence

We now come to a particularly interesting canon. It has had considerable attention in canonical circles, especially since Edward Peters published a significant article on the canon and its implications in *Studia Canonica.*[34]

> **Canon 277 §1** Clerics are obliged to observe perfect and perpetual continence for the sake of the kingdom of heaven and therefore are bound to celibacy which is a special gift of God by which sacred ministers can adhere more easily to Christ with an undivided heart and are able to dedicate themselves more freely to the service of God and humanity.

As we proceed, we must keep c. 17 in mind: "Ecclesiastical laws must be understood in accord with the proper meaning of the words considered in their text and context. If the meaning remains doubtful and obscure, recourse must be made to parallel places, if there are such, to the purpose and circumstances of the law, and to the mind of the legislator."

From the outset we must consider the "proper meaning of the words" *continence*, *chastity*, and *celibacy*. Celibacy is the willed acceptance of remaining unmarried. Chastity is the proper use of human sexual gift within one's state of life; it is as appropriate to speak of "married chastity" as it is "celibate chastity." Continence is to abstain from sexual activity, regardless of one's state of life. The crux of the issue is this: c. 277 states the longstanding Tradition of clerical continence in the West; the canon applies, without any stated exception, to all clergy. In short, it seems that following ordination, married clergy and their wives are obliged to abstain completely and permanently ("perfect and perpetual") from sexual relations. Even before Peters wrote his 2005 article in *Studia Canonica*, several scholars had made this observation.

Frankly, however, most theologians, bishops, and deacons who heard of it simply dismissed the idea out of hand. The reasons for this dismissive attitude generally revolved around several points. First, this claim was never made in any of the magisterial documents that related to the renewal of a diaconate permanently exercised. It was not contained in any document of Vatican II or in any act of the postconciliar papal magisterium vis-à-vis the renewed deaconate. There were no texts from the Roman curia that discussed this, even as late as February 1998 when the Congregation for Catholic Education and the Congregation for the Clergy issued jointly the *Basic Norms for the Formation of Permanent Deacons* and the *Directory for the Ministry and Life of Permanent Deacons*. Popes and curial officials, while not ignoring other canonical and theological dimensions of the renewal, were simply silent on this most significant issue! It seems highly unusual that such a profound matter would simply be "presumed" by Church authority. The "mind of the legislator" or the *mens ecclesiae* seemed straightforward enough: that no such demand was being placed on these new married deacons. No deacon formation programs anywhere in the world considered c. 277 as applying to married deacon candidates and their wives. And so, for most bishops and deacons, the invocation of c. 277 §1 simply seemed irrelevant to the renewal. I think most people read the canon "in reverse." The canon speaks first of the obligation to continence, and, because of this, the obligation of celibacy. Since it was already well established that deacons could now be selected from men who were already married, how could they be obliged to continence? Right or wrong, that seems to be the way most observers understood the matter.

I first became aware of the general argument in 2002 when I joined the senior staff of the USCCB in Washington. A theologian had submitted a paper on the issue to the conference on the subject with the request that the bishops immediately correct this oversight and ensure that all deacons and candidates be made aware of the requirement of perfect and perpetual continence. Upon review it was ultimately decided that the paper's position was incorrect and that no action would be taken. Several years later, Peters published his article in *Studia Canonica*. Both in his article and in subsequent writing on the subject, Peters stresses that his analysis is based on the law itself, especially c. 17. His focus is on "the proper meaning of the words in their text and context." He points out that "this study is not, consequently, broadly historical, sacramental, or comparative (with Eastern canon law in particular)."

The language of the canon itself is clear. "Clerics [obviously including deacons] are bound to perfect and perpetual continence for the sake of the kingdom of heaven and therefore are bound to celibacy." On the strength of strict textual analysis, Peters is correct. However, two things need to be considered about the canon in context. First, we must examine other canons to see if any offer mitigation of the obligation. Second, there is that nagging mention of being bound to celibacy. We already know that most deacons are not bound to celibacy and are, in fact, married. Therefore, we must examine the relationship of the two obligations contained in the canon. This is the crux of Peters's position as I understand it: the law states all clerics are bound to continence, but not all clerics are bound by celibacy. But does this mean that even married deacons are still bound by continence?

First, we examine the law to find if there is any mitigation of the obligations of c. 277 §1. Other canons in this section, for example, legislate that clerics are obliged to wear clerical attire, that they are to avoid secular occupations, and so forth. Many of these things simply could not apply to permanent deacons, who most often work in the secular world. (I was a career Navy officer; it would have been problematic to wear clerical attire while on duty.) So, near the end of this section of the Code we find c. 288, and it reads, "The prescripts of cc. 284, 285, §§3 and 4, 286, and 287, §2 do not bind permanent deacons unless particular law establishes otherwise." Interestingly, c. 277 §1 is not there. The law does not appear to mitigate the canon for married deacons.

Peters points out that during the preparation of the new Code, such mitigation was included. However, for no stated reason, Pope

John Paul II removed it prior to the promulgation of the Code. The absence of such an exemption with no rationale is not dispositive; it's simply not there. No one in authority has explained why it is not there. We might infer a couple of responses. One can infer that Peters's conclusion is correct and that married clerics are bound to continence. There are no mitigating conditions or canons. Two, one can infer that those responsible felt that such a statement was not necessary because of other statements in the Code itself that would indicate this obligation did not bind married clerics.

Could mitigation lie within c. 277 §1 itself? After it imposes the obligation to continence, the canon goes on to use an especially important, and I submit, critically important Latin word, *ideoque*. *Ideoque* has a variety of meanings, most usually translated as "therefore." Clerics are bound to continence, and because of that obligation, they are bound to celibacy. As Peters points out, the foundational obligation is that of continence; celibacy is a secondary obligation flowing from the first. And, in my opinion, therein lies the mitigation. Since clerical celibacy flows from the desire for clergy to be continent, then the removal of the requirement for celibacy for certain clerics would also convey the mitigation for the obligation to continence. If the Latin Church wishes all its clergy to be continent, then all its clergy must be celibate. If there is a category of clerics for which celibacy is not obligatory, then it seems reasonable to infer that the Church does not wish to impose continence either. This is certainly reflected in the lived experience of deacons, their wives, and their bishops for more than fifty years of the renewed diaconate.

Peters prefers to speak of the longstanding practice of continence and celibacy in the Latin Church. A review of the 1917 Code, however, reveals no direct mention of an obligation to clerical continence. It speaks of clerical celibacy, of course, but not clerical continence as a distinct or even foundational virtue. In fact, 1917 c. 124 §1, a parallel to the 1983 c. 277 §1, reads that "clerics constituted in major orders are prohibited from marriage and are bound by the obligation of observing chastity, so that those sinning against this are sacrilegious, with due regard for the prescription of canon 214 §1." There is some scholarship indicating that what the 1917 Code refers to as "chastity" is more accurately described as "continence," but even if one exchanges those terms in the 1917 Code, c. 124 (all three sections of it) is clearly more focused on the law of clerical celibacy itself. Since major clerics were to be celibate, they would of course and consequently be continent ("chaste" in the language of the 1917 Code). The order is reversed in the 1983 Code wherein the obligation for continence leads to clerical celibacy (*ideoque*). If the 1983 Code had simply adapted the phrasing of 1917 c. 124 §1, there would be no confusion.

Under the provisions of c. 17, are there other canons we might consult on this issue? I submit that cc. 1384 and 1385 pertain.

> **Canon 1134** From a valid marriage there arises between the spouses a bond which by its nature is perpetual and exclusive. Moreover, a special sacrament strengthens and, as it were, consecrates the spouses in a Christian marriage for the duties and dignity of their state.
>
> **Canon 1135** Each spouse has an equal duty and right to those things which belong to the partnership of conjugal life.

Married deacons and their spouses at no point surrender anything covered by these canons. Note, that in the case of matrimony, a sacred sacrament, the same adjective is used as we find in c. 277: "perpetual" (*perpetua*). Celibate clergy are bound to perpetual continence (a discipline); married clergy share a perpetual sacramental bond with their spouses in which they acquire duties and rights for the whole of life.

Also, Peters's analysis deliberately focuses solely on the language of the law in the West. In an exchange with the author, he maintained that "Eastern law is not an issue here. I am talking about the law and tradition of the West. I don't know why so many people assume that, where East and West disagree, the East must have it right (that is not your claim, I know); but it's a debate I don't enter or need to enter. I am talking about Western canon law."[35] I respond, however, that we are dealing with the Tradition of the entire Church, and not solely the Latin Church. The renewal of the diaconate is taking place throughout all the Churches *sui iuris*, and so I contend that we can and should consult the *CCEO* as well. What's more, the Eastern traditions have longstanding experience with both married and celibate clergy. It is not that I believe the *CCEO* is "correct," and the *CIC* is not; I simply believe we should, as St. John Paul II taught, "breathe with both lungs" and seek the wisdom of the entire Tradition. If clerical continence is a fundamental value of the Church, it should be reflected in the Eastern traditions as well. We have already seen the observation of Chorbishop Faris that "in light of c. 17, the parallel passages of the Eastern code can contribute to the interpretation of ambiguous passages in the Latin code. Further, the Eastern code can serve as a supplementary source of law for the Latin Church."[36]

The Eastern canons on this issue are straightforward. First, there is no mention whatsoever of continence, clerical or otherwise, in any part of the Eastern Code. Second, in the section of the law pertaining to clerics three canons pertain:

> *CCEO*, c. 373: Clerical celibacy chosen for the sake of the kingdom of heaven and suited to the priesthood is to be greatly esteemed everywhere, as supported by the tradition of the whole Church; likewise, the hallowed practice of married clerics in the primitive Church and in the tradition of the Eastern Churches throughout the ages is to be held in honor.
>
> *CCEO*, c. 374: Clerics, celibate or married, are to excel in the virtue of chastity; it is for the particular law to establish suitable means for pursuing this end.
>
> *CCEO*, c. 375: In leading family life and in educating children, married clergy are to show an outstanding example to other Christian faithful.

I find it interesting that none of these canons invokes continence. As noted in our definitions above, a celibate cleric would be bound to continence, and all clerics are bound to chastity, but those are not the same thing. Not only are we speaking of the same Catholic Church here, but we must also acknowledge that the Eastern Catholic Churches have as venerable a history as the Latin Church (and in some ways even more ancient), so an appeal to any historical connection between clerical continence and celibacy must account for this silence on that very point in the Code of Canons for the Eastern Churches.

A final thought on this matter: law serves the Church. Law is to reflect the theology of the Church. As the Church and its theology changes, so too must the law. So, to interpret the law, it seems to me as a theologian that we must first look at the theological sources for the law. Such a theological hermeneutic seems to me quite obvious. So, when considering the renewed diaconate, what has the Church had to say about all this outside of the law? Expressed differently: What is the context of the renewal of the diaconate against which we may assess the law? As mentioned above, at no point, in any conciliar or postconciliar magisterial document has there ever been a single statement that married deacons were to remain continent following ordination. It is not in any of the Council documents, it is not in any papal statements, nor is there any mention of it in any of the several documents promulgated by the Holy See concerning the nature and exercise of the permanent deacon. In fact, married deacons have been encouraged to be completely faithful and diligent in carrying out all the responsibilities, duties, and dimensions of family life. For many deacons and their wives who have had children after ordination, there has been no public outcry that some kind of canon has been violated, nor has such a deacon been dealt with by means of loss of faculties or suspension from ministry. If such a connection as posited by Peters was of such importance to the Latin Church (it clearly is not in the Eastern Churches), you would think that someone in authority would have acted accordingly. In this case, theological and pastoral praxis seems to provide a powerful hermeneutic for approaching the law.

From a theological perspective, there is yet one other issue to consider. While this canon is dealing with a specific question related to the sacrament of orders, we simply cannot ignore the fact that the canon is related to yet another sacrament: the sacrament of matrimony. While, again, we cannot devote the time this relationship demands in this chapter, the question must still be raised. How is matrimony valued in relationship to orders? Let me be clear: no one is suggesting that marital sexual relations are the most fundamental value of matrimony. Every married couple abstains from sexual activity on occasion, due to illness and other factors. And yet, valuing "perfect and perpetual continence" over and above a normal, sexually active matrimonial life is not consistent with the sacramental language the Church uses about matrimony.

Some years ago, while serving on active duty in the Navy, I was also assigned as deacon of the military chapel where we lived. One evening, my wife and I were eating dinner with the three Catholic chaplains also assigned to the chapel. All three men were well-educated and experienced priests, and we were having interesting conversations on ministry, including my own experience as a married deacon. My wife excused herself for a few moments, and in her absence, the senior priest turned to me and said, "The only difference between our ministry and yours is that you can fornicate." To say I was stunned would be an understatement. For him, it all boiled down to sex. What's more, he referred to the relations of a husband and wife as "fornication"! It was clear that the other two priests were chagrined and embarrassed by his comment. I couldn't remain at the table any longer and left, found my wife, and went home. At no point that evening or ever did Father apologize for his statement. The other two priests apologized on his behalf (not that they needed to), but not him.

I recount this story simply to say that the Church's attitudes toward things change over time. Furthermore, we must consider how the Church lives out the wonderful claims we make about ourselves and our sacraments. Even if a teaching is beautifully written and artfully crafted with precision, how does that teaching reflect the actual experience of people "on the ground"? Does every Catholic in every parish truly see matrimony as a sacrament equal in effect to orders? Does every Catholic in every parish believe the beautiful language of the *Catechism* about matrimony? Why, as many observers have noted, do we raise to the altar those married people who either forsake marital relations or enter religious life after the death of a spouse? It seems to many people that sex is still understood as "dirty" and that purity, especially ministerial purity, demands abstention. In short, even if Peters is correct that continence is a fundamental value going all the way back to the beginning of Christianity, it could be that this is no longer the case in the lived experience of the Church. Now seems the time to consider a canonical position more reflective of that experience and the contemporary theology of the Church.

Therefore, it seems to me that, clearly, the mind of the universal Church is such that there is no expectation of clerical continence by married deacons. For example, when in 2011 the U.S. Conference of Catholic Bishops (USCCB) requested an interpretation on this matter from the Pontifical Council for Legislative Texts, the response was that "the current canonical discipline does not require married permanent deacons, as long as their marriage lasts, to observe the obligation of perfect and perpetual continence established by can. 277, § 1 *CIC* for clerics in general."[37] Nonetheless, I agree with Peters that the canon should be rewritten to remove any ambiguity or lack of clarity. All of this leads to the following recommendation.

Recommendation #7:
Delete c. 277 §1. Replace with the following canons adapted from *CCEO* 373–75.

NEW canon 277 §1 Clerical celibacy chosen for the sake of the kingdom of heaven is to be greatly esteemed everywhere, as supported by the tradition of the whole Church; likewise, the hallowed practice of married clerics in the history and tradition of the Church is to be held in honor.

RETAIN CURRENT canon 277 §2 and §3

NEW canon 278 Clerics, celibate or married, are to excel in the virtue of chastity; it is for particular law to establish suitable means for pursuing this end.

NEW canon 279 In leading family life and in educating children, married clergy are to show an outstanding example to other Christian faithful.

F. Concluding Rights and Obligations and the "Permanent Deacon" Exception

The following canons are significant on a couple of levels. Although written to pertain to all clerics, they are—in whole or in part—"waived" for "permanent deacons" by c. 288. A more precise methodology would include any adaptation deemed necessary within each canon itself.

> **Canon 284** Clerics are to wear suitable ecclesiastical garb according to the norms issued by the conference of bishops and according to legitimate local customs.

This is one of the two most asked questions from deacons (the other being concerned with deacons and the sacrament of anointing of the sick). First, this canon is not referring to the deacon's liturgical vesture; it pertains to clothing worn outside the sanctuary. Second, the obligation to wear clerical attire is removed for deacons by c. 288, but that does not *forbid* a deacon from wearing clerical attire. The Code of Canon Law does not designate what "suitable ecclesiastical garb" is supposed to be; that is left to particular law established by an episcopal conference or diocesan bishop. Pastoral practice around the country varies widely. Some bishops absolutely forbid permanent deacons from ever wearing clerical attire. Other bishops permit it on a case-by-case basis, still others permit it under certain conditions, and some leave the matter completely up to the deacons. Some dioceses have decreed that deacons wear a distinctive color (other than black) in their clerical attire, and still others make no such decision. In the United States, the episcopal conference has consistently decided against establishing a national norm on the matter, since the individual bishops of the conference prefer to leave that decision to each diocesan bishop. This is due to the great diversity of need and practice around the country. It is also interesting that the Eastern canons are completely silent on the matter.

The reason to "waive" the obligation of wearing clerical garb for deacons employed outside the Church is to avoid competing obligations. Most deacons are employed in various jobs, careers, and professions, many of which have their own required dress code. In short, the canon is not intended to deprive deacons of the responsibility to wear suitable clerical garb; it is to free them to be able to respond to the demands of their various obligations.

Recommendation #8:
Adapt c. 284 as follows:

> **Canon 284** Clerics are to wear suitable ecclesiastical garb according to the norms issued by the conference of bishops and according to legitimate local customs and adaptations as particular law dictates.

Moving to the other canons included in c. 288's "waiver" for deacons, I have included the necessary language within each canon, thus eliminating the need for c. 288.

Recommendation #9:
Adapt c. 285 as follows:

> **Canon 285 §1** Clerics are to refrain completely from all those things that are unbecoming to their state, according to the prescripts of particular law.
>
> **§2** Clerics are to avoid those things that, although not unbecoming, are nevertheless foreign to the clerical state.
>
> **§3** Clerics are forbidden to assume public offices that entail a participation in the exercise of civil power, although deacons not destined for the presbyterate may do so with the permission of their ordinary.
>
> **§4** Without the permission of their ordinary, they are not to take on the management of goods belonging to laypersons or secular offices that entail an obligation of rendering accounts. They are prohibited from giving surety even with their own goods without consultation with their proper ordinary. They also are to refrain from signing promissory notes, namely, those through which they assume an obligation to make payment on demand. Married clerics are not bound by this canon.

Recommendation #10:
Adapt c. 286 as follows:

Canon 286 Clerics are prohibited from conducting business or trade personally or through others, for their own advantage or that of others, except with the permission of legitimate ecclesiastical authority. Married clerics responsible for the economic welfare of themselves and their families are not bound by this canon; the provisions of c. 281 §3 apply.

Given the responsibilities all clergy share for building up the Body of Christ, and given that deacons are official preachers and teachers of the word of God, it seems appropriate that deacons *not be* exempted from c. 287 §2. This is particularly true during the current state of polarized politics. No specific change is necessary to c. 287 itself; the deletion of c. 288 will take care of that.

Canon 287 §1 Most especially, clerics are always to foster the peace and harmony based on justice which are to be observed among people.

§2 They are not to have an active part in political parties and in governing labor unions unless, in the judgment of competent ecclesiastical authority, the protection of the rights of the Church or the promotion of the common good requires it.

Recommendation #11:
Delete, *in toto*, c. 288.

Canon 288 The prescripts of cc. 284, 285, §§3 and 4, 286, and 287, §2 do not bind permanent deacons unless particular law establishes otherwise.

II. The Deacon and the Teaching Function of the Church (*Munus Docendi*)

One of the most powerful moments in the ordination of a deacon occurs after the newly ordained deacon is vested for the first time in stole and dalmatic. He then returns to the bishop and, kneeling before him, receives the Book of the Gospels. The bishop directs, "Receive the Gospel of Christ, whose herald you have become. Believe what you read, teach what you believe, and practice what you teach." This "Deacon's Charge" inspires and challenges every deacon in his spirituality and in ministry. So now we turn to the canons related to the deacon and the ministry of the word.

> **Canon 757** It is proper for presbyters, who are co-workers of the bishops, to proclaim the gospel of God; this duty binds especially pastors and others to whom the care of souls is entrusted with respect to the people committed to them. It is also for deacons to serve the people of God in the ministry of the word in communion with the bishop and his presbyterium.

It is significant that the canon mentions "others to whom the care of souls is entrusted," recalling our earlier discussion about the phrase "care of souls" in *LG* 29. The language of this canon is problematic. Yes, presbyters are coworkers of the bishops, and it is proper for them to "proclaim the gospel of God." However, so too are deacons—ordained by the bishop alone for his service (*non ad sacerdotium sed in ministerio episcopi*) and presented by the bishop with the Book of the Gospels. Deacons, as we have seen, are ordained *pro cura animarum* even if it is not the *cura plena* of c. 150. This canon need not distinguish between presbyters and deacons in this regard, and a revised canon would make this clear.

Recommendation #12:
Replace c. 757 with the following new text, taken completely from *CCEO* 596:

> **REVISED canon 757** The office of teaching in the name of the Church belongs only to bishops; but that function is shared, according to the norm of law, both by those who have been made collaborators of the bishops by sacred orders and by those who, though not in sacred orders, have received the mandate to teach.

The following canon is easily remedied by expanding the final term.

Recommendation #13:
Change c. 762 by deleting the final word "priests" and replacing it with "all sacred ministers."

> **REVISED canon 762** Sacred ministers, among whose principal duties is the proclamation of the gospel of God to all, are to hold the function of preaching in esteem since the people of God are first brought together by the word of the living God, which it is certainly right to require from the mouth of all sacred ministers.

III. The Deacon and the Sanctifying Function of the Church (*Munus Sanctificandi*)

The *munus sanctificandi* of the deacon is found not only in the canons but also in the liturgical books themselves, following the texts of the Second Vatican Council. Therefore, our review will be necessarily brief. There are no changes to be made to the canons, with the possible exception of c. 1003.

Canon 835 assigns to each *ordo* its sanctifying functions, and "deacons have a part in celebration of the divine worship in accord with the prescriptions of the law." While the Eastern Code does not specify the role of deacons in the parallel canon, deacons are included in the canons outlining the responsibilities of all clerics. For example, *CCEO* 381 §2 directs,

> Unless constrained by a just impediment, clerics are bound by the obligation to provide assistance to the Christian faithful out of the spiritual goods of the Church, especially the word of God and the sacraments, when they ask for them at appropriate times, are properly disposed, and are not prohibited by law from receiving them.

The documents of Vatican II (in particular, *Lumen Gentium*), other canons, and the liturgical books themselves identify particular diaconal functions. According to *Lumen Gentium* 29, for example, the deacon is to

> administer baptism solemnly; care for the eucharist and give holy communion; assist at and bless marriages in the name of the Church; carry viaticum to the dying; read the Scriptures to the people and exhort and instruct them; preside over worship and prayer; administer sacramentals; officiate at funeral and burial rites.

Baptism by a deacon is covered by c. 861 §1, which states that "the ordinary minister of baptism is a bishop, presbyter or deacon." This is a change from the 1917 Code in which the deacon was an extraordinary minister of baptism. Likewise, the deacon as ordinary minister of holy communion (also a change from the 1917 Code, which considered the deacon an extraordinary minister) is covered by c. 910 §1, and the deacon is also a "minister of exposition of the Most Holy Sacrament and the Eucharistic benediction" according to c. 943, still another change from the 1917 Code, in which only a priest could impart the benediction. Although *Lumen Gentium* spoke of the deacon as an ordinary minister of viaticum, the law (c. 911 §2) obliges certain priests (those who are not pastors or chaplains), deacons, and other ministers to this ministry only "in the case of necessity or with the presumed permission of the pastor, chaplain, or superior, who must be notified afterwards." It is not clear why this restriction should apply to any cleric and, although I am not making a specific recommendation in this regard, I would request this restriction be lifted. Most deacons are involved in various forms of hospital ministry and are often called upon in a patient's last moments. The deacon's pastoral availability is often greater than others', and ministering viaticum to the dying is one of the ways we may minister to them, especially since deacons are not currently permitted to celebrate the sacrament of anointing of the sick. On a practical level, I am not aware of any problem in this regard; namely, where any "pastor, chaplain, or superior" would object to any cleric performing this ministry. It is precisely for this reason that I am suggesting that the language of the canon should reflect that reality.

Canon 1003 §1, which pertains to the minister of the anointing of the sick, specifically restricts administration of this sacrament to those in sacerdotal orders, and the Eastern Code (739 §1) repeats this restriction. Deacons and lay ecclesial ministers have become increasingly active in ministries to the sick and aged, and several episcopal conferences have unsuccessfully sought approval to extend this faculty to deacons. The development of c. 1003 is illuminating. Frederick McManus observed,

> In the last states of the revision, an unsuccessful effort was made to remove the words *valide* (much debated in the process of revision) and *omnis et solus* from the text of paragraph one, which follows canon 938, §1 of the 1917 *Code* closely. The omission was proposed on the grounds that the statement cannot be supported historically, at least for the first eight centuries....The redacting commission preferred to retain the 1917 text.
>
> This canon precludes, at least for the present time and discipline, the celebration of the sacrament by deacons.... This restriction is partly because of a desire to retain the relationship of the sacrament to the anointing mentioned in the letter of James, which speaks of presbyters or elders, who are understood to be those in positions of authority in the local Christian community.[38]

Given the great pastoral need, and the fact that our history shows certain flexibility in this matter, especially in the first eight centuries, as Father McManus noted, it is recommended that c. 1003 be adapted as follows:

Recommendation #14:
Revise c. 1003 as follows:

REVISED canon 1003 §1 Every priest and, in case of necessity, every deacon validly administers the anointing of the sick.

§2 All priests to whom the care of souls has been entrusted have the duty and right of administering the

> anointing of the sick for the faithful entrusted to their pastoral office. For a reasonable cause, any other priest or, in case of necessity, any deacon can administer this sacrament with at least the presumed consent of the priest mentioned above.
>
> **§3** Any priest or deacon is permitted to carry blessed oil with him so that he is able to administer the sacrament of the anointing of the sick in a case of necessity.

Of course, this leads to the question of auricular confession as part of the last rites of confession, anointing of the sick, and viaticum. The recommendation above does not address the issue of the sacrament of reconciliation. It is sometimes pointed out that the sacrament of anointing of the sick itself (with or without auricular confession) forgives sins and, therefore, deacons cannot be eligible to administer this sacrament. However, it should go without saying that forgiveness comes from God alone, and that deacons are ordinary ministers of the sacrament of baptism itself, which also forgives all sins. It seems that, in an analogous way, deacons could therefore administer the sacrament of anointing of the sick, especially in cases of necessity.

Canons 1079 and 1080 give deacons (and priests) the faculty to dispense from certain impediments to marriage "in danger of death" (c. 1079) or "when all is prepared for the wedding" (c. 1080). Canon 1108 specifies the local ordinary and the pastor, or a priest or deacon delegated by either of them, as the authorized witness to marriage. Regarding sacramentals, c. 1168 authorizes clerics and certain laypersons to minister sacramentals, and c. 1169 specifies that "a deacon can impart only those blessings which are expressly permitted to him by law." Finally, no canon specifically delineates the role of the deacon as a minister at funeral or burial rites, but this role is included in the liturgical books, as provided for under c. 835.

IV. The Deacon and the Church's Ministry of Governing (*Munus Regendi*)

It is difficult to provide a clear-cut canonical description of the deacon's governing functions. As discussed above, however, the bishops at Vatican II nonetheless included the technical term *pro cura animarum* in *LG* 29. We also referred to John Beal's observation that this is "a phrase with historic associations with the power of jurisdiction."[39]

It is possible to distinguish distinct levels of *cura animarum.* Consider c. 150:

> **Canon 150** An office which entails the full care of souls and for whose fulfillment the exercise of the priestly order is required cannot be conferred validly on one who is not yet a priest.

While this canon specifies offices that require the *full* care of souls (necessitating a priest), other canons refer to persons other than priests who share in some degree in the care of souls. James Provost identifies, for example, coadjutor and auxiliary bishops, parochial vicars, "deacons and lay persons involved in the care of souls [e.g., c. 517 §2], some chaplains."[40] From the earliest days of the diaconate, deacons have been "dedicated to works of charity *and functions of administration*" (*LG* 29; emphasis added). Functions of administration frequently fall into the category of administrative governance, although they never constitute the capacity for *full* care of souls. A recent Instruction from the Congregation for the Clergy notes, "There are many ecclesial tasks, therefore, that can be entrusted to a deacon, namely, all those that do not involve the full care of souls [citing c. 150]. The Code of Canon Law, however, determines which offices are reserved to the priest and those that can also be entrusted to the lay faithful, while there is no indication of any particular office in which the deacon's ministry can find specific expression."[41] This lacuna needs to be addressed: What are particular offices for the deacon to exercise the diaconal *cura animarum*?

The same instruction also speaks of the administration of temporal goods as a governance for deacons.

In any case, the history of the diaconate recalls that it was established within the framework of a ministerial vision of the Church, as an ordained ministry at the service of the Word and of Charity; this latter context includes the administration of goods. The twofold mission of the deacon is expressed in the liturgical sphere, where he is called to proclaim the gospel and to serve at the eucharistic table.

These references can help identify the specific tasks of a deacon, adding value to that which is proper to the diaconate, with a view to promoting the diaconal ministry.[42]

Paul VI's 1967 *motu proprio*, *Sacrum Diaconatus Ordinem*, provided the norms for the renewal of the diaconate. He expanded the duties described in *LG* 29, resulting in eleven sets of diaconal functions (*SDO* 581–82). Nearly all of them involve leadership: the deacon is said to "preside, direct, guide, foster, aid, teach, preach, administer." Several of these functions are directly related to areas traditionally associated with acts of governance:

- To preside over the offices of religious worship and prayer services when there is no priest present,
- To do charitable, administrative, and welfare work in the name of the hierarchy, and
- To legitimately guide outlying communities of Christians in the name of the pastor and the bishop.

With this in mind, let us quickly review some related canons. Canon 483 §2 (*CCEO* 253) permits deacons, as clerics, to serve as diocesan chancellors and notaries. Similarly, Canon 512 §1 (*CCEO* 273) refers to clerics being a part of a bishop's diocesan pastoral council; while deacons are not mentioned explicitly, they are also not excluded; unless particular law restricts membership of the diocesan pastoral council to the laity, deacons may serve in this capacity. Canon 536 §1 (*CCEO* 295) addresses the establishment of parish pastoral councils; the pastor is to preside, while "those who share in pastoral care by virtue of their office in the parish" are involved in the council in order to assist "in fostering pastoral activity"; this would include all clerics assigned to the parish by their bishop. The 1998 *Directory on the Ministry and Life of Permanent Deacons* specifies, "Where the bishop has deemed it opportune to institute parish pastoral councils, deacons appointed to participate in the pastoral care of such parishes are members of these councils by right."[43]

Canon 1421 (*CCEO* 1087), c. 1428 §2 (*CCEO* 1093), and c. 1435 (*CCEO* 1099) include deacons (when qualified) as judges and various court officials.[44] Mention has already been made under the deacon's sanctifying function of his authority to dispense under certain conditions (under the Latin Code only; deacons do not have this authority in the *CCEO*). Canon 517 deserves special attention. On the one hand, the role of the deacon under this canon is an extraordinary diaconal function, since most deacons do not ordinarily or routinely serve in this capacity. On the other hand, deacons are given a definite precedence under the law and in the 1998 dicasterial documents on the diaconate, and it is enlightening to review the history and rationale offered for this precedence.

> **Canon 517 §1** When circumstances require it, the pastoral care of a parish or of different parishes together can be entrusted to several priests *in solidum*, with the requirement, however, that in exercising pastoral care one of them must be the moderator, namely, the one who is to direct the joint action and to answer for it to the bishop.
>
> **§2** If, because of a lack of priests, the diocesan bishop has decided that participation in the exercise of the pastoral care of a parish is to be entrusted to a deacon, to another person who is not a priest, or to a community of persons, he is to appoint some priest who, provided with the powers and faculties of a pastor, is to direct the pastoral care.

Canon 517 was new to the 1983 Code and there is no parallel canon in the *CCEO*. The point to the canon ensures that full pastoral care is provided through the assignment of pastors to every parish, even when those parishes may not have the presence of a resident pastor. The history of the canon is illustrative.

The canon addresses the need for some person to provide for the *cura animarum* in each parish. Since only a priest can supply *full* care, provisions must be made to provide some priest with that responsibility, even if that priest is not resident in the parish. Furthermore, if the priest is not resident, someone else must coordinate day-to-day pastoral life. From the beginning of the Code revision process, the possibility was considered that there might be insufficient numbers of presbyters to pastor every parish, leading to the drafting of the following text, discussed by the Pontifical Commission for the Revision of the Code of Canon Law, February 15–20, 1971.

> If, in unusual circumstances, according to the norm of law, a participation in the exercise of the pastoral care of a parish is entrusted to a person not signed with the sacerdotal character [*personae sacerdotali charactere non insignitae*], or to a community of persons, a priest is to be designated to oversee [*moderetur*] the pastoral care, as would the proper pastor of the parish.[45]

The primary purpose of the canon was to provide the parish with a priest to oversee the pastoral care of a parish. It is only in the subordinate clause of the canon that is found the provision of on-scene pastoral leadership by someone other than a priest. During the discussion, the text was amended to clarify the proper authority to make such an assignment, and the approved text now begins,

> If, because of a lack of priests, a diocesan bishop has determined that participation in the exercise of the pastoral care of a parish is to be entrusted to some person....[46]

At the next session in 1971, discussions focused on the juridical status of the priest-moderator, suggesting that he be assigned "with all the rights and obligations of a pastor."[47] However, the commission concluded that, while certainly the moderator would have the rights of a pastor, he would not have all the obligations; the revision ultimately approved at this session reads,

> [The diocesan bishop] is to designate a priest who, with the rights of a proper pastor, shall oversee [*moderetur*] the pastoral care.[48]

This canon was not considered again for five years. In March 1976, two amendments were accepted. First, the verb "designate" was changed to "appoint," and "with the rights of a proper pastor" was changed to "having the power of a pastor" [*potestate parochi gaudens*]. The approved text reads,

> The diocesan bishop is to appoint a priest who, having the power of a pastor....[49]

Again, the principal concern was on the nature and responsibilities of the priest-moderator, not on the daily administrator. This is also the first use of the term *potestas* in the canon.

Deacons were first mentioned in connection with the canon in May 1980. "If, because of a lack of priests, the diocesan bishop has determined that participation in the exercise of the pastoral care of a parish is to be entrusted to some deacon or even [*etiam*] to a lay member of the Christian faithful or to a group of them, he is to appoint...."[50] John McCarthy explains: "This revised text is significant because it not only mentions explicitly the possibility of a deacon functioning as the on-site assistant but, by inclusion of the word 'even' [*etiam*], seems to suggest that a deacon would be preferable in that role to a lay person or group of persons."[51] For reasons left undocumented, however, many of the revisions of this session do not appear in the resulting *schema*, including the reference to deacons.

In response to the 1980 *schema*, a *relatio* was prepared that addressed this proposed canon.[52] One bishop requested the text be modified to address the fact that the person appointed to provide on-scene pastoral care does so "in an extraordinary and temporary manner."[53] Furthermore, the bishop stated that "pastoral ministries can be entrusted to lay persons only in this way."[54] The next recommendation came from then Bishop Bernadin, who suggested that the words "to a deacon" be added (one could say, restored, since mention of the deacon had previously been suggested, then deleted from the *schema*). The response of the Code Commission to Bishop Bernadin's suggestion, especially considering the previous recommendation about the *extraordinary and temporary* nature of a layperson's appointment to this task, is interesting. The commission responded that a specific inclusion of deacons was not necessary because it is clear that

> deacons always have, in a certain ordinary and permanent way [*modo quidem ordinario et permanenti*], "participation in the exercise of the pastoral care of a parish." The

> norm of this § concerns only a participation entrusted to other members of the Christian faithful who have received no grade of the ministerial priesthood [*qui nullum gradum sacerdotii ministerialis receperunt*].[55]

The focus of this response as it pertains to the on-scene provider of pastoral care is on the concession of an extraordinary participation in governance to laypersons in such situations. Deacons need no such concession since they already enjoy, by virtue of diaconal ordination, an ordinary and permanent participation in this exercise of governance.

When the final text of the canon was prepared, however, the reference to deacons was left intact and included. No explanation is offered for the inclusion. However, whereas the text of the previous draft that referred to deacons inferred a distinction between deacons and laity who might be entrusted with pastoral care ("the diocesan bishop [may entrust] the pastoral care of a parish to some deacon or *even* [*etiam*] to some member of the Christian faithful"), the final text does not include this distinction. It reads simply that pastoral care may be entrusted "to a deacon, to another person, or to a community of persons." Again, no explanation is provided. McCarthy concludes reasonably, that "it could well be, however, that the omission stems from the response given in the *Relatio complectens synthesim*: deacons have priority as a consequence of ordination,"[56] an ordination that gives deacons a certain ordinary and permanent responsibility for pastoral care.

Subsequent Vatican documents reach the same conclusion. The 1997 interdicasterial instruction, *Ecclesiae de Mysterio*,[57] addresses the provisions of *CIC* 517 §2. Significantly, this Instruction was approved by John Paul II *in forma specifica*, thereby making it law:

> The right understanding and application of this canon… requires that this exceptional provision be used only with strict adherence to conditions contained in it. These are:
>
> a) *a shortage of priests* [emphasis in text] and not for reasons of convenience or ambiguous "advancement of the laity," etc.;

> b) this is *a share in the exercise of the pastoral care* [emphasis in text] and not de facto directing, coordinating, moderating or governing the parish; these competencies, according to the canon, are the competencies of a presbyter alone.
>
> Because these are exceptional cases, before employing them, other possibilities should be considered, e.g., using the services of retired presbyters still capable of such service, or entrusting several parishes to one priest or to "several priests jointly."
>
> *In any event, the preference which this canon gives to deacons cannot be overlooked* [emphasis added].[58]

In 1998, the Congregation for the Clergy included this law in in its *Directory* on the diaconate. In dealing with this canon, the Congregation asserts,

> Where permanent deacons participate in the pastoral care of parishes which do not, because of a shortage, have the immediate benefit of a parish priest, they always have precedence over the nonordained faithful....When deacons are available, participation in the pastoral care of the faithful may not be entrusted to a lay person or to a community of lay persons.[59]

The development of this canon, therefore, even though it refers to an extraordinary diaconal function, demonstrates an underlying presupposition that deacons exercise some *ordinary* responsibility for the care of souls that goes beyond the responsibility of the baptized faithful. Since the deacon is not ordained to a sacerdotal order, his exercise of governance is limited to offices and functions not requiring "the priestly character" such as pastor or parochial vicar. And yet, the deacon is given a certain canonical precedence over the laity when pastoral leadership is required in the absence of a presbyter. The nature of this preference demands attention. Could it be that in this canon the diaconate is still perceived as a participation in the ministerial priesthood as it was for so many centuries prior to Vatican II? The fact is that deacons are now the largest group of ministers serving in this capacity, and it would be good to have a conversation on the rationale for canonical preference.

Conclusion

Here are the fourteen recommendations discussed above, in table format for ease of reading. I believe that the recommendations developed in this chapter, along with the other reflections on deacons in the existing Code, might be a first attempt to respond to Father Provost's dream of a more systematic and comprehensive approach to the diaconate in the law. It also positions the deacon to better exercise his ministries with humility, precision, and care.

Proposed Revisions to the Code of Canon Law

Recommendation #1: Insert four new canons after c. 231; adapted from *CCEO* 323–26:

NEW canon 232 §1 Sacred ministers, who are also called clerics, are Christian faithful who, chosen by the competent ecclesiastical authority, are constituted through a gift of the Holy Spirit received in sacred ordination to be ministers of the Church participating in the mission and power of Christ, Servant and Pastor.

§2 In virtue of sacred ordination clerics are distinguished from the other Christian faithful by divine institution.

NEW canon 233 Clerics joined among themselves by hierarchical communion and constituted in various degrees participate in diverse ways in the one ecclesiastical ministry of divine origin.

NEW canon 234 In virtue of sacred ordination clerics are distinguished as bishops, presbyters, and deacons.

NEW canon 235 Clerics are constituted into the degrees of orders by sacred ordination itself; but they cannot exercise that power except according to the norm of law.

Note: These are new canons being inserted at the beginning of the section on "Sacred Ministers or Clerics." The existing canons (232–36) are retained and renumbered, unless otherwise indicated.

Recommendation #2: Revise c. 384 as follows:

NEW canon 384 With special solicitude, a diocesan bishop is to attend to his clergy and listen to them as assistants and counselors. He is to protect their rights and take care that they correctly fulfill the obligations proper to their state and that the means and institutions that they need to foster spiritual and intellectual life are available to them. He also is to take care that provision is made for their decent support and social assistance, according to the norm of law.

§1 Deacons, ordained "not to the priesthood but to the service of the bishop," enjoy a unique relationship to the diocesan bishop as his particular assistants and advisors in a *diakonia* of Word, Sacrament, and Charity. The diocesan bishop is to establish means to encourage and nurture this relationship so as to extend his own ministry to all.

§2 The diocesan bishop is to see that the families of his clerics, if they are married, be provided with adequate support, appropriate protection, and social security in addition to health insurance according to the norm of law.

Recommendation #3: Delete current cc. 1008–9.

Recommendation #4: Rewrite (and renumber) current c. 236, adapting *CCEO* 354. Notice: the current two subcanons (1° and 2°) are deleted.

REVISED canon 236 The formation of deacons not destined for the priesthood is to be appropriately adapted from the norms given above so that the curriculum of studies extends at least three years keeping in mind the traditions of the Latin Church concerning the service of the Word, Sacrament, and Charity, as determined and defined by the conference of bishops.

Recommendation #5: Rewrite current cc. 129 and 274 as follows:

Canon 129 §1 Through episcopal ordination, bishops exercise fully the power of governance, which exists in the Church by divine institution and is also called the power of jurisdiction. Through ordination, presbyters and deacons are qualified, according to the norm of the prescripts of the law, for the power of governance as determined by the diocesan bishop.

§2 Lay members of the Christian faithful also exercise this same power as authorized and determined by the diocesan bishop.

Canon 274 §1 Clerics exercise the power of orders as determined by their order; they may obtain offices for whose exercise the power of ecclesiastical governance is required.

Recommendation #6: Adapt c. 276 §2.3 from *CCEO* 377:

REVISED canon 276 §2.3 All clerics must celebrate the Liturgy of the Hours according to the particular law of the regional episcopal conference or the diocesan bishop.

Recommendation #7: Delete c. 277 §1. Replace with the following canons adapted from *CCEO* 373–75.

NEW canon 277 §1 Clerical celibacy chosen for the sake of the kingdom of heaven is to be greatly esteemed everywhere, as supported by the tradition of the whole Church; likewise, the hallowed practice of married clerics in the primitive Church and in the tradition of the Eastern Catholic Churches throughout the ages is to be held in honor.

RETAIN CURRENT canon 277 §2 and §3

NEW canon 278 Clerics, celibate or married, are to excel in the virtue of chastity; it is for particular law to establish suitable means for pursuing this end.

NEW canon 279 In leading family life and in educating children, married clergy are to show an outstanding example to other Christian faithful.

Recommendation #8: Adapt c. 284 as follows:

Canon 284 Clerics are to wear suitable ecclesiastical garb according to the norms issued by the conference of bishops and according to legitimate local customs and adaptations as particular law dictates.

Recommendation #9: Adapt c. 285 as follows:

Canon 285 §1 Clerics are to refrain completely from all those things that are unbecoming to their state, according to the prescripts of particular law.

§2 Clerics are to avoid those things that, although not unbecoming, are nevertheless foreign to the clerical state.

§3 Clerics are forbidden to assume public offices that entail a participation in the exercise of civil power, although deacons not destined for the presbyterate may do so with the permission of their ordinary.

§4 Without the permission of their ordinary, they are not to take on the management of goods belonging to laypersons or secular offices that entail an obligation of rendering accounts. They are prohibited from giving surety even with their own goods without consultation with their proper ordinary. They also are to refrain from signing promissory notes, namely, those through which they assume an obligation to make payment on demand. Married clerics are not bound by this canon.

Recommendation #10: Adapt c. 286 as follows:

Canon 286 Clerics are prohibited from conducting business or trade personally or through others, for their own advantage or that of others, except with the permission of legitimate ecclesiastical authority. Married clerics responsible for the economic welfare of themselves and their families are not bound by this canon; the provisions of c. 281 §3 apply.

Canon 287 §1 Most especially, clerics are always to foster the peace and harmony based on justice which are to be observed among people.

§2 They are not to have an active part in political parties and in governing labor unions unless, in the judgment of competent ecclesiastical authority, the protection of the rights of the Church or the promotion of the common good requires it.

Recommendation #11: Delete, *in toto*, c. 288.

Canon 288 The prescripts of cc. 284, 285, §§3 and 4, 286, and 287, §2 do not bind permanent deacons unless particular law establishes otherwise.

Recommendation #12: Replace c. 757 with the following new text, taken completely from *CCEO* 596:

REVISED canon 757 The office of teaching in the name of the Church belongs only to bishops; but that function is shared, according to the norm of law, both by those who have been made collaborators of the bishops by sacred orders and by those who, though not in sacred orders, have received the mandate to teach.

Recommendation #13: Change c. 762 by deleting the final word "priests" and replacing it with "all sacred ministers."

Canon 762 Sacred ministers, among whose principal duties is the proclamation of the gospel of God to all, are to hold the function of preaching in esteem since the people of God are first brought together by the word of the living God, which it is certainly right to require from the mouth of all sacred ministers.

Recommendation #14: Revise c. 1003 as follows:

REVISED canon 1003 §1 Every priest and, in case of necessity, every deacon validly administers the anointing of the sick.

§2 All priests to whom the care of souls has been entrusted have the duty and right of administering the anointing of the sick for the faithful entrusted to their pastoral office. For a reasonable cause, any other priest or, in case of necessity, any deacon can administer this sacrament with at least the presumed consent of the priest mentioned above.

§3 Any priest or deacon is permitted to carry blessed oil with him so that he is able to administer the sacrament of the anointing of the sick in a case of necessity.

CHAPTER SIX

ORDAINING DEACONS IN A HUMBLE CHURCH

Proposed Revisions to the Rite of Ordination

Introduction

Some years ago, I wrote about diaconate ordination; this chapter builds on that foundation. As I wrote then, "The liturgy itself is an indispensable source for theology. Through the symbolic discourse of sacramental celebration, the Church is re-created, and we come to a deeper understanding of God's presence and action in the life of the Church."[1] How we pray reflects who we are, and who we are affects how we pray. Who are we as a humble Church when we designate a disciple to serve us in an order of ministry? In both the Latin and Eastern Catholic Churches, the liturgical assembly declares its "worthiness" (*axios*).[2] But worthy for what? To do what? How are our ministers identified, selected, formed, and designated? From the time of the patristic era through the Second Vatican Council and beyond, the ordained have been said to act both *in persona Christ* and *in nomine Ecclesiae*. What is being done "in our name" when a person is ordained? And who are we when a person is ordained on our behalf? Specific to the thesis of our current project—that humility is the lens through which we see and experience Church—we may ask, "How does a humble Church ordain?"

We have already referenced Father Komonchak and his concern over the gap between the things we say about the Church and the reality of the Church people actually experience. Nowhere is that gap more apparent than in our rites of ordination. What I wrote all those years ago remains accurate here. "The purpose of this chapter, then, is to examine the rite of diaconal ordination to gain insights about what this might teach us about the nature of the Church, the nature and role of her deacons, and what all of this means in the Church and world today. Through the symbolic discourse of the ordination rite, what is the Church attempting to say and to do and to be?"[3] And, building on Komonchak, we will be concerned with closing the gap between our symbolic discourse and our lived experience.

I write from the perspective of the Latin Church. The proposals for change are for the Latin Church. However, as I did in the previous chapter on canon law, I will draw upon the insights of Eastern Catholic ordination traditions to consider ways in which Eastern practice might enhance and improve the symbology of the Latin ordination rite.

Rites of ordinations have always been works in progress. Over the centuries they have taken many forms as the Church has sought to express what ordination signifies. Our symbols communicate. If they are to communicate effectively, they must be precise, accurate, and honest, resonating with people's experience and need. As David Power once wrote, "One norm for the interpretation of symbols is stated in the axiom: symbols articulate and transform experience. It demands attention to the interaction between experience and symbol."[4]

In the following section I will develop several principles that inform the proposed revisions.

The Roman Pontifical and the Ordination of Deacons

The 2012 Edition of the Roman Pontifical summarizes important themes behind the ordination of deacons. We will consider two of them: first, the theological foundations for the ordination of deacons, and second, principles to guide adaptation and liturgical reform.

Holy Orders in General

"Through sacred ordination certain of the Christian faithful are appointed in the name of Christ and receive the gift of the Holy Spirit to shepherd the Church with the word and grace of God."[5] Vatican II consistently teaches about the "shepherding" role of the ordained. For example, this reference from the General Introduction cites *Lumen Gentium* 11: "Those of the faithful who are consecrated by Holy Orders are appointed to feed the Church in Christ's name with the word and the grace of God." *LG* 18 builds on this theme:

> For the nurturing and constant growth of the People of God, Christ the Lord instituted in His Church a variety of ministries, which work for the good of the whole body. For those ministers, who are endowed with sacred power, serve their brethren, so that all who are of the People of God...may arrive at salvation.
>
> This Sacred Council...teaches and declares that Jesus Christ, the eternal Shepherd, established His holy Church, having sent forth the apostles as He Himself had been sent by the Father; and He willed that their successors, namely the bishops, should be shepherds in His Church even to the consummation of the world.

The Apostolic Role of the Bishop and His Deacons and Presbyters

The role of shepherd falls in its fullest to the bishops, as successors of the apostles and "sharers in his consecration and mission." This apostolic ministry is then shared with two orders of ministry to support and extend the ministry of the bishop: presbyters and deacons. The ministry of these subordinate orders derives from the bishop. They are "assistant shepherds" of a sort. As the General Instruction puts it, "[The bishops] in turn have lawfully handed on the office of their ministry in several grades to different individuals in the Church. Thus, the divinely established ecclesiastical ministry is exercised in different Orders by those who even from antiquity have been called Bishops, Priests, and Deacons" (*LG* 28). Following these general comments on the apostolic ministry, the General Instruction offers specific observations on each of the orders.

Deacons, Bishops, and *Diakonia*

In the paragraph on the order of deacons, we read that deacons "receive the laying on of hands not for the Priesthood but for the ministry. Strengthened by sacramental grace, they serve the People of God in the *diakonia* of liturgy, word, and charity, in communion with the Bishop and his presbyterate." This section repeats verbatim the teaching of *LG* 29. It is unfortunate, as I have written before, that the Council made use of the later texts based on the *Statuta Ecclesiae*, rather than the far older *Traditio Apostolica*. By using the later texts to refer to the fact that deacons are ordained *non ad sacerdotium, sed ad ministerium*, the Council and the revised pontifical perpetuate the problem of a generic and unspecific *ministerium*. Far more helpful would have been the ancient teaching of the *Apostolic Tradition*, which specifies the character of the deacon's service: the deacon is ordained *non ad sacerdotium sed in ministerio episcopi*. The deacon, on whom hands are laid by the bishop alone to signify the unique relationship between the bishop and his deacons, is ordained specifically and concretely *into* the ministry of the bishop. Pierre Jounel wrote, "All ordination rituals that have been used in the [Roman] Church flow from that given by Hippolytus.... The Roman liturgy has always prescribed the rites to which the Apostolic Tradition assigns normative value."[6] Making use of the more ancient and "normative" text would go a long way to providing clarity about the nature and role of the diaconate.

Deacons and the Sacramentality of Their Ordination

We discussed the sacramentality of the diaconate in chapter 4. Here we simply review some highlights as presented in the General Instruction of the Roman Pontifical (GIRP). Over the last thirty years there has been a gradual development of a theology of holy orders that distinguishes two modes of participation in the one sacrament: the sacerdotal and the diaconal. As we discussed in chapter 4, the Church still ordains seminarians to the diaconate before ordination to the presbyterate, and bishops are still chosen from the presbyterate. Since all ordinations are permanent in sacramental effect, presbyters and bishops are also still deacons. I have referred to this holdover from the *cursus honorum* as the "apprentice" model of the diaconate. But since 1967 the apprentice model is no longer the norm: the diaconate no longer finds its sacramental end in ordination to the sacerdotal orders. The rite of ordination of deacons must take this "new norm" of a mature, vocational diaconate—a "full and equal order"—into account.

Adaptations for Different Regions and Circumstances

Part 3 of the General Introduction directs, "It belongs to the Conferences of Bishops to adapt the rites of Ordination of a Bishop, of Priests, and of Deacons to the needs of the particular regions, so that, after the Apostolic See has confirmed the decisions of a Conference, the rites may be used in the region of that Conference."[7] Specifically regarding the ordination of deacons, episcopal conferences may

a) establish in what way the community indicates its "assent" to the election of the candidates (Deacons, nos. 198, 226, 264, 305);
b) direct that additional questions be included during the examination of candidates (Deacons, nos. 200, 228, 268, 309);
c) "specify the form by which the elect for the Diaconate and the Priesthood are to promise respect and obedience" (Deacons, nos. 125, 153, 201, 228, 269, 271, 310, 312);[8]
d) develop some additional act to demonstrate an unmarried candidate's commitment to the obligation of celibacy;
e) approve additional liturgical music;
f) finally, conferences may propose other adaptations to the Holy See. Specifically excluded from adaptation, however, are the act of laying on of hands and the prayer of ordination, and the "general structure of the

rites and the proper character of each element are to be retained."[9]

The proposals that follow fall within these parameters.

General Principles for Reform

Ecclesia: Semper Idem, Semper Reformanda

The Church is mystery. From the beginning, Christians have struggled to find the balance between necessary continuity and change. A ship or aircraft maneuvers best when in proper trim, when things are in balance; the barque of Peter is no different. A saying commonly associated with St. Augustine is that the Church is "always reforming" (*semper reformanda*). But reform can be frightening to many people, particularly those who seek order, predictability, and constancy. Cardinal Alfredo Ottaviani took *Semper idem* as his episcopal motto—"always the same." Many agree with him even today. While some people embrace change as a normal part of life, including Church life, others accept change only reluctantly and only when no other option is available.

The more optimistic of these worldviews was expressed by St. John Newman when he wrote about what happens to a "great idea": "In time it enters upon strange territory; points of controversy alter their bearing; parties rise and fall around it; dangers and hopes appear in new relations; and old principles reappear under new forms. *It changes with them in order to remain the same. In a higher world it is otherwise, but here below to live is to change, and to be perfect is to have changed often.*"[10] Newman is not writing in naïve terms, but in words that reflect life as it is lived. Particularly important is his observation that a great idea changes with time and circumstance precisely in order to remain the same. For example, the "great idea" of the Trinity developed over time, making use of extrabiblical language and philosophical concepts to express the relationships between God and humanity through the covenants God made with the ancient Israelites and the new covenant in Christ. God has not changed; in fact, that is one of the critical elements of the developing doctrine: to express to contemporaries the ancient truth that "I will be your God and you will be my people." Newman is not writing about change for change's sake alone. He describes change as something that helps us express ancient truths in contemporary ways.

When considering matters of the liturgy, and sacraments in particular, we must attend to this balance of constancy and change. Scholars have researched the history of the Latin Rite extensively and its development over the centuries. To what extent must our reflections be bound to that history? That depends on two things. First, if the proposed revision touches on some matter of dogma (e.g., the bread and wine to be used during the Eucharist), the historical evidence will be crucial and, to a greater or lesser degree, binding. Second are those revisions that are historically, culturally, and even geographically conditioned, and that may have little to do with dogma. An example here would be the current promise of obedience. The intent behind the gesture is profound and vital, but the form used in the modern rite is problematic. It derives from medieval oaths of fealty that would have been recognizable and particularly meaningful in the context of medieval feudalism but seem anachronistic today. In short, then, while we must respect the lessons of history, we are not always restricted to it.

The Primacy of Sacramental Initiation

Our sacramental call to ministry starts with baptism. In the Latin rite of ordination, the ordinand vests in an alb. The alb is the foundational vestment for all the baptized: altar servers wear them; newly baptized adults wear them; bishops, deacons, and presbyters wear them. Even the pope wears them. The alb signifies the white garment given at baptism: "You have become a new creation and have clothed yourself in Christ. May this white garment be a sign to you of your Christian dignity." It is over this foundation (the baptismal alb) that we who are ordained place the vestments unique to our office: the stole and dalmatic for the deacon, the stole and chasuble for the presbyter, and the bishop wears them all. Theologically, it is over the foundation of sacramental initiation that ordination to the specific ministries of bishop, deacon, and presbyter takes place.

In baptism, we are immersed into the very life of the Trinity, filled with and anointed by the Holy Spirit. Consecrated with sacred chrism, we are charged, "Almighty God, the Father of our Lord Jesus Christ, has freed you from sin, given you new birth by water and the Holy Spirit and joined you to his people. He now anoints you with the chrism of salvation, so that you may remain members of Christ, Priest, Prophet, and King unto eternal life." Now joined to Christ in his own identity as priest, prophet, and king, the newly baptized shares in Christ's mission and ministry. Vatican II teaches in its "Decree on the Apostolate of Lay People,"

> The faithful who by baptism are incorporated into Christ, are placed in the People of God, and in their own way share the priestly, prophetic and kingly office of Christ, and to the best of their ability carry on the mission of the whole Christian people in the Church and in the world [*LG* 31]....As sharers in the role of Christ the Priest, Prophet, and King, the laity have an active part to play in the life and activity of the Church (*AA* 10).[11]

This universal commission to service based upon sacramental initiation into the dynamic life of the Trinity sustains the conclusion that "no member of the Church ought to be purely passive, simply the recipient of someone else's ministrations. Everyone is to serve and to be served."[12] "Serving"—more properly, *diakonia*—is not the province of a particular order of ministry, but of all disciples. It is, in fact, the entire Church's responsibility to serve. John Paul II, in his 1987 address to the diaconate community gathered in Detroit made the following observation:

> The service of the deacon is the Church's service sacramentalized. Yours is not just one ministry among others, but it is truly meant to be, as Paul VI described it, a "driving force" for the Church's *diakonia*. You are meant to be living signs of the servanthood of Christ's Church.[13]

Similarly, in addressing the deacons of the Archdiocese of Chicago, Cardinal Joseph Bernardin wrote,

> This does not mean that the deacon has a monopoly on service in the Church. Others can carry out many tasks he performs in the community, and his ordination is not intended to exclude others from performing those tasks. *All* in the Church are to serve but by the liturgical consecration and empowerment of *some* of us, that is, the deacons, this call and response to serve is made visible and effective. So, the deacon is a sign and instrument of that manifold service without which the Church cannot be the sign and instrument of the risen Lord Jesus. In other words…[the deacon] is meant to be an eloquent reminder to each of us of what we, too, should be doing, what we must continually strive to become, in accord with our own God-given gifts.[14]

This insight from Cardinal Bernardin is often overlooked, especially in cultures in which compartmentalization of responsibility is commonplace. Deacons are not ordained to serve so that others don't have to; they are to inspire, cajole, model, nurture, support—to lead—each member of the Church to respond to the grace of baptism in service of others. Put simply, the deacon visits the sick, feeds the hungry, clothes the naked, consoles mourners, and all the rest because he is a baptized disciple of Christ. The deacon participates in pastoral servant leadership as his bishop and canon law dictates because he is ordained into the apostolic ministry of the bishop.

At the ordination of a deacon, all aspects of this theology of initiation come into play. The act of ordination itself must be understood within the larger context and framework of initiation. Ordination should not be focused on what some writers have termed the "status elevation" of the ordinand. The sacramental significance of the ministerial (i.e., ordained) diaconate finds its true meaning within the broader servant Church.

The Role of the People of God in the Ordination of a Deacon

With all that being said, we recognize that an ordination is a corporate act of the whole assembly called together by God through baptism.

The liturgy of ordination, especially within the sacramental framework of the Eucharist, is to engage the full, conscious, and active participation (both internally and externally) of all of the faithful, as called for by the bishops of the Second Vatican Council (see *Sacrosanctum Consilium* 14, 19). "Such participation by the Christian people as 'a chosen race, a royal priesthood, a holy nation, a redeemed people' (1 Pet. 2:9; cf. 2:4–5), is their right and duty by reason of their baptism" (*Sacrosanctum Concilium* 14).

In the proposed revisions to the ordination rite that follow, it is crucial to keep this fundamental principle of reform in mind. "In the restoration and promotion of the sacred liturgy, this full and active participation by all the people is the aim to be considered before all else." Proposals to address the participation of the faithful are much more than merely finding something for people to do! Lest anyone think this is a farfetched notion, consider the following.

I was visiting another diocese, speaking with some lay leaders about the renewal of the diaconate. One of the leaders mentioned that she thought it was nice of the pastor to "find things for the deacon to do" during Mass, like reading the Gospel. Even more frequent, however, is the comment of many priests before Mass that "we don't need you here at Mass today, Deacon. We've got everything covered." The perception is that Father and selected lay ministers can do everything and that the deacon's ministry is simply an option when there is a desire for more solemnity. When deacons hear such things, responses range from anger and frustration to disappointment and depression.

The meaning of ordination is found precisely in establishing the ordained as a person with a specific, concrete role to play within an established community of faith. It is that community that is calling on the bishop to ordain this candidate; they are not merely going to "receive" passively the ministrations of the newly ordained. It is, indeed, their "right and duty" to be the foundation upon which this ordination occurs. For this reason, as many members of the Church as possible should be present and active in the ordination. The ordination should take place at a date, time, and place that permits that participation. The current rite states this clearly; however, in practice, the involvement of the laity is minimal. In most ordinations, laypersons (usually family members of the ordinand) proclaim the readings (other than the Gospel, of course), and bring the gifts of bread and wine to the bishop. Some bishops will acknowledge the families of the ordinands during his homily or at some other point in the liturgy.

Such participation—while certainly appropriate—is inadequate to signify the theological significance of the entire diocesan Church in the ordination. When contrasted, for example, with the ordination rituals of the Eastern Catholic traditions, this lacuna is striking. Throughout the Eastern ordination, the assembly has vocal responses that affirm and support the liturgical action. In one example from the Byzantine Tradition, the bishop literally vests the deacon, assisted by other clergy. As he places the sticharion over the new deacon's head, the bishop cries out, "Axios!" and this cry is repeated by the rest of the clergy and then by the people. Immediately, the bishop places the orarion on the new deacon, again crying out, "Axios!" followed by the clergy and then the faithful. Finally, the bishop vests the deacon with the epimanikia, crying out "Axios!" echoed by the clergy and the faithful. Feeling the "full, conscious, and active participation" is palpable.

Another consideration about the timing of the ordination concerns when it takes place during the ordination Mass itself. Current praxis of both East and West offer significant insights. In the Latin Church until 1972, ordinations to the minor orders (porter, lector, exorcist, acolyte) and the major orders (subdeacon, deacon, presbyter) took place at different times during the Mass. Then the newly ordained could exercise his ministry for the first time. For example, a subdeacon was ordained before the Epistle so he could proclaim the Epistle; a deacon was ordained before the Gospel so he could proclaim the Gospel. After postconciliar changes to the ordinals, followed by the structural reforms made to the sacrament of holy orders by St. Paul VI in 1972, this placement was revised.[15] Now in the Latin ordination rite, the ordination takes place following the proclamation of the Gospel. By contrast, in the Byzantine Tradition, the deacon's ordination takes place after the anaphora; in the Maronite ordination rite, ordination takes place after the bishop's and concelebrants' communion but before the communion of the assembly.

Is this something the Latin Church should consider? The position of the ordination following the Gospel seems to emphasize a bridging between Word and Eucharist; the Eastern practice appears to emphasize the Eucharist itself. This is made explicit in the post-ordination rites of vesting and handing on the instruments of the order. In the Byzantine Tradition, the new deacon is kneeling at the altar with his head bowed down on his crossed arms on the altar. The bishop places first the diskos and then the chalice (each with the consecrated species) on the bowed head of the deacon. There is no analogous rite in Latin practice. Such differences are entirely legitimate, of course; they help demonstrate the sacramental richness and diversity of our common faith. Still, would the Latin ordination rite benefit from a change of location within the Eucharist?

The Theology of the Diaconate

As discussed in chapter 4 and elsewhere, there is only one order of deacons. There is no such thing as a "permanent diaconate" as distinguished from a "transitional diaconate." Once ordained, the ordinand remains in the order of deacons permanently. Some deacons may later be ordained into the presbyterate and even into the episcopate, but they remain deacons. All deacons are permanent in our theology, just as all presbyters are permanent and all bishops are permanent. The liturgy should never refer to "permanent" or "transitional" deacons—just deacons.

Next, the order of deacons is not a "lesser order" to the presbyterate; it is an order *distinct* from the presbyterate. Until 1972, the diaconate *was* a subordinate order according to the *cursus honorum*, where men "ascended" up a ladder of minor and major orders on the way to the presbyterate. Further, according to the 1917 Code of Canon Law, bishops were not to ordain anyone to a lesser order if he did not have a reasonable presumption that he would ordain that man to the presbyterate at some point. That all changed with the Second Vatican Council. Following the Council, a man could be ordained a deacon and remain in that order without moving on to the presbyterate. This was a break with the Tradition, even though a vestige of the old *cursus honorum* remains in the form of seminarians who are still ordained to the diaconate before ordination as presbyters. We will discuss this situation further in chapter 7.

The normative form of the Order of Deacons is that of the so-called permanent diaconate. The overwhelming majority of the world's deacons serve within the context of home, family, and work, and the rite of ordination should better reflect that fact. Today, for example, more than 95 percent of the world's deacons are married men with families and secular occupations. Just as most presbyters in the Latin Church are celibate and their celibacy is to be acknowledged and honored, most deacons are married, and their sacramental state of matrimony should be recognized and honored. This, of course, must be done while not making a particular state of life seem preferable over another within the ministry. For example, married presbyters within the Latin Church, while in the minority of Latin priests, are not to be seen as some sort of second-class priests, nor are celibate deacons second-class deacons. Whatever one's state of life, we honor them all, with no implication that only one state of life is inherent to a particular order.

The ministry of the deacon revolves around the three traditional *munera* of Word, Sacrament (sometimes referred to by the more general term *Liturgy*), and Charity. The U.S. bishops have, since 1971, spoken of the inherent unity of the triple *munus*, and that "no one is to be ordained who is not committed to all three." The deacon is ordained for all three; it is indeed within the unity and balanced exercise of these ministries that the theological significance and expression of the diaconate are to be found. In the current Latin ordination rite, however, there is scant attention paid to the balanced exercise of the triple *munus*. I will address this further in the proposed revisions.

Language of status elevation, while greatly reduced in the 1990 rite, is still found, particularly in the suggested homily; future revisions will need to take this into account. Finally, and perhaps most significantly, the unique relationship of the deacon with his bishop, attested to so strongly in Scripture and the patristics and already discussed above, must be emphasized. To this point, I have highlighted several areas that may be clarified in future revisions of the rite.

Proposed Rite of Ordination of Deacons

Introductory Rites and Liturgy of the Word

Those to be ordained wear the alb and, if the situation warrants, the amice and cincture.

The introductory rites and the Liturgy of the Word up to and including the Gospel reading continue in the usual way.

After the Gospel reading, the deacon reverently places the Book of Gospels back on the altar, where it remains until it is presented to the newly ordained deacons.

[**COMMENTARY**: Consistent with the longstanding practice of the Latin Church, the ordinand is vested in an alb. The alb represents the white garment of our common baptism and so the current practice is retained.]

Ordination

The bishop, if necessary, goes to the seat prepared for the Ordination, and the presentation of the candidates take place.

Election of the Candidates

The candidates are called by a deacon:

Let those to be ordained deacons come forward.

Then their names are called individually by the deacon. Each one answers:

Present.

Each candidate goes to the bishop, to whom he makes a sign of reverence.

When the candidates are in their place before the bishop, the priest designated by the bishop says:

Most Reverend Father, holy Mother Church asks you to ordain these men, our brothers, to the responsibility of the diaconate.

The bishop asks:

Do you know them to be worthy?

A designated member of the lay faithful answers:

After inquiry among the Christian people and upon the recommendation of those responsible, I testify that they have been found worthy.

Bishop:

Relying on the help of the Lord God and our Savior Jesus Christ, we choose these, our brothers, for the Order of Deacons.

All present say:

Thanks be to God.

[**COMMENTARY**: In the current rite, candidates are called from the assembly by a deacon. They are presented to the bishop by a priest designated for that task, who asks the bishop to ordain them deacons, and then attests to their worthiness. In common practice, the presentation and attestation is actually done by a deacon, usually the diocesan director of the diaconate office. Ordination is an act of the entire Church, and to that end, it seems appropriate that representatives of all orders, including the order of the baptized, should be involved to the greatest extent possible. This is especially true at the outset of the rite, since the deacon is destined to serve in the name of Christ and the bishop all the faithful. Therefore, the proposal retains the calling of the candidates by a deacon. The presentation to the bishop should be done by a presbyter, as currently indicated in the ritual. However, the attestation of worthiness should be done by a layperson, woman or man, designated for that responsibility by the bishop. In this way, the order of the baptized, the order of bishops, the order of deacons, and the order of presbyters are all involved. The designated member of the faithful should be someone who exercises some form of public ministry in the

Church. He or she might, for example, be a member of the diocesan pastoral council, a member of the diocesan staff, or the director of a diocesan ministry such as Catholic Charities. At the bishop's discretion, this representative might also be drawn from various parish leadership positions.]

Homily

Then the bishop, while all are seated, gives the homily. Taking his theme from the biblical readings just proclaimed in the Liturgy of the Word, he addresses the people and the elect on the office of deacon. He may use these or similar words:

Beloved brothers and sisters: since these elect, our relatives and friends, are now to be ordained to the Order of Deacons, let us first acknowledge the life of the Church which has brought them here. We recognize now the loving parents and other family members of these elect; we recognize the loving and supportive spouses and children of these elect; and we recognize the many communities of the faithful who have nurtured these elect and brought them to this day. With great affection and appreciation we thank you and hold you all in Christian love and ask God's blessing upon you.

Moving forward, it is important for all of us to consider carefully the nature of this Order of ministry to which these elect are about to be ordained.

Strengthened by the gift of the Holy Spirit, they are uniquely bound to the bishop, who alone ordains them. From ancient times, the deacons have served as principal assistants to the bishop, leading one ancient writer to proclaim that the relationship of the bishop to his deacons should be like "one soul in two bodies." They will help the bishop in his ministry of the Word, of the Altar, and of Charity, showing themselves to be servants of all. As assigned by the bishop, they will assist the pastors of souls within our parishes or serve within other diocesan institutions.

As ministers of the Word, they will proclaim the Gospel, and preach, teach and exhort believers and unbelievers alike.

As ministers of the Altar, they will prepare the sacrifice, and distribute the Lord's Body and Blood to the faithful. They will preside over public prayer, administer Baptism, assist at and bless Marriages, bring Viaticum to the dying, and conduct funeral rites.

As ministers of Charity, consecrated by the laying on of hands that comes down to us from the Apostles and bound more closely to the service of the altar, they will perform works of charity in the name of the bishop.

With the help of God, they are to go about all these duties in such a way that you will recognize them as disciples of him who came not to be served, but to serve.

Now, dear sons, you are to be ordained to the Order of the Diaconate. The Lord has set an example that just as he himself has done, you also should do.

As deacons, that is, as ministers of Jesus Christ, who came among his disciples as one who served, do the will of God from the heart: serve the people in love and joy as you would the Lord.

Since, by your own free choice, you present yourselves to the Order of Deacons, you should be men of good reputation, filled with wisdom and the Holy Spirit, as were those chosen by the Apostles for the ministry of charity.

For those of you who are married, remember that marriage you share with your wife is an eschatological sign of the relationship of Christ and the Church. With perfect humility, renew now your own commitment to your marriage, and may it be a source of enlightenment, strength and affirmation of your vocations to holy matrimony and to holy orders.

As for those of you who will exercise your ministry committed to celibacy, know that celibacy is both a sign of pastoral charity and an inspiration to it, as well as a

source of fruitfulness in the world. Compelled by a sincere love of Christ the Lord and living in this state with total dedication, cling to Christ with your whole heart.

May all of you be firmly rooted and grounded in faith and show yourselves beyond reproach before God and man, as is proper for the ministers of Christ and the stewards of God's mysteries. Never allow yourselves to be turned away from the hope offered by the Gospel. Now you are not only hearers of this Gospel but also its ministers. Holding the mystery of faith with a clear conscience, express by your actions the word of God which your lips proclaim, so that the Christian people, brought to life by the Spirit, may be a pure offering accepted by God. Then on the last day, when you go out to meet the Lord you will be able to hear him say, "Well done, good and faithful servant, enter into the joy of your Lord."

[**COMMENTARY**: The ordination homily provided in the rite is merely suggestive, and most bishops in actual practice prepare their own homily for each ordination. Nonetheless, the Church does give the bishop certain elements that he should consider in preparing the homily. In the proposed revision, the bishop begins by acknowledging the role that the families, friends, and fellow parishioners have played in nurturing the specific vocations of the candidates. Most bishops currently do this during their homilies; I am simply including this explicitly in the suggested homily and placing at the very beginning of the homily. This is for two reasons: it recognizes the foundational role of the entire Church in this process, and, by placing it first in the homily, it avoids coming across as an afterthought if it is done later.

Next, the bishop turns to the meaning of the diaconate itself, and the revised text emphasizes the unique relationship of the deacon to the bishop, drawing upon the ancient Tradition of the Church. The bishop then explains that it is under his authority that the deacon exercises a *diakonia* of Word, Sacrament, and Charity. There are brief sections on each of the triple *munera*, slightly expanded from the current homily.

A huge lacuna in the current suggested homily, and indeed, in the rite itself, is that there is no substantive reference to the fact that most deacons (well over 95 percent) serve within the sacramental context of marriage and family life. The current revision corrects that omission, and places it prior to an exhortation on the celibate life. Also eliminated is the use of language that suggests that married deacons are more "trammeled" in their ability to follow Christ. This section is an attempt to honor both states of life equally.]

Promise of the Elect

After the homily, the elect alone will rise and stand before the bishop, who questions all of them together:

Dear sons, before you enter the Order of the Diaconate, you must declare before the people your intention to undertake this office.

Do you resolve to be consecrated for the Church's ministry by the laying on of my hands and the gift of the Holy Spirit?

Together, all the elect answer:

I do.

Bishop:

Do you resolve to discharge the office of deacon with humble charity in order to assist the bishop and to benefit the Christian people?

Elect:

I do.

Bishop:

Do you resolve to hold fast to the mystery of faith with a clear conscience, as the Apostle urges, and to proclaim this faith in word and deed according to the Gospel and Church's tradition?

Elect:

I do.

The following is asked of all married elect.

Bishop:

Those of you who will serve within the sacrament of Matrimony: Do you resolve to keep forever this sacramental sign of your dedication to Christ the Lord for the sake of the Kingdom of Heaven, in the service of God and neighbor?

Married Elect:

I do.

The following is asked even of those who are professed religious. It is omitted if only elect who are married are to be ordained.

Bishop:

Those of you who are prepared to embrace the celibate state: do you resolve to keep forever this commitment as a sign of your dedication to Christ the Lord for the sake of the Kingdom of Heaven, in the service of God and man?

Unmarried elect:

I do.

Bishop:

Do [all of] you resolve to maintain and deepen the spirit of prayer that is proper to your way of life and, in keeping with this spirit and what is required of you, to celebrate faithfully the Liturgy of the Hours with and for the People of God and indeed the whole world?

Elect:

I do.

Bishop:

Do you resolve to conform your life always to the example of Christ, of whose Body and Blood you are ministers at the altar?

Elect:

I do, with the help of God.

[The following promise of respect and obedience may be adapted by the episcopal conference. The following formulation is offered as one possible form.]

Each ordinand goes to the bishop and, kneeling before him, places his joined hands between those of the bishop.

If the bishop is the elect's Ordinary, he asks:

Do you promise respect and obedience to me and my successors?

Elect:

I do.

If the bishop is not the elect's Ordinary, he asks:

Do you promise respect and obedience to your Ordinary?

Elect:

I do.

If the elect is a religious, the bishop asks:

Do you promise respect and obedience to the diocesan bishop and to your legitimate superior?

Elect:

I do.

The candidate stands, turns and faces the assembly. The assembly rises. The bishop addresses the assembly:

My brothers and sisters, will you accept this your brother in his new role as a Deacon of our diocesan Church?

Assembly:

We do.

The bishop always concludes, addressing the assembly:

May God bless us all in this commitment and may God who has begun the good work in you bring it to fulfillment.

[**COMMENTARY**: The existing promises remain largely intact, with some exceptions. For example, the promise "to assist the Bishop and the priests" is changed "to assist the Bishop." This is the primary responsibility of the deacon; if the deacon is assigned by the bishop to serve in a particular parish or other ministry that is overseen by a priest, that resulting relationship is covered by the nature of the office itself and as a result of the deacon's obedience to the bishop. The concern here is that to retain language that suggests that the presbyteral order is inherently supervisory to the diaconate is not accurate, reflecting an older norm when the diaconate was merely transitory to the presbyterate. The diaconate and presbyterate each flow from the ministry of the bishop. To the extent that deacons serve under the direct authority of a pastor, they do so because the bishop has assigned them to that ministry, not because the diaconate is inherently inferior to the presbyterate.

An additional promise has been added to address the state of life of the ordinand. One promise for those who are married acknowledges and emphasizes the significance of the sacrament of matrimony lived by the ordinand and his wife. There is then a promise for those who will serve within the discipline of the celibate state. Neither state of life is presented as greater or lesser than the other.

Additional promises may be added at the discretion of the diocesan bishop or the episcopal conference.

The promise of obedience has been adapted to convey a richer sense of the new relationship that is being established not only with the diocesan bishop (or religious superior) but with the entire diocesan Church. As mentioned above, the GIRP delegates episcopal conferences "to specify the form by which the elect for the Diaconate and the Priesthood are to promise respect and obedience" (GIRP 11). The longstanding rite of obedience owes its origins to feudalism, and several authors have critiqued its current form for that reason. Furthermore, the flexibility offered by the GIRP provides the opportunity for significant creative cultural adaptation: there can be differing forms in different regions, and such adaptability is essential.]

Litany of Supplication

All remain standing. After putting aside the miter, the bishop stands, faces the people, and, with hands joined, invites them to pray:

My dear people,
Let us pray that God the all-powerful Father
will mercifully pour out the grace of his blessing on these, his servants, whom in his kindness he raises to the sacred Order of Deacons.

The elect prostrate themselves and the litany is sung; all respond. On Sundays and during the season of Easter, all in the assembly remain standing. On other days, however, they kneel, in which case a deacon says:

Let us kneel.

At the proper place in the litany, there may be added names of other Saints (for example, the Patron Saint, the Titular of the church, the Founder of the church, the Patron Saints of the ones to be ordained) or the petitions suitable to the occasion.

Lord, have mercy	Lord, have mercy
Christ, have mercy	Christ, have mercy
Lord, have mercy	Lord, have mercy
Holy Mary, Mother of God	pray for us
Saint Michael	pray for us
Holy angels of God	pray for us
Saint John the Baptist	pray for us
Saint Joseph	pray for us
Saint Peter and Saint Paul	pray for us
Saint Andrew	pray for us
Saint John	pray for us
Saint Mary Magdalene	pray for us
Saint Stephen	pray for us
Saint Ignatius of Antioch	pray for us
Saint Lawrence	pray for us
Saint Vincent	pray for us
Saint Perpetua and Saint Felicity	pray for us
Saint Agnes	pray for us
Saint Gregory	pray for us
Saint Augustine	pray for us
Saint Athanasius	pray for us
Saint Basil	pray for us
Saint Ephrem	pray for us
Saint Martin	pray for us
Saint Benedict	pray for us
Saint Francis	pray for us
Saint Dominic	pray for us
Saint Francis Xavier	pray for us
Saint John Vianney	pray for us
Saint Catherine of Sienna	pray for us
Saint Teresa of Jesus	pray for us
All holy men and women, Saints of God	pray for us

Lord, be merciful	Lord, deliver us, we pray
From all evil	Lord, deliver us, we pray
From every sin	Lord, deliver us, we pray
From everlasting death	Lord, deliver us, we pray
By your incarnation	Lord, deliver us, we pray
By your death and resurrection	Lord, deliver us, we pray
By the outpouring of the Holy Spirit	Lord, deliver us, we pray
Lord, be merciful	Lord, deliver us, we pray
From all evil	Lord, deliver us, we pray
From every sin	Lord, deliver us, we pray
From everlasting death	Lord, deliver us, we pray
By your incarnation	Lord, deliver us, we pray
By your death and resurrection	Lord, deliver us, we pray
By the outpouring of the Holy Spirit	Lord, deliver us, we pray
Be merciful to us sinners	Lord, we ask you, hear our prayer
Govern and protect your holy Church	Lord, we ask you, hear our prayer
Keep the Pope and all the ordained in faithful service to your Church	Lord, we ask you, hear our prayer
Bless these chosen men	Lord, we ask you, hear our prayer
Bless and sanctify these chosen men	Lord, we ask you, hear our prayer
Bless, sanctify, and consecrate these chosen men	Lord, we ask you, hear our prayer
Bless, sanctify, and comfort the families of these chosen men	Lord, we ask you, hear our prayer
Bring all peoples together in peace and true harmony	Lord, we ask you, hear our prayer
Comfort with your mercy the troubled and the afflicted	Lord, we ask you, hear our prayer
Strengthen all of us and keep us in your holy service	Lord, we ask you, hear our prayer
Jesus, Son of the living God	Lord, we ask you, hear our prayer
Christ, hear us	Christ, hear us
Christ, graciously hear us	Christ, graciously hear us

After the singing of the litany, the Bishop standing, with hands out-stretched, sings or says:

Lord God,
mercifully hear our prayers
and graciously accompany with your help
what we undertake by virtue of our office.
Sanctify by your blessing these men we present,
for in our judgment we believe them worthy
to exercise sacred ministries.
Through Christ our Lord.

All answer:

Amen.

Deacon (if the people are kneeling):

Let us stand.

All rise.

[**COMMENTARY**: The Litany remains largely unchanged. However, near the end of the Litany, an intercession praying for the families of the ordinands is included.]

Laying on of Hands and Prayer of Ordination

The elect rise. One by one they go to the bishop, who stands at his chair wearing the miter, and kneel before him.

The bishop lays his hands on the head of each of them, without saying anything.

With the elect kneeling before him, the bishop puts aside the miter, and with hands outstretched, he sings or says the prayer of Ordination:

Draw near, we pray, Almighty God,
giver of every grace,

who apportion every order and assign every office;
who remain unchanged,
but make all things new.
In your eternal providence,
you make provision for every age.
as you order all creation
through him who is your word,
your power and your wisdom,
Jesus Christ, your Son, our Lord.

You grant that the Church, his Body,
adorned with manifold heavenly graces,
drawn together in the diversity of its members,
and united by a wondrous bond through the Holy Spirit,
should grow and spread forth
to build up a new temple
and, as once you chose the sons of Levi
to minister in the former tabernacle,
so now you establish three ranks of ministers
in their sacred offices to serve in your name.

And so, in the first days of your Church,
Through the inspiration of the Holy Spirit,
Your Son's Apostles appointed seven men of
good repute
to assist them in the daily ministry,
that they might devote themselves more fully
to prayer and preaching of the word.
By prayer and the laying on of hands
they entrusted to those chosen men the ministry of
serving at table.

We beseech you, Lord:
look with favor on these servants of yours
who will minister at your holy altar
and whom we now dedicate to the office
of deacon.

Send forth upon them, Lord, we pray,
the Holy Spirit, that they may be strengthened
by the gift of your sevenfold grace
for the faithful carrying out
of the work of the ministry.

May there abound in them every Gospel virtue:
unfeigned love,
concern for the sick and poor,
unassuming authority,
the purity of innocence,
and the observance of spiritual discipline.
May your commandments shine forth in their conduct,
so that by the example of their way of life
they may inspire the imitation of your holy people.
In offering the witness of a clear conscience,
may they remain strong and steadfast in Christ,
so that by imitating on earth your Son,
who came not to be served but to serve,
they may be found worthy to reign in heaven with him,
who lives and reigns with you in the unity of the
Holy Spirit,
God for ever and ever.

All answer:

Amen.

[**COMMENTARY**: No changes.]

Post Ordination Rites

Vesting and the Altar

After the prayer of Ordination, all sit. The bishop puts on the miter and the newly ordained stand.

Bishop:

Receive the stole of the deacon, the sign of your joyful sharing in the ordained ministry, in the name of the Father, and of the Son, and of the Holy Spirit.

All respond:

Amen.

Following the bishop's direction, assisting deacons place the deacon's stole on each of them. After the deacons have received the stole, the bishop continues:

Receive the dalmatic of the deacon, the dalmatic of justice, the vestment of joy, in the name of the Father, and of the Son, and of the Holy Spirit.

All respond:

Amen.

Following the bishop's direction, assisting deacons place the deacon's dalmatic on each of them.

When the newly ordained are vested, they process to the altar, where they individually reverence the altar with a kiss. They then return to stand in front of the bishop.

[**COMMENTARY**: Multiple sources, including the current rite of ordination, refer to the fact that, after ordination, the ordinand is "more closely tied to the altar." In the current rite, however, the deacon's participation in the Church's ministry of sacrament is not expressly communicated. The rite of vesting the new deacon in the Mass vestments of the deacon points to that ministry, but I believe its actual significance is minimized. When researching this section of the rite, I found the Eastern Catholic practices particularly significant. In the Latin Catholic Tradition, vesting of the newly ordained is done in an almost cursory, albeit joyful, way. The newly ordained rises and is vested by another deacon or priest, assisted in some cases by family members. There is nothing said or done to indicate the significance of the new identity of the deacon as reflected in the use of these vestments. The Eastern traditions are much more helpful. In the Byzantine Tradition, for example, the bishop himself initiates the vesting with sticharion, orarion, and epimanikia (cuffs). I am proposing a middle position. The assisting clergy take their position as now, but it is the bishop who begins the process by directing, "Receive the stole," and later, "Receive the dalmatic." The assisting clergy then help with the actual vesting.

The East offers us an even more stunning witness of the deacon's role at the altar. For the act of ordination, the candidate kneels at the altar, places his extended arms in the form of a cross on the altar. He then bows, with his head placed face down onto his crossed arms. The bishop lays his hand on the deacon's head for the ordination. The deacon remains in this position, however, while the bishop places first the diskos and then the chalice on the deacon's head. It is particularly significant to recall that in the Eastern traditions, the ordination is taking place after the anaphora but before communion, so the eucharistic species are already consecrated. The symbol is clear: the newly ordained deacon, at the altar, is now responsible for the sacred elements at that altar. In the proposed revision, after the deaconis vested, he proceeds to the center of the altar and, for the first time, reverences the altar with a kiss. He then returns to his place in front of the bishop.]

Book of the Gospels

Vested as deacons, and now tied more closely to the altar, the newly ordained go to the bishop individually and kneel before him. He places the Book of Gospels in the hands of each one and says:

Receive the Gospel of Christ, whose herald you have become.

Believe what you read,
teach what you believe,
and practice what you teach.

[**COMMENTARY**: No changes to the current rite.]

Anointing

The bishop receives a linen gremial. If circumstances so suggest, he instructs the people. Then he anoints with holy chrism the palms of each new deacon as he kneels before him. The bishop says:

Consecrate the hands of this deacon, we beseech You, O Lord, and sanctify them through this anointing and blessing, that whatever they bless is blessed, and whatever they sanctify is sanctified. Through Christ our Lord.

All:

Amen.

Then, the bishop and the newly Ordained wash their hands.

[**COMMENTARY**: The contrast between East and West on the question of anointing is interesting. In the Eastern ordination rites of bishops, presbyters, and deacons, there are no anointings with sacred chrism. In the Latin Church, bishops are anointed on the head, presbyters are anointed on the hands, and there is no anointing of the deacon. Let us begin by examining the texts used for the episcopal and presbyteral anointings.

At the bishop's ordination, the consecrating bishop addresses the ordinand: "May God, who made you a sharer of the High Priesthood of Christ, himself pour out upon you the oil of mystical anointing and make you fruitful with an abundance of spiritual blessings." At a presbyter's anointing, the bishop says, "The Lord Jesus Christ, whom the Father anointed with the Spirit and power, guard and preserve you, that you may sanctify the Christian people and offer sacrifice to God." The anointing with holy chrism is not tied to any particular function of the bishop or the priest but serves as a sign of divine protection and providence.

It seems appropriate that an anointing of the deacon would be appropriate in the Latin Tradition. In examining ancient ordinals to see if anointing of the deacon was part of our ritual history, one example stood out, the pontifical of Archbishop Egbert, the archbishop of York from 732 to 766.[16] Historians debate the dating of this text, with some scholars suggesting it was composed long after Egbert, perhaps as late as the fourteenth century. Nonetheless, whether from the eighth or the fourteenth centuries, the pontifical contains several interesting elements, including a diaconal anointing. Not surprisingly, the text refers to the "ordinations" of gatekeepers, lectors, acolytes, subdeacons, deacons, and presbyters. During the ordination of a deacon, we find the normal acts of investiture with the stole, the handing over of the Book of the Gospels, the laying on of hands by the bishop alone, and the prayer of ordination.

However, in a section entitled *Consecratio Diaconi*, we find an extensive body of prayers surrounding the anointing of the deacon, followed by a short section entitled *Consecratio manuum Diaconi de oleo sancto et chrisma*. The bishop anoints the hands of the new deacon with the following prayer: "Consecrentur manus iste, quaesumus Domine, et sanctificentur per istam unctionem, nostramque benedictionem, ut quaecumque benedixerint benedicta sint, et quaecumque sanctificaverint sanctificata sint."[17] For comparison, the section on the ordination of presbyters is structured similarly, containing rites of both ordination and consecration. The new presbyter has his hands anointed in a manner like the deacon, to which is added a further anointing on his head. Now, it would be wrong to extrapolate that such a practice was in any way universal throughout the Latin Church; on the other hand, there seems to have been no problem with its inclusion in the rite, or any objections raised to it. In fact, if the text comes from the twelfth to fourteenth centuries, it becomes even more dramatic since this was a time of considerable shifting in the theology of ordained ministry. For this reason, therefore, the proposed revision contains a rite of anointing of the new deacon's hands, using a slightly adapted version of the prayer from the pontifical of Archbishop Egbert.

I realize that the addition of this anointing will be controversial. Nonetheless, I think that for a number of reasons, its addition is warranted. First, it signifies the anointing of all three orders of the Latin Church; it is, in this regard, a sign of the unity of all three orders in the one sacrament. Second, it consecrates the deacon to his participation in the triple *munera*. Third, the prayers associated with each anointing (bishop, presbyter, deacon) are distinct, so there should be no confusion about the purpose of the anointing. There is no confusion between the anointing of a bishop and that of a presbyter; there need not be with an anointing of the deacon, with much to be gained for the good of the newly ordained and for the people he will serve.]

Pastoral Staff

After washing his hands, each newly ordained deacon again kneels before the bishop. The bishop receives the pastoral staff. Holding the staff, the bishop invites the Deacon to grasp the staff together with him. The bishop says:

My beloved son, share with me in the pastoral care of the Christian people. Exercise your ministry as Deacon with humility, mercy, and compassion, in the name of the Father and of the Son and of the Holy Spirit.

All:

Amen.

[**COMMENTARY**: As mentioned above, the current rite contains no explicit connection to the deacon's exercise of the ministry of Charity. Given the unique relationship of the deacon to the bishop, signified by the fact that only the bishop lays hands on the deacon, and that the deacon is ordained specifically to share in the bishop's ministry (*non ad sacerdotium sed ad ministerium episcopi*), the proposed rite adds a short ritual. With the new deacon kneeling in front of the bishop, the bishop takes up his pastoral staff. He extends it toward the new deacon, who grasps it with the bishop so that both are holding it; the bishop does not relinquish it, nor is it being given to the deacon! Rather, the bishop and the deacon are holding it together. The prayer associated with this gesture exhorts the deacon to share in the pastoral care of the people. After the prayer, the new deacon lets go of the staff and stands for the fraternal kiss.]

The Greeting of Peace

Lastly, the bishop gives each of the newly ordained the fraternal kiss, saying:

Peace be with you.

The newly ordained responds:

And with your spirit.

All the deacons present, or at least some of them, approach the newly ordained and do likewise.

[**COMMENTARY**: No change to the current rite.]

Presentation to the Assembly

Following the greeting of peace, the bishop instructs the new deacons to face the assembly of the faithful. He presents the newly ordained to them, and the people respond with applause or other customary action.

[**COMMENTARY**: This is another opportunity for the assembly to indicate their approval of the ordination.]

Liturgy of the Eucharist

Mass continues in the usual manner. The newly ordained deacon assumes his proper role at the Eucharist. If more than one deacon has been ordained, one assumes this role and the others join with the Order of Deacons present. The Profession of Faith is said when called for by the rubrics; the Prayer of the Faithful (Universal Prayer) is omitted.

In the Eucharistic Prayer mention is made of the newly ordained deacons according to the following formulas.

a) In Eucharistic Prayer I, the bishop says the following proper form of *Hanc igitur*:

This, then, is the oblation of our service,
and that of your whole family,
which we also offer for your servants,
whom you have kindly advanced to the Order of
the Diaconate.
We beg you graciously to accept it, Lord,
and in your mercy to preserve in them the gifts you
have given, that what they have received from your divine goodness, they may fulfill by the aid of your divine grace.
[Through Christ our Lord. Amen.]

b) In the intercessions of Eucharistic Prayer II, at the prescribed place, the following is inserted:

Remember, Lord, your Church spread throughout
the world: and perfect her in love
together with [NAME], our Pope,
and [NAME], our bishop,
Remember also these, your servants,
whom you have willed today to provide as ministers of the Church, and all the clergy.
Remember also our brothers and sisters…

c) In the intercessions of Eucharistic Prayer III, at the prescribed place, the following is inserted:

May you graciously strengthen in faith and love
your pilgrim Church on earth:
together with [NAME], our Pope, [NAME], our bishop, with the Order of Bishops and these, your servants,
ordained today to be ministers of the Church,
with all the clergy,
and the entire people you claim as your own.
Be mercifully attentive to the prayers of the family you have allowed to stand here before you...

d) In the intercessions of Eucharistic Prayer IV, at the prescribed place, the following is inserted:

And so Lord, remember now all those for whom we
make this oblation:
especially your servant, [NAME], our Pope, [NAME], our bishop,
the entire Order of Bishops,
and these, your servants,
whom you have graciously chosen today
to serve your people as deacons,
as well as all the clergy.
Remember also those who take part in the offering, those here present, all your people,
and all who seek you with a sincere heart.
Remember all those who have died...

Some of the newly ordained deacons assist the bishop in giving Communion to the faithful, especially as ministers of the chalice.

A liturgical song of thanksgiving may be sung after the completion of the distribution of Communion. The Prayer after Communion follows the song.

Concluding Rite

The following blessing may be used in place of the usual blessing. A deacon may say the following invitation:

Bow down for the blessing.

Or he may use similar words.

Then, the bishop, with hands extended over the newly ordained and the people, gives the blessing:

My dear brothers and sons, you have been made worthy to enter the Holy Order of the diaconate by the coming of the holy and life-creating Spirit. For it is not by the laying on of my hands, but by God's abundant mercies that grace is given to serve. May God keep you free from sin and give you grace to stand humbly before all and receive the reward promised to the good and faithful servant.

Response:

Amen.

Bishop:

May God who has called you to the service of others in
his Church give to you a great zeal for all people through a
ministry of Word, Sacrament, and Charity,
especially for the poor and the suffering.

All answer:

Amen.

Bishop:

May God who has charged you to preach the Gospel
of Christ help you to live by his word
and thus bear him sincere and fervent witness.

All answer:

Amen.

Bishop:

May God who appointed you stewards of his mysteries make you imitators of his Son, Jesus Christ, and ministers of unity and peace in the world.

All answer:

Amen.

Bishop:

And may almighty God bless all of you gathered here, + the Father, + and the Son, + and the Holy Spirit.

All answer:

Amen.

After the blessing and following the dismissal of the people by the deacon, the procession returns to the vesting room in the usual way.

CHAPTER SEVEN

RECURRING QUESTIONS ON THE DIACONATE

Some questions about the diaconate never seem to go away. In this chapter, I will review some of them with a view toward where we might go in the future. I do not presume to provide definitive responses to these questions. It remains for others in authority to do that. These are merely my personal responses, tentative as they are, to these recurring questions. The demands of the future will require ongoing creative responses to these and many other questions, always prayerfully under the guidance of the Spirit.

> The home of God is among mortals.
> He will dwell with them;
> they will be his peoples,
> and God himself will be with them;
> he will wipe every tear from their eyes.
> Death will be no more;
> mourning and crying and pain will be no more,
> for the first things have passed away.
> And the one who was seated on the throne said, "See, I am making all things new." (Rev 21:3–5).

God is doing the work; we cooperate in it. In the language of Vatican II, we are coresponsible.[1] We now turn to these recurring questions: (1) deacons and clerical attire; (2) deacons and the anointing of the sick; (3) women and the diaconate; (4) deacons and priests.

Deacons and Clerical Attire

Whether or not deacons wear clerical attire may seem trivial. In light of the harsher realities of life, this is true. And yet, there are several important considerations behind it that demand attention. The concern is not over wearing the liturgical vestments proper to the deacon; it is about wearing distinctive clerical attire outside the sanctuary. The Catholic bishops of the United States have consistently maintained since 1971 that their preference was that deacons should dress like the people they serve. (At least one smart-eyed observer has noted that deacons are ordained to serve the bishop, so they should dress like the bishop!) In the United States, each bishop determines the policy on clerical dress within his diocese, and those policies vary significantly among the 196 dioceses and eparchies throughout the country. There have been several attempts to establish a regional or national policy, but all such proposals failed; the bishops want to reserve that decision to themselves.

What are the issues? Those in favor of deacons wearing clerical attire cite the need for easy identification of the deacon as a cleric. They recount instances where wearing the collar resulted in people approaching the deacon for help because he was identifiable as a cleric; without the collar, such an opportunity would not have happened. Those who resist wearing clerical garb offer a couple of concerns. Perhaps the most oft-heard concern is the "we-don't-want-to-cause-confusion" argument. Another stated concern is that clerical attire risks incipient clericalism if worn as a sign of status or power. Before dealing with these issues, let's review what the law says.

Canon law (c. 284) states that "clerics are to wear suitable ecclesiastical garb according to the norms issued by the conference of bishops and according to legitimate local customs." Canon 288 relieves the permanent deacon of that obligation. In other words, current canon law does not forbid permanent deacons from wearing the collar; it simply removes the obligation to do so. Since permanent deacons generally work in secular jobs, occupations, and careers, the obligation to wear clerical garb would conflict with the performance of those responsibilities. For example, I was serving on active duty as a line officer (not a chaplain) in the Navy when I was ordained.

My obligation to wear the military uniform would conflict with a concurrent obligation to wear clerical garb. A deacon serving as a judge, a police officer, or many other professions would have similar conflicts. It is helpful to remember that the reason behind the exemption from this obligation is not to "take away" some prerogative of the (permanent) deacon. It is to avoid these types of conflicts not generally experienced by presbyters or bishops. The law removes such a potential conflict.

The USCCB has issued complementary norms on c. 284 concerning appropriate ecclesiastical garb for "clerics" (which includes bishops, deacons, and presbyters):

> The National Conference of Catholic Bishops, in accord with the prescriptions of canon 284, hereby decrees that without prejudice to the provisions of canon 288, clerics are to dress in conformity with their sacred calling.
>
> In liturgical rites, clerics shall wear the vesture prescribed in the proper liturgical books. Outside liturgical functions, a black suit and Roman collar are the usual attire for priests. The use of the cassock is at the discretion of the cleric. In the case of religious clerics, the determinations of their proper institutes or societies are to be observed with regard to wearing the religious habit.[2]

Notice that the "black suit and Roman collar" is specified for presbyters, but that the cassock is appropriate for all clerics. In a rather bizarre example, one diocese permits (permanent) deacons to wear the cassock but without a collar. In the same diocese, priests, seminarians (even those not yet ordained deacons), and so-called transitional deacons, may wear the cassock with the collar.

Finally, the USCCB provides a particular law on deacons in its *National Directory for the Formation, Ministry, and Life of Permanent Deacons in the United States*:

> The *Code of Canon Law* does not oblige permanent deacons to wear an ecclesiastical garb. Further, because they are prominent and active in secular professions and society, the USCCB specifies that permanent deacons should

> resemble the lay faithful in dress and matters of lifestyle. Each diocesan bishop should, however, determine and promulgate any exceptions to this law, as well as specify the appropriate clerical attire if it is to be worn.[3]

Turning to history, we find some interesting things. When did Catholic clerics begin to wear distinctive garb, and more importantly, why? It is well known that early Christian officeholders wore no special attire. Things changed quickly when Constantine came to power, and Christian ministers, especially bishops, began to function as officials of the Roman Empire. Liturgical vesture gradually came into use and reflected life in the Eastern and Western parts of the empire. The meanings behind the deacon's liturgical vestments have their origins in service: the servant's tunic known as the dalmatic and the stole worn diagonally (in the Latin Church) to keep the right hand free to serve. What clergy wore outside the sanctuary eventually became a subject of concern. Clergy and laity alike began to adopt newer, shorter clothing styles, and some bishops felt these were inappropriate for the clergy. This was far more than simple concern for propriety. For example, in 428, Pope Celestine wrote to some Gallic bishops, "We should be distinguished from the common people by our learning, not by our clothes; by our conduct, not by our dress; by cleanness of mind, not by the care we spend upon our person."[4]

Bishops wanted their clergy to wear simple, modest, and humble clothing that was symbolic of the cleric's state of life. Not unlike Augustine's description of a sacrament as an outward sign of inward grace, bishops stressed that their clergy should reflect in their outward appearance their inward spirituality. Using Celestine's terminology, clergy should be recognized by their learning, conduct, and cleanness of mind and so should dress accordingly. This has been a consistent theme up to the present day.

Universal Church law has never explicitly decreed what clerics should wear outside the sanctuary, only that clerics should wear distinctive garb; specifics were left to individual bishops. For most regions, this meant wearing the ankle-length black cassock, but there was still considerable variety in practice depending on location and culture. In one well-known example, in Japan, St. Francis

Xavier directed that his fellow missionary priests adopt the orange (saffron) robes associated with Buddhist monks so that they would be recognizable as holy men. In tropical climates, the black cassock was replaced by a white one, better suited to the high temperatures.

It is interesting to note that throughout most of Christian history, a "collar" is not mentioned. The collar is a much more recent innovation, tracing its roots to the Protestant Tradition following the Reformation of the sixteenth century. Eventually, Catholic clerics began to wear it as well. In the United States, the Third Plenary Council of Baltimore in 1884 decreed that priests wear the cassock when at home and a plain long frock coat, with a collar, when away from home or traveling.

We now return to the several issues mentioned above: the need for easy identification of the minister, the concern over possible confusion between priest and deacon, and concern that distinctive garb might be perceived as a status symbol. Being identifiable as a minister of the Gospel is undoubtedly reasonable. We can make a strong case that in today's world, and with our renewed commitment to evangelization, such ready identification supports that mission. What remains is to determine the appropriate specific form such identification takes. I do not presume to suggest a particular solution. For centuries this has been rightly the responsibility of the local bishop, but there are several things those local bishops should keep in mind when considering their options.

No one doubts the truth of Celestine's observation that what matters most is one's interior life. Nonetheless, even in a poor and humble Church, those who serve in its name should be identifiable somehow. In our contemporary age with its attendant crises, one wonders if the familiar cassock and collar have become a more confusing and even problematic sign for many. Ecclesiastical garb is supposed to convey simplicity, modesty, and humility. We must ask ourselves if that is still what is communicated by cassock or black suit and collar. Many people worldwide associate those outward signs with abuse, malfeasance of office, hypocrisy, arrogance, and sinfulness. At least as many people would run from those signs of clerical office as would run toward them for assistance.

The bottom line is this. Celestine was correct: what matters most is living outwardly the interior values of Christian discipleship. This is how we will be recognized. "I give you a new commandment, that you love one another. Just as I have loved you, you also should love one another. By this everyone will know that you are my disciples, if you have love for one another" (John 13:34–35). Jesus knew that this witness would be countercultural: even then, people who loved each other would be noteworthy! This is a good reminder for all of us today, in light of the violence, anger, and vitriol so prevalent around us. The ministers serving such loving people of God should embody this love in every aspect of ministry and life.

Then there is the "confusion" argument. This is the eye-roller most frequently heard. Simply stated, we hear that "people will be confused" if deacons wore the collar. They claim that people will think the deacon is a priest. The confusion might lead people to believe that the deacon could hear their confession or serve some other priestly purpose. Deacons generally scoff at such an argument because of its inconsistent application. Not only do seminary deacons (so-called transitional deacons) wear the collar, so do seminarians who have yet to be ordained at all. Seminarians who have not been ordained should not be wearing clerical attire in the first place. This practice is a holdover from the pre-1972 seminary system. Seminarians in the major seminary became clerics through the rite of tonsure. Since they were clerics, they began wearing the cassock and collar; some seminaries used the expression that, after tonsure, seminarians would "take the soutane"—the French name for a cassock. Since 1972, "becoming a cleric" has been attached to diaconal ordination. There is no good reason, and many bad ones, for young, nonordained seminarians to wear clerical attire. Returning to our question, however, we can simply observe that, just as seminarians and transitional deacons can easily explain their role if needed, so too can "permanent" deacons. It also implies that the laity can't tell the difference. The conclusion that permanent deacons should not wear the collar because it might confuse the laity is fatally flawed.

Finally, there is the concern over the possible use of clerical garb as a sign of an elevated status, a way to identify oneself as standing above others as part of a superior clerical caste. Notice that this concern begins with the valid problem already cited of ministerial identification. The difference is found in motivation: does the cleric seek to be identified for the good of another or for oneself? One thinks of Jesus's words, describing the hypocrisy of the scribes and Pharisees: "They do all their deeds to be seen by others; for they make their phylacteries broad and their fringes long. They love to have the place of honor at banquets and the best seats in the synagogues, and to be greeted with respect in the marketplaces, and to have people call them rabbi" (Matt 23:5–7). To be clear, I am not claiming that the wearing of clerical attire is inherently a sign of clericalism, any more than Jesus was saying the scribes and Pharisees shouldn't do good deeds, attend banquets, or pray in public. What Jesus is condemning is the hypocrisy of doing good things for wrong and self-aggrandizing reasons. The same applies to the wearing of clerical attire.

I have lived and ministered in dioceses in which deacons wore clerical garb and others where it was forbidden. One archdiocesan policy is concise and accurate. "If in the judgment of the deacon, the wearing of clerical attire will enhance his ministry, he may do so." I find this particularly helpful in ministry. It presumes the good will, judgment, and professional ministerial competence of the deacon. For example, I was serving in a diocese where the use of the collar was discouraged. I began taking communion to nursing homes in the area. One elderly lady was unable to come to our communion service but always put her name on the list to receive communion afterward. She was almost catatonic and usually in her wheelchair. The first day I approached her, she looked up at me, then, shaking her head, looked back down. She never spoke. Just that quick look up and back down, shaking her head in the negative. I later discovered in talking with other people who were also taking communion to that home that this was a common experience with them as well. Unless, they said, it was one of the priests who sometimes visited. They would approach her, she would look up—and receive communion. It was clear: she was looking for the collar. No collar, no communion. I was serving on the diocesan staff, so the next day I went to see the bishop and told him the story. I asked him if he'd mind if I began wearing a clerical collar on those days I visited that home. He gave his permission readily. My new friend at the nursing home received communion every time after I started wearing the collar.

The simple act of wearing the collar meant that this hurting believer would receive communion.

Deacons and the Anointing of the Sick

Another recurring question for the diaconate concerns the sacrament of anointing of the sick. In these days of presbyterates spread thin, it is far more common to find deacons as the ordained ministers present when this sacrament is needed. Deacons are frequently the on-scene representatives of the Church, ministering to the families as well as the patient. The consolation of the sacrament of anointing is unavailable if a priest is unavailable. Since the renewal of the diaconate, bishops, theologians, and canon lawyers have questioned whether, under certain conditions, deacons might celebrate the sacrament.

The critical issue, of course, is the forgiveness of sin. Although the sacrament is no longer restricted to those in imminent danger of death as *extrema unctio* ("final anointing"), let us first discuss it within the context of the "last rites." This umbrella term refers to three components: sacramental reconciliation, anointing of the sick, and viaticum. Under current canon law, the deacon is an ordinary minister of viaticum, so we will set that aside for the moment. We begin with sacramental reconciliation, which, of course, requires the ministry of a priest (presbyter or bishop). The question is sometimes asked, "What if the patient is comatose and unable to go to confession? Why couldn't a deacon proceed with the anointing?" The reasoning offered is that, while a priest is necessary for sacramental confession, the actual anointing of the sick is not an act of sacramental reconciliation. The answer relies on testing that theory. Is the sacrament of anointing of the sick, in and of itself and even in the absence of sacramental reconciliation, an act of forgiveness of sins?

Bishops and priests—let alone deacons—do not forgive sins. God forgives sins. It is always God acting through the instrumentality of the minister in all the Church's sacraments. For example, traditional Catholic teaching stresses that during baptism, it is Christ who is baptizing. In baptism, Christ forgives all sins. Looking closer at baptism, we remember that the minister of baptism is ordinarily any bishop, deacon, or presbyter, and in emergencies, a layperson may do so. And these laypersons need not be Catholic, as long as they use water, the trinitarian formula, and intend to do what the Church intends. In every case, whether administered by a cleric or layperson, the sins of the newly baptized are washed away. It seems reasonable to consider the sacrament of anointing of the sick in the same way. Just as God forgives all sins during every valid celebration of the gateway sacrament of baptism, regardless of the human minister, why could not the same understanding be applied to the anointing of the sick?

The Congregation for the Doctrine of Faith acknowledged the pastoral need but unfortunately chose to address this question only indirectly in its "Note on the Minister of the Sacrament of the Anointing of the Sick" of February 11, 2005.[5] In the associated commentary, we read,

> In these last decades, theological tendencies have appeared, which cast doubt on the Church's teaching that the minister of the Sacrament of the Anointing of the Sick "*est omnis et solus sacerdos*." The approach to the subject has been mainly pastoral, with special consideration for those regions in which the shortage of priests makes it difficult to administer the Sacrament promptly, whereas the problem could be overcome if permanent deacons and even qualified lay people could be delegated to administer the Sacrament.

The commentary and conclusion of the Note focus exclusively on the pastoral and liturgical history related to the minister of the sacrament. For example, "all the Rituals of the Sacrament of the Anointing of the Sick have, moreover, always presumed that the minister of the Sacrament be either a bishop or a priest. Therefore, they never contemplated the possibility that the minister be a deacon or a layperson."[6] This "we've-always-done-it-this-way" argument is not convincing.

The question becomes even more complex when one reads the conclusion of the Note. "The doctrine which holds that the minister of the Sacrament of the Anointing of the Sick '*est omnis et solus sacerdos*' enjoys such a degree of theological certainty that it must be described as a doctrine '*definitive tenenda*.'" The Note concludes that should a deacon or layman attempt to administer the sacrament, it would be a crime to be penalized under canon law.

In the end, the Note did not address the pastoral issue it highlighted at its outset. The pastoral need for the sacrament remains with no clear plan to do anything about it. In light of the need, and if only priests can fill that need, what is being done to ordain significantly more priests to do so? The Note is silent about that. Simply repeating the longstanding practice of restricting the sacrament's administration to priests alone does nothing to meet people's real needs and their right to the Church's sacraments. Canon 213 holds that "the Christian faithful have the right to receive assistance from the sacred pastors out of the spiritual goods of the Church, especially the word of God and the sacraments." Without a pastoral plan that either increases the number and availability of priests or else opens up the administration of the sacrament to other ministers, Church authority is essentially kicking the can down the road and failing to adequately address pastoral needs at a critical moment in a believer's life and death. The Note identifies the problem and then does nothing to meet it. The challenge remains to this day. The humble Church serves, and, as we have discussed in an earlier chapter, creates structures to facilitate solutions to the problems people face.

If deacons could be delegated to administer the sacrament, even extraordinarily, pastoral needs could be met more readily. Those who are seriously ill and their families often feel great frustration and anger when no priest is available to celebrate the sacrament. In light of the overall shortage of priests, deacons and lay ministers in hospital ministry struggle to find an available priest to help out. It's not that priests don't want to be there for their people; rather, there simply aren't enough priests to go around. Expanding the pool of eligible ministers would help; there is no doubt that the problem could be ameliorated. I recognize that the longstanding Tradition of the Church has been to restrict the administration of this sacrament to priests alone. However, perhaps it is time to reconsider that practice for the common good of all. I repeat that this suggested approach seems analogous to our approach to baptism, our most fundamental sacrament. All sins are forgiven by God through baptism, regardless of the minister of the sacrament. The same understanding could be applied here. The facts remain: (1) the pastoral need for the sacrament persists; (2) the current practice of the Church cannot adequately meet that need; and (3) the people of God have a right to the sacrament. I am reminded of a classic sentence from *LG* 29. The bishops wrote, "Since these duties, so very necessary to the life of the Church [*ad vitam Ecclesiae summopere necessaria*], can be fulfilled only with difficulty in many regions in accordance with the discipline of the Latin Church as it exists today, the diaconate can in the future be restored as a proper and permanent rank of the hierarchy" (*LG* 29). The "duties" enumerated in the text do not, of course, include the anointing of the sick. Nonetheless, the pastoral rationale of this statement is clear. When sacred duties "so very necessary to the life of the Church" can only be fulfilled with difficulty, the Church must be creative and courageous in its response. In the case of Vatican II, it was to renew a diaconate to be permanently exercised. It is not unreasonable to suggest that similar creativity and courage are required now regarding the sacrament of the sick.

Women and the Diaconate

The Church has been discussing whether women might be admitted to the contemporary diaconate since Vatican II. For many people, Pope Paul VI and Pope John Paul II answered the question in the negative, so there is no need to pursue the matter further.[7] However, these texts address the specific question of ordaining women to the presbyterate; they are silent on the diaconate. In fact, because of this silence, many bishops and theologians raised the question of whether this teaching also extended to the diaconate. Had John Paul II or Cardinal Ratzinger simply responded in the affirmative that *OS* applied to all three orders within the sacrament of holy orders and that the Church lacked the authority to admit women to the diaconate, the discussion would have moved in a different direction. However, that's not what happened. Instead, Cardinal Ratzinger put the question of the diaconate on two successive agendas of the

International Theological Commission (ITC) for their study. Nearly ten years of research followed, with the ITC finally concluding in 2003, "In the light of these elements which have been set out in the present historico-theological research document, it pertains to the ministry of discernment which the Lord established in his Church to pronounce authoritatively on this question."[8] In other words: the ITC concluded that ordaining women to the diaconate remained an open question. Pope Francis continued this process by establishing two successive papal commissions to study the question of women in the diaconate. The first commission could not reach a recommendation. The second commission is still working, and it is unclear at this writing what its conclusions and recommendations might be.

Therefore, the question of women in the diaconate is an open question to which the "Church's ministry of discernment" has yet to render a decision. Many theologians have entered the lists, researching the history and theology of women who served in diaconal roles, in addition to the work of the ITC and the two papal commissions on the topic. For nearly thirty years, the Church has been examining this issue. It is not unusual for some people to criticize this discussion because they believe Popes Paul VI and John Paul II have already "ruled" on it. The truth is that the Church has not made any definitive decision on the question, and loyal, faithful Catholics can and should reflect upon it. Space does not permit us to review all existing research,[9] but I want to take up three critical points.

First, as we have seen in chapter 4, the Church distinguishes the sacerdotal orders of the episcopate and the presbyterate on the one hand and the diaconate on the other. What applies to one order does not necessarily apply to another, so that one's capacity to be ordained to the diaconate no longer implies an ability to be ordained to the presbyterate. Is this contemporary distinction sufficient to permit the ordination of women to the diaconate?

We have one sacrament of holy orders, yet the Church has traditionally maintained a fundamental distinctiveness between each order. If one focuses on the unity of orders, then one could argue that an inability to ordain a person to one order would make ordination to any order impossible. If the focus is on the diversity within the sacrament, one might argue that we risk losing the unity of the sacrament as participation in the one priesthood of Christ. The question is whether the traditional distinctiveness of the diaconate from the priesthood ("deacons are ordained not to the priesthood...") is sufficient to ordain women to the diaconate, even if women are not ordained to the priesthood. Given the renewed attention paid theologically, catechetically, and canonically to the distinctive nature of the diaconate, I believe the Church should be as generous as possible with God's gift of the diaconate to the Church.

Second, when discussing the possibility of ordaining women to the diaconate, the initial response is generally an appeal to history. Did the Church ordain women in the past? Were women in a diaconal ministry "ordained" with the same meaning we have for ordination today? What was the historical practice of the Church, both East and West? History tells us clearly that women were involved in ministries identified by their communities as diaconal. These various diaconal ministries, like those exercised by their male counterparts, varied from place to place. Rites of ordination or blessing also varied greatly. However, whether the theological understanding of their status is the same as our understanding today is largely irrelevant. What matters is how their communities understood their ministry. Consider how we approach similar matters today. In the nineteenth century, country doctors or small-town attorneys rarely had much if any formal education, and yet they were considered physicians and lawyers by their communities. If an ancient community under the leadership of their bishop identified a male or female person as a deacon, that's what should matter. To say that such a person was not a deacon simply because they were perhaps not ordained in the same way we mean today would be anachronistic.

As valuable as history can be, it is not dispositive, at least in this case. We did many things in the past that we no longer do, and there are many things we did not do then that we do now. History is valuable, but contemporary decisions about who enters ordained ministry are questions of theology. As we have already seen in chapter 4, the conciliar discussions of October 1963 focused on the sacramental grace of the sacrament, which benefits the entire Church as well as those who minister in its name. This was particularly obvious in the writings and interventions of German Cardinal Julius

August Döpfner of Munich-Freising and Belgian Cardinal Leo-Josef Suenens of Malines-Brussels.

In 1995, the Canon Law Society of America took up the question in a study entitled "The Canonical Implications of Ordaining Women to the Permanent Diaconate."

> Today, is diaconal ordination of women necessary or at least useful for promoting the mission of evangelization and pastoral care which Christ entrusted to the Church to carry out in the world, particularly in the United States? Does the breadth and diversity of the Church's communion embrace the possibility of ordination of women to the permanent diaconate in at least some local areas of the communion, much as ordination of men to the permanent diaconate has become an option in some local areas of the Church without it being necessarily embraced by all areas of the Church?[10]

Considering the mission of the Church to evangelize, it is difficult to imagine how the Church would not benefit from the inclusion of the graced presence of women in the diaconate. The CLSA study of 1995 further anticipated the conclusion of the ITC's study text of 2003 when it concluded that "the supreme authority of the Church is competent to decide to ordain women to the permanent diaconate."

> The amount of adjustments in law which would be required to open the permanent diaconate to women are within the authority of the Church to make and are relatively few in number. The practical effect, however, would be to open up ordained ministry as permanent deacons to women, enabling them to receive all seven sacraments and making them capable of assuming offices which entail the exercise of the diaconal order and of ecclesiastical jurisdiction, which are now closed to women because they are closed to lay persons.[11]

Third, if the Church's "ministry of discernment" decides to ordain women to the diaconate, the implementation should be straightforward. When the diaconate was renewed after Vatican II, the bishops in council agreed that each national episcopal conference would determine the need for deacons and request authority from the Holy See for their preparation and ordination. In 1968, the U.S. Conference of Catholic Bishops requested such authority. Once received, the bishops decided that the final authority of whether permanent deacons, married and unmarried, would be ordained rested with each diocesan bishop. Some bishops eagerly embraced the diaconate and began ordaining men right away, while other bishops waited awhile or even decided against the idea. A similar process could work in the situation of women in the diaconate. Episcopal conferences could make the national decision but leave the diocesan implementation to each bishop. The process of individual discernment of a vocation to the diaconate and the application process for formation, the formation process itself, and policies for postordination ministry, life, and ongoing formation should need little if any adjustment. Those elements are covered substantively in the *National Directory for the Formation, Ministry, and Life of Permanent Deacons in the United States of America.*

Deacons and Priests

As we have seen, bishops ordain deacons *in ministerio episcopi*: into the particular service of the bishop's own *diakonia* of Word, Sacrament, and Charity. Ordination is about relationships, and first on the deacon's list of ecclesial relationships is his unique relationship with his bishop. Nonetheless, in most cases, priests are deacons' closest collaborators in ministry. Bishops tend to assign deacons to parish ministry, with possible additional assignments outside the parish. But in that parish assignment, of course, deacons exercise their ministry under the pastor's direction. Again, it's all about relationships, in this case, the deacon's relationship with the pastor. If there are other presbyters and deacons assigned to the same parish, they are all indeed brothers and partners in ministry, united by their shared participations in the one sacrament of orders. In *Pastores Dabo Vobis*, John Paul II wrote, "The ordained ministry has a radical 'communitarian form' and can only be carried out as 'a collective work.'"[12] While he was writing on priestly formation, his comments about ordained ministry as a whole make them appropriate to the diaconate as well.

When I speak with diocesan presbyterates or individual priests, I often find considerable confusion or uncertainty about the nature of the diaconate. Also, priests have had vastly different experiences with deacons. Some priests are thrilled with their relationships with their deacons and their deacons' competence in ministry. The experience of other priests—well, not so much. When deacons gather, they share the other side of the coin. Some pastors won't schedule the deacon to preach. Others restrict the deacon to a narrow swath of his potential ministry. Still others treat deacons as extraordinary ministers who are called into service in emergencies.

The bottom line is that this relationship between ordained brothers is critically important, not only for the health of the priest and deacon but also for the community they jointly serve. I was once assigned to a wonderful parish with a priest friend whom I'd known for years. However, this would be his first assignment as pastor, and the parish had never had a deacon before. We were beginning our new assignments within weeks of each other. The previous pastor had been beloved, and we were following in his enormous footsteps. One of the greatest compliments we received some months later will remain with me forever. It was after Mass one Sunday. A parishioner approached me and said, "Deacon, you know how much we all loved our retired pastor," he began, and I started to feel a little nervous. "But you and Father have brought something so special to our parish—joy! You two clearly like and respect each other, and you both are so joyful in your ministries. It's infectious! Thank you so much!" It was never more evident to me just how vital the relationship between priests and deacons is and how that relationship can affect the dynamic of the entire parish. The bottom line: ordination is all about relationships, the "communitarian form" alluded to in *Presbyterorum Ordinis*.

Using the *National Directory* as a guide, we will examine some specific aspects of the relationship between presbyters and deacons: sacramental nature, spirituality, and formation.[13] The sacramental nature of the diaconate, as with presbyters and bishops, flows from ordination itself. Sharing this sacramental nature establishes new ecclesial relationships for all three orders. Of course, chief among these relationships is the deacon's relationship to the bishop, followed by his relationship to the priesthood. "Deacons exercise their ministry in communion not only with their diocesan bishop but also with the priests who serve the diocesan Church." Echoing the *Directory for the Ministry and Life of Permanent Deacons* from the Congregation for Clergy, it is written, "The diaconate is not an abridged or substitute form of the priesthood; it is a full order in its own right."[14] What exactly does that mean, that the diaconate is a "full order"? I take this to mean that the deacon, while in a unique and dependent relationship with the bishop, has his own proper duties and responsibilities. He is not simply a substitute when another minister is unavailable. The Congregation for Clergy makes this clear:

> In every case, it is important, however, that deacons fully exercise their ministry, in preaching, in the liturgy, and in charity to the extent that circumstances permit. They should not be relegated to marginal duties, be made merely to act as substitutes, nor discharge duties normally entrusted to non-ordained members of the faithful. Only in this way will the true identity of permanent deacons as ministers of Christ become apparent, and the impression avoided that deacons are simply laypeople particularly involved in the life of the Church.[15]

This is an important lesson. A parish secretary once contacted me at the USCCB about what procedures they should follow to hire a permanent deacon for the parish. They had a position description prepared and were wondering if there were specific publications I would recommend in which they could place their ad. I explained that deacons, like priests, are given assignments by their bishop and are not hired by the parish. She was amazed, then acknowledged that they would, of course, never go out and try to "hire" a pastor, but since this was "just a deacon," they thought they could do it this way. This is why these few sections in the *National Directory* are so important: the diaconate is ultimately an "order in its own right," responsible to the bishop for extending the bishop's ministry beyond the boundaries of a particular parish. A mutual understanding of the sacramental nature of our orders is the foundation of the relationship between deacon and presbyter.

The *National Directory* observes that "priests should be informed about the sacramental identity of the deacon, the nature of diaconal spirituality and the specific functions the deacons will perform within the diocesan Church" (no. 58). A southern diocese had invited me to spend several days with the priests, updating them on the theology and spirituality of the diaconate. The first morning's session had focused on the historical background to the renewal of the diaconate. I had ended the session by talking about the influence on the diaconate of the surviving priest prisoners at Dachau following the Second World War. The experience of these men and their work leading up to the Second Vatican Council was profoundly influential, particularly with the question of renewing the diaconate. Following this session, one of the older priests pulled me aside and asked to speak with me privately. He was quite agitated. He told me that no one had ever instructed the priests of the diocese about the diaconate before now, even though deacons had been present in the diocese for more than a quarter-century. He mentioned that he had simply seen deacons as minor helpers around the parish, little more than janitors. He grew even more disturbed after learning of the "Dachau connection" to the diaconate. He confessed that he had been treating the deacons of the diocese "like dirt on my shoes"—and how could he ever make amends to the deacons? It was a powerful moment, and I was humbled by his honesty and moved by his emotion.

This encounter demonstrates how much we owe our priests if we expect them to be partners with deacons as brothers in ordained ministry. If "priests should be informed about the sacramental identity of the deacon," how is that done? The *National Directory* reminds bishops that it is their responsibility to teach the diocese, including the presbyterate, about the diaconate:

> The bishop promotes "a suitable catechesis" throughout the diocesan Church to help the lay faithful, religious, and

> clergy to have a richer and firmer sense about the deacon's identity, function, and role within the Church's ministry. In fact, such a catechesis is also "an opportunity for the bishop, priests, religious, and laity to discern the needs and challenges of the local Church, to consider the types of services needed in order to meet them, to tailor a diaconal program to address them, and to begin the process of considering which men in the church might be called upon to undertake diaconal ministry."[16]

That catechesis can take place in various ways. There needs to be education on the diaconate in the seminary curriculum. Clergy training days or convocations are prime opportunities, and they should include background and regular updates on the diocesan diaconate. In addition, there are today many good books, articles, and other resources that can be made available, even online, for ongoing education of the clergy. What might the bishop and his staff include in this catechesis? Let me suggest three categories.

First, a substantive look at the history of the diaconate, especially the Conciliar renewal, should be provided. This gives a sense of the vision of the Council regarding the diaconate. Members of religious orders and societies speak of engaging the vision of their founders. The bishops of Vatican II are the "founders" of the modern diaconate; their vision is vital.

A second critical element concerns the various functions of the deacon as spelled out in canon law, liturgical law, and particular law from the USCCB and the diocesan bishop. There are many things the deacon can and should be doing that are often overlooked in light of the routine operations of the parish. As part of this review, however, it is necessary to avoid the trap of simply talking about the functional aspects of the deacon's ministry. As Church, we recognize the danger of approaching the ordained ministry of the priest and bishop from purely functional perspectives: the priest and bishop are more than the sum of their functions. So, too, is the deacon.

Finally, the bishop must make clear to the presbyterate his vision of the diaconate as part of the overall pastoral plan of ministry in the diocese. For example, when the deacon is assigned to a parish by the bishop, it is with the presumption that the deacon will exercise all facets of ministry: that he will be a minister of the word, preaching and teaching; that he will be a minister of sacrament, assisting at Mass in his proper role, celebrating baptisms, witnessing marriages, and leading the people in prayer; and that he will be a minister of the Church's charity, providing and coordinating efforts to meet the various needs of parishioners following the corporal and spiritual works of mercy. He does all of this in obedience to the bishop, as he promised at ordination, and in collaborative communion with the pastor and any other deacons and presbyters assigned to the parish.

The bishop must make clear that the deacon's mission, wherever he is assigned, is the mission of the whole Church: evangelization. The deacon must evangelize and serve the evangelistic efforts of everyone else; after all, St. John Paul II called deacons "Active Apostles of the New Evangelization."[17] Evangelization is not limited to ministries of the word. Evangelization cuts across all three *munera* of Word, Sacrament, and Charity. There is an "inherent unity" between the *munera*, as the U.S. bishops remind us in the *National Directory*. It is probably better to refer to it as a single *munus* that consists of three integrated functions. The U.S. bishops have cautioned repeatedly since 1971, "The diaconal ministries, distinguished above, are not to be separated; the deacon is ordained for them all, and no one should be ordained who is not prepared to undertake each in some way."[18]

Just as the spirituality of the priest flows from his baptism, ordination, and the exercise of ministry, so too is the spirituality of the deacon. Like the priest, the deacon is called to a permanent and public life of service to the Church. The deacon's spirituality is further shaped by the various states of life in which he lives. The majority of deacons are also married with children and then grandchildren; the sacrament of matrimony serves as a vital human and spiritual context within which the married deacon develops and serves in official ministry. This dual sacramentality can offer a powerful witness to the rest of the Church. Conversely, a smaller but no less significant number of deacons serve in the celibate state. While similar to the celibacy lived by priests, the context in which diaconal celibacy is lived is usually quite different, living in the secular workplace and venues other than the ecclesial. So, while there are many similarities among the spirituality of priests, deacons, and bishops, there are also significant distinctions; each order needs to be aware of these distinctions.

These insights are all vital as deacons and pastors develop the details of the deacons' parochial duties. In some cases, for example, pastors perceive the deacons through the lens of social justice ministry only, while minimizing the deacons' responsibilities in Word and Sacrament. The deacon must exercise all three elements of the *munus* in the most balanced way possible. It is precisely in this integrated *diakonia* that the sacramental power of the diaconate is revealed. We will discuss this in greater detail in the next chapter.

The relationship between priests and deacons begins when pastors are asked to identify possible candidates for the diaconate. Do these potential candidates exhibit signs of a sacred vocation? Are they people with whom other pastors, priests, deacons, and lay leaders can work in a fraternal and collaborative way across a diverse set of ministries? Does he possess the same kinds of gifts and skills that you would seek in any other professional and competent minister? Is he a man who can exercise servant leadership and, as a servant leader, work well with you and the rest of the pastoral team? If a person does *not* have this kind of potential, regardless of his spirituality or his education, he will not be a good deacon, any more than a prospective applicant for the seminary who does not have these skills will not be a good priest. There is no reason to lower one's professional and ministerial standards for the diaconate any more than one should lower standards for the presbyterate. The people we serve have a right to nothing less.

But the responsibilities for fraternal understanding are most definitely not one way. That's not how relationships work. Deacons should do all they can to develop their relationships with our brother clergy. If we expect our priests, for example, to understand who we are, personally and ministerially, we should work to understand their background, hopes, and dreams. That's what brothers do. We show concern and interest in every aspect of each other's lives. Deacons should try to appreciate the strengths and weaknesses of the priests' formation and seminary experience, challenges they might be facing in their own families, and so on. In the German literature on the diaconate from the 1940s and 1950s, prison camp survivors and theologians offered many reasons to support the need for a renewed diaconate. While these writers generally listed the renewed diaconate's functions, at least one Dachau survivor added one I believe is particularly significant. Wilhelm Schamoni observed that the deacon could serve as a friend and moral support to the priest; I would add that friendship and moral support flows from priest to deacon, too. As brothers, we share a common family with similar joys and stressors. We must both work to be there for each other. Perhaps a deacon and pastor will not become best friends, but they can still have close relationships that encourage, engage, and nurture both.

Conclusion

This chapter has examined specific recurring questions about the ministry and life of deacons. While appropriate Church authorities may address these particular questions in the future, these issues contain essential elements that will persist. How the Church faces the world, how the Church and its ministers are recognized in the world, how we approach ministry with courageous humility to find creative ways to reintroduce a secularized world, and how the Church's ministers model Christian discipleship through their own interactions and fraternal relationships—all these concerns will travel with us into an uncertain future. As I said at the outset of the chapter, these are my personal reflections on the recurring issues. As the saying goes, "Your mileage may vary." My thoughts are based on the comments received and questions asked over many years, the shared experiences of many priests and deacons, and my personal experiences first as a lay minister and later as a deacon. These issues and many others will only be addressed adequately when the Church's understanding of the diaconate matures—only when the diaconate is recognizable and recognized as a "full and equal Order," and not an "abridged or substitute form of the priesthood." In the final chapter, we will consider a path forward to this end, tapping the as-yet-unrealized potential of the renewed diaconate.

CHAPTER EIGHT

CONCLUDING REFLECTIONS

Tapping the Potential of the Diaconate

Introduction: "A Full and Equal Order"

In the last chapter, we encountered the term "full order in its own right" by the bishops of the United States, speaking of the diaconate.[1] Deacons are neither "minipriests" nor "super laymen." They have their own rightful duties, responsibilities, and ministries. Another term emerges in certain studies about the renewed order, that the diaconate is "a full and equal order." This is particularly evident in James Barnett's *The Diaconate: A Full and Equal Order*.[2] The notion of "the equality" of an order adds a further dimension to our reflection. In particular, this is best understood to mean that the diaconate is "equal" in the sense of maturity of purpose. It means that the renewed diaconate has moved beyond its somewhat tentative beginnings right after the Council. Indeed, "equality" does not refer to equality of function or governance: the diaconate is subordinate to the bishop and depends upon the bishop for the exercise of ministry. Nonetheless, the order of deacons is equal to the other two orders in the communion of holy orders and its mature exercise of *diakonia*. In short, the diaconate has left its years of apprenticeship behind.

If one examines the contemporary renewal of the diaconate, it is easy to see how things have progressed. Here, in the United States, we have moved far from the first couple of years, when several bishops ordained men they had known previously and considered good candidates for the diaconate; formation for these first candidates (ordained in 1969 and 1970) was essentially nonexistent. By 1971 the Bishops' Committee on the Permanent Diaconate of the National Conference of Catholic Bishops[3] had created some fundamental principles for formation. That was also the same year that several dioceses ordained their first large classes of permanent deacons. In those early years, the formation process was usually two years or less; this remained relatively common until the 1983 Code of Canon Law specified three years. The bishops issued more comprehensive guidelines for formation based on the new law in 1984. By then, dozens of dioceses had renewed the diaconate, and formation became more comprehensive and systematic. In 1995, the United States Conference of Catholic Bishops formally removed "permanent" from the office title, now to be known as the Secretariat for the Diaconate. This action was taken because the bishops wanted to stress that there is only one diaconate, which is permanent, and therefore to use the term was redundant. This secretariat remained in place until the restructuring of the USCCB in 2008 when the Secretariat for the Diaconate was rolled into the new Secretariat for the Clergy, Consecrated Life, and Vocations.

With the 1998 publication of two documents from the Holy See, one on the formation and the second on the ministry and life of deacons, the U.S. bishops began work on the *National Directory*, which was published in 2005. A second edition of the *National Directory* was published in 2021. The number of deacons in the United States and worldwide has continued to rise throughout the past six decades. We have grown from zero permanent deacons in 1967 to nearly fifty thousand permanent deacons worldwide.

It is not only the numbers that have grown steadily throughout the years. As deacons themselves have learned and developed through experience the fine points of diaconal ministry, the Church itself became reacquainted with the contemporary forms of this ancient ministry. As in any relationship, there have been growing pains. The diaconate has progressed steadily, if unevenly: from the pioneering early years, through decades of maturation, to a point where we are on the threshold of a fully realized diaconate. Experience with the diaconate has not been universal or linear but rather quite diverse, regionalized, and cyclical. For example, some smaller countries have fewer deacons than might a single diocese in the United States. In other countries, to take another example, deacons are found much more involved in civil government. I once attended an international gathering of deacons where one of the other delegates was the minister of transportation for his country. Even in the United States, there has been great unevenness. One bishop might ordain deacons, while his successor decides not to do so. While the Church has gained much through the renewal of the diaconate, we have much more to do to actualize the order's full potential.

In this chapter, we reflect on the ongoing maturation of the diaconate. In the foreword to Barnett's classic text, the late Anglican scholar-priest Reginald H. Fuller wrote of "the abolition of the apprentice diaconate and the recovery of the Office [of Deacon] in its primitive authenticity."[4] I believe that Fuller is using "apprentice diaconate" in two crucial ways. First, that term can refer to the seminary diaconate, sometimes erroneously referred to as a "transitional" diaconate. This model is, of course, an apprenticeship leading to the priesthood. Second, "apprentice diaconate" can refer to a more general misperception that sees *all* deacons as apprentices. After my ordination, a member of my own family observed that the ordination "was almost like a real ordination." I have been asked after Mass when my ordination (to the priesthood) would take place. I have had priests tell me that "being a deacon" is not a proper vocation; that as a married man, my vocation is to be husband and father, and that being a deacon is little more than a hobby. The false premise, of course, is that we only get one vocation in life or that we can't have more than one vocation at a time.

Fuller also refers to the recovery of the diaconate in its "primitive authenticity." By this, I believe he means that the ancient diaconate functioned in its own right, linked to the bishop's authority, of course, but with no hint of "apprenticeship" or sense that the diaconate was some kind of "abridged" form of the priesthood. This chapter considers what the future might hold for an authentic, full, and equal diaconate. I believe that the following five topics will be important to that future.

Considerations for the Future

Eliminate the Practice of a Seminary ("Transitional") Diaconate

It is time to leave our apprenticeship behind. As we have seen throughout this text, there is but one diaconate, just as there is one presbyterate and one episcopate. What's more, all ordinations are permanent, even when speaking of seminary deacons destined for the priesthood. Sacramentally, there is no such thing as a transitional diaconate, and to talk of "permanent" deacons is redundant, just as we do not speak of "permanent" priests or "permanent" bishops. We do not refer to some presbyters as "transitional priests" if they later become bishops. (Imagine a conversation that goes something like this: "Oh, I knew Bishop Tom when he was serving as a transitional priest in our parish." To continue to speak of a transitional diaconate is just as nonsensical.) As many writers on the diaconate have concluded over the last fifty years, there is simply no sufficient reason to retain the practice of ordaining men discerning a vocation to the presbyterate to another order entirely. I cannot stress this last point strongly enough. The seminary is designed for one purpose: to aid in the discernment and formation of priestly, not diaconal, vocations. The diaconate and the presbyterate, as we have seen, are related but distinct participations in the sacrament of orders. Seminarians are not discerning, nor are they in formation for, a vocation to the order of deacons. There is no theological reason to continue the practice of ordaining seminarians to the diaconate.

Some might ask, "If service is part of the priesthood, what's wrong with seminarians spending a year as a deacon before ordination to the presbyterate?" Unfortunately, such an argument is misplaced. This argument presumes that such a year of diaconate would, in fact, be diaconal. The current practice of a seminary-based diaconate bears little resemblance to the diaconate as exercised outside the seminary. Most seminarian deacons spend much less than a year between diaconal ordination and presbyterate. Most of that time is spent within the seminary, not in parish or other diaconal ministries. Instead, their experience is limited mainly to liturgical ministry within the seminary. As we have stressed throughout, the sacramental significance of the diaconate is found in the balanced and integrated exercise of the triple *munus* of Word, Sacrament, and Charity. Gibaut and others have amply documented that the whole rationale for the practice of ordaining seminarians to the diaconate was supposed to be practical and pastoral: to give prospective priests the training and experience they needed for the priesthood. Is the current practice helpful for preparation and probation? It is the contention of many of us that it is not.

Gibaut, in his comprehensive study of the development of the *cursus honorum*, proposes that "the *cursus honorum* arose fundamentally to serve a pastoral need, not a theological need, specifically the preparation and probation of the clergy. From the beginnings of the legislation in the fourth century through to the Gregorian reforms of the eleventh and to the Reformation and Counter-Reformation of the sixteenth century, preparation and probation seem to be the consistent rationale for the clerical *cursus*."[5] But that path was not always followed. He summarizes that "history indicates countless presbyters who were never deacons; such clerics were nonetheless true presbyters."[6]

There is a fascinating insight from the Council of Trent (1545–63) that relates to this very issue. By the sixteenth century, the diaconate was already a largely ceremonial transitory phase before ordination to the priesthood. The bishops knew that they wanted to do something about that. At a minimum, they wanted to restore "the functions of holy orders from the deacon to the porter."[7] Near the end of the Council, they reviewed a text that included the following:

> It is fully apparent that the many necessary and sacred services were committed to the order of deacons, which is distinct from other ministries of the church and next to the priesthood. They are the eyes of the bishops and special ministers of the church whose works, whether in the celebration of the sacred mysteries or in the administration of the church, should always be present.[8]

Given the largely ceremonial experience of the diaconate most of the bishops would have had at the time, it is noteworthy how passionate this passage is about the deacon's relationship with the bishop as well as his extraliturgical roles.

Then, on June 2, 1563, Bishop Giovanni Carlo Bovio, the forty-one-year-old bishop of Ostuni, offered an interesting suggestion:

> I desire that the functions of subdeacon and deacon, diligently culled from the sayings of the holy Fathers and conciliar decrees, be restored, especially those of deacons. The church has always used their services, not only in ministering at the altar but also in baptism, in the care of the sick, of widows, and the suffering. Finally, all the needs of the people are placed before the bishop by deacons.
>
> I also desire...a longer period between orders, at least three or four years, in which he may minister in his order and serve well in his office, and then be allowed to proceed to a higher order.[9]

Edward Echlin referred to this recommendation as a call for a "temporary permanent" diaconate.[10]

Bishop Bovio was objecting to the practice of treating the diaconate as a mere short-term step to priesthood. He wanted the diaconate to be exercised to its fullest, exercising its associated ministries, and for a more extended time. In other words, he wanted a true and proper order of ministry that may, but not necessarily, lead to the presbyterate. Unfortunately, these discussions and debates did not make their way into the final texts from the Council, and nothing changed concerning the diaconate. Perhaps, one could say that with the development and growth of the seminary system following the Council, the practice of ordaining seminarians to the priesthood became even more firmly ensconced.

Moving into the twentieth century, we arrive at the 1917 Code of Canon Law.[11] This Code documented the approach taken to the seminary diaconate up to the legislative changes made by St. Paul VI in 1972 when he implemented the postconciliar diaconate. In every instance, the deacon in the 1917 Code was either not permitted certain functions that are now allowed or was designated as an extraordinary minister of those functions. For example, in this Code, the deacon was not authorized to preach; however, there seemed to be some latitude on this matter since bishops and pastors could involve "other suitable men" in preaching and catechetical ministry if the need arose. The deacon was an extraordinary minister of baptism and in the distribution of communion. Deacons could expose the Blessed Sacrament, but the actual Benediction was reserved to a presbyter. The deacon was not even an extraordinary witness of matrimony, nor was he capable of granting dispensations. "Deacons and lectors" were permitted to bless as described in the liturgical books, but they were not included as celebrants of funeral rites. Deacons could not serve as judges in any capacity. There were simply no comparable canons addressing deacons as presiders at the Liturgy of the Hours or leading a parish in the absence of a presbyter. These functions are treated differently in the 1983 Code, which has its own shortcomings, as we documented in chapter 5. In short, the 1917 Code provided canonical support for an apprentice diaconate for future priests.

Two paths forward are possible. The first would be to adapt Bishop Covio's recommendation from the Council of Trent. He recommended a more extended period of service as a deacon before ordination to the presbyterate. While he suggested a minimum of three or four years, I would push that out to a minimum of ten years. Formation for diaconal ordination should not be the province of the seminary; the candidate for diaconate should be part of the diocesan diaconate formation process along with other (nonseminary) candidates discerning vocations to the diaconate. Seminaries are places for priestly formation.

The current seminary practice of ordaining men to the diaconate without substantive discernment and formation for the diaconate only minimizes and dismisses the vocational and sacramental significance of the deacon. To be ordained deacon and then not have the opportunity to serve in a meaningful way as a deacon makes this minimization complete. All deacons, following proper discernment and formation, should receive assignments from the bishop. At the end of this period of extended regular ministry as a deacon, a deacon who may possess signs of a priestly vocation may pursue the application, selection, and discernment process for the priesthood. No one should be ordained to any order who has not demonstrated the signs of a vocation to that order. Having a vocation to one order does not guarantee a vocation to another. Having a vocation to the presbyterate does not mean one has a vocation to the diaconate, and a vocation to the diaconate does not mean one has a vocation to the presbyterate. If a man is to be ordained deacon, there must be time to discern that specific vocation properly and be formed appropriately for that order.

A second approach is, in my opinion, preferred. Remove the ordination of seminarians to the diaconate altogether. As the history of sequential ordination demonstrates, it simply is unnecessary. Furthermore, it is harmful and detrimental to the organic development of the order of deacons. Just as we do not have two expressions of priesthood, we do not need two forms of the diaconate. As long as a seminary model of diaconate exists—an apprentice model by design—the diaconate will never reach its full potential as the "full order" the Church's documents describe. The seminary diaconate distorts and minimizes the sign that the diaconate is supposed to be in service to the Church. It is time to make official what has become commonplace in practice: there is simply no justification—theologically, academically, or pastorally—to ordain seminarians to the diaconate. It is time to leave the apprentice diaconate to history.

The Purpose of the Diaconate within the Mosaic of Ministry

The renewal of the diaconate was just one of the reforms regarding ministry on the agenda of the Second Vatican Council. It also considered other aspects of the sacrament of holy orders, such as the nature and ministry of bishops. Further discussions on ministry, which did not necessarily make their way into the conciliar documents, were addressed after the Council. Pope Paul VI implemented some of these discussions in 1972 with *Ministeria Quaedam* and *Ad Pascendum*. Combined with 1967's *Sacrum Diaconatus Ordinem*, both the sacrament of holy orders as structured in the Latin Church and lay ministries were realigned. Under Pope Francis, lay ministries continue to evolve. With *Spiritus Domini* on January 10, 2021, the pope revised canon law to include laywomen as well as laymen in the ministries of lector and acolyte (established in *Ministeria Quedam*). On May 10, 2021, Pope Francis added to these instituted lay ministries when he included the ancient office of the catechist as a stable, instituted ministry. In *Antiquum Ministerium*, he provides some interesting context:

> At times, the charisms that the Spirit constantly pours out on the baptized took on a visible and tangible form of immediate service to the Christian community, one recognized as an indispensable *diakonia* for the community. The Apostle Paul authoritatively attests to this when he states that "there are different kinds of spiritual gifts but the same Spirit; there are different forms of service but the same Lord; there are different workings but the same God who produces all of them in everyone. To each individual the manifestation of the Spirit is given for some benefit.... But one and the same Spirit produces all of these, distributing them individually to each person as he wishes" (1 Cor 12:4–11). (no. 2)[12]

Diakonia, as we have seen repeatedly, is not restricted in its exercise to the diaconate. *Diakonia* is a service on behalf of the community, one of the "visible and tangible" forms of direct service using the varied charisms the Holy Spirit pours out on all the baptized. The "prime minister" of *diakonia*, the original minister of *diakonia*, the one who "orders" ministry, is the bishop. Within the mosaic of ministries described by St. Paul, we must consider how the charism of the diaconate fits into the larger pattern of the Church's ministry.

The bishops of Vatican II explained the purpose of ordained ministry in the Church in paragraph 18 of *Lumen Gentium*:

> For the nurturing and constant growth of the People of God, Christ the Lord instituted in His Church a variety of ministries which work for the good of the whole body. For these ministers, strengthened with sacred power, are dedicated to serving their sisters and brothers so that all

> who are part of the People of God, and therefore enjoy true Christian dignity, may, through their free and well-ordered efforts towards a common goal, attain to salvation.

In 1998, the Congregation for Clergy and the Congregation for Catholic Education began their documents on the diaconate by quoting the same passage.

The point is this: the diaconate is one of the three ordained ministries of the Church, all of which exist "for the nurturing and constant growth" of the people of God. The deacon serves in a particular way through a balanced *diakonia* of Word, Sacrament, and Charity. The simple question is, Are our words and actions building up the body of Christ or tearing it down? The mission of the whole Church is to evangelize, to spread the good news of God's saving love, to introduce the entire world to Christ, the Word of God. The role of the ordained—bishops, deacons, presbyters—is to serve and build up the people of God for that mission through their unique participations in the apostolic ministry. According to *Lumen Gentium* 29, deacons do this through the integrated exercise of Word, Sacrament, and Charity. In the words of Pope Paul VI, the role of the deacon is to animate the Church's service, with John Paul II adding that deacons are the Church's service sacramentalized. Through baptism, we are all evangelists; through ordination, deacons are "active apostles of the new evangelization," according to John Paul II.

In humility, then, we must ask, Are our actions building up or tearing down? When preaching and teaching, is the deacon proclaiming opinion or fact? Do we think and act with the Church? Do we constantly seek the truth? All of this goes beyond the content of our discourse. It includes how that content is delivered. Is the message delivered in a way that mocks, belittles, condescends, or abuses, especially those who may be struggling with particular issues? Of course, it is necessary to challenge ourselves and our listeners at times; Christ's message is itself challenging. However, a humble servant of a humble Church offers the challenge with humility.

When serving at community prayer, whether assisting at the Eucharist or presiding at other sacraments and prayer services, does the deacon's *ars celebrandi* turn people's attention to the Lord? Is the deacon himself "transparent"? Can he say, with St. Paul, "I have been crucified with Christ; and it is no longer I who live, but it is Christ who lives in me" (Gal 2:19–20). And when serving the poor, the lonely, the abandoned, the abused, do we do so with a view, not only to address the immediate needs but also to take steps to deal with the underlying causes of those needs?

Perhaps one of our greatest needs today is to heal the breach caused by the virulent polarization in our Church and world. Things are made even more challenging—and anonymous—with high-tech devices and social media. I have maintained a blog for quite a while now, although I don't post very regularly. However, not long ago, I posted a note that offered prayer and support for Pope Francis. I was stunned by the overwhelmingly negative responses I received, most from self-identified Catholics! Of all the topics I had tackled on the blog over several years, I had never experienced such vitriol. A friend and fellow blogger was as stunned as I. He joked, "Catholic Deacon Writes in Support of the Pope! Film at 11!"

In the months that followed, I struggled with my own reactions to these responses. At first, I was defensive and felt a sense of righteous indignation. But then, I began—finally—to question my original post. Had my words been appropriate? Was the tone of the post—as some commenters claimed—condescending? Of course, writing in support of the pope was a good thing to do, but *how* had I done that? What I intended by my words became relatively unimportant; what mattered more was how they were received. In other words, was I responsible to some degree for generating the negative responses in the first place? Was I building up or tearing down? To answer this question demands more than a stated positive intention. It requires a regular examination of conscience. To build up the people of God remains the goal of all we do as deacons.

The Angelic Ministry of the Deacon: "Humble Go-Between"

In the future, the Church's ministers will need to be creative and courageous in meeting situations, needs, and challenges for which we have no model today. In this section, I will offer some thoughts on the myriad ways deacons have been envisioned and imagined over time. Our sources are Scripture and Tradition.

While the New Testament refers to deacons, it tells us precious little about their ministry. For example, the identification of St. Stephen and the rest of the seven as deacons is not scriptural. It remains for the patristic writers to make that connection; the identification is from Tradition, not Scripture. Indeed, the Church's Tradition is a principal source for information on deacons and the diaconate, as we shall review shortly. Before turning to that Tradition, however, we must consider the scriptural words associated with the diaconate and their meaning. The cognate words used in association with the deacon and the diaconate (διακουέω, διακουία, διάκουος) are used in a variety of contexts, sometimes having nothing to do with Christian ministry. Nonetheless, these terms provide a critical lens for interpreting the diaconal identity of the Church and its ministers.

As discussions about a renewed diaconate became more common in the nineteenth and early twentieth centuries, scholarly efforts to probe the linguistic insights of these "deacon" words became more crucial, even before the renewal of the diaconate itself. For example, what kind of service is *diakonia* compared to other types of service? What is the difference between *diakonos* and *doulos*? In the early twentieth century, German scholars Herman Beyer and Wilhelm Brandt conducted research that influenced the field for decades.[13] Their work emerged against the backdrop of a Church struggling to find its identity in a modern world and within the ecumenical context of deacons seen primarily as ministers of charity.

Nineteenth-century Christians were concerned with matters of ecclesial reform as the world faced new challenges brought about by a world entering a new, modern age.[14] The political, governmental, philosophical, and social dimensions of life were all undergoing significant change. In the United States of 1800, for example, Catholics were the smallest Christian Church. By 1900, Catholics had become the largest Christian Church in the country, due almost entirely to the several waves of immigration from Europe. Around 1840, Catholics in Germany and France began to investigate how best to move forward, especially in meeting the real-world needs of their parishioners. It is about this time that we find modern movements of liturgical and catechetical reform. Many parishioners had already given up trying to survive in the "old country" and had emigrated, looking for better opportunities. German Lutherans, drawing on Scripture, began to envision a renewed biblical office of the deacon. In their view, these deacons would focus on charitable work. Catholic Church leaders began considering a similar approach, with deacons who would focus on the social ministry of the Church. The charitable organization Caritas was formed during this time, and by the end of the nineteenth century, the Catholic bishops of Germany demanded a Caritas organization in each diocese. It would become one of the most influential organizations in the renewal of the diaconate at Vatican II.

It is against this background that we turn to the work of Beyer and Brandt. In examining the biblical meaning of *diakonia* and its related terms, these scholars concluded that they denote "humble service… 1) something to do with waiting or attending on a person; 2) service that was common, ordinary—that is, there was nothing special about it, and 3) that the service involved menial tasks."[15] This understanding of *diakonia* still permeates many formation programs, assignment policies for deacons, and popular understanding. In the late 1980s, when I was in formation for ordination, we were tasked with developing a "diaconal" project for our parish. I asked our pastor what needs he saw that could benefit from the project. He told me that he really wanted help setting up a viable adult faith formation program for the parish. I developed one, wrote up a description of it, and submitted it to our formation director. He read it over and handed it back, saying, "It's not diaconal enough." I asked him what he meant. I believed that it was diaconal since it involved evangelization and met a parish need (the pastor was thrilled, by the way). The director responded that the deacon's ministry was about rolling up our sleeves and getting our hands dirty, feeding the hungry, clothing the naked, and so on. The understanding was that ministries of Word and Sacrament were not as "diaconal" as a direct ministry of charity.

Things were beginning to change, however. After Pope John Paul II promulgated the revised Code of Canon Law in 1983, the bishops in the United States decided to develop new deacon formation guidelines that incorporated provisions from the new Code.

Released in 1984, the guidelines insisted that "the diaconal ministries, distinguished above, are not to be separated; the deacon is ordained for them all, and no one should be ordained who is not prepared to undertake each in some way."[16] The 2005 and 2021 editions of the *National Directory for the Formation, Ministry, and Life of Permanent Deacons in the United States* repeats that teaching, citing the earlier guidelines. Specifically, there is "an inherent unity" between and among the deacon's ministries of Word, Sacrament, and Charity.

Against this background, theologian John N. Collins offered an exhaustive semantic survey of the *diakon* word groups in 1990, challenging the long-held positions of Beyer and Brandt.[17] Where they had focused on the "humble service" of a waiter, Collins put the waiter in motion, an agent who bridges the kitchen and the diners. This service is less about humble service than it is about the actions of the go-between. This new and highly nuanced approach hit the diaconate community in the United States like a bombshell. Gatherings of the National Association of Deacon Directors, for example, held discussions on the matter. Many bishops and diocesan deacon directors felt that Collins's work went too far, minimizing or even dismissing the notion of humble service as the hallmark of the deacon's ministry. Others held the opposing view, seeing biblical *diakonia* in a new, more expansive way. The "waiter-as-humble-servant" model of Breyer and Brandt gave way to a model of legate, ambassador, or go-between. Anyone writing on the diaconate today must take Collins's work into account. One of the finest contemporary analyses of the biblical concept of *diakonia*—in dialogue with Collins—is W. Shawn McKnight's *Understanding the Diaconate*. Bishop McKnight's nuanced analysis is invaluable.[18]

In the early years following the appearance of Collins's work, some observers tended to adopt an either-or response to it. For example, if a bishop assigned a deacon to a ministry of "humble service" such as staffing a soup kitchen, he might be criticized for continuing to be caught up in the old "humble service" model. Documents from the Holy See or the USCCB were often critiqued for the same perceived flaw. Instead, I maintain that, while Collins is undoubtedly correct that biblical *diakonia* is a much richer concept than "humble service," it cannot be said that humble service is *excluded* from the concept. Our response, in my opinion, should be both-and. The longstanding Tradition of the Church consistently sees humble service as part of *diakonia*, something that all Christians are called to in virtue of baptism. Even an emissary or a go-between (Collins) needs to exercise his or her mission with humility. The emissary, after all, is not speaking their own message but proclaiming the message of the one who sent him or her. I think we can all agree that the linguistic analysis represented by Beyer and Brandt needed correction and that Collins has done much to offer that correction.

However, Tradition goes beyond biblical linguistic analysis. For example, the history of the diaconate, from its early "golden age" through the Middle Ages and beyond, reveals deacons (and others, of course) serving the poor and those in need. The legend of St. Lawrence, the third-century archdeacon of Rome, demonstrates the deacon's responsibility for the temporalities of the Church and the care of those in need. Deacons are described as emissaries, carrying messages from their bishop to another, or representing their bishop in councils. Deacons are involved in catechesis (e.g., Deogratias of Carthage), preaching (Quodvultdeus of Carthage), and administration. These are just a handful of examples; the patristic literature is replete with others. Even as late as the sixteenth century, we find English Cardinal Reginald Pole, while still a deacon, presiding over the first session of the Council of Trent as the pope's legate. I concur wholeheartedly with Bishop McKnight's observation:

> We need to balance Collins's description of ministry as a noble charge with its also being a humble service. These two are not contradictory but complementary, because Christian *diakonia* has a Christological character. Jesus has already set the pattern of ministry, a pattern attested again and again in the scriptures. While Son of God, as commissioned by his Father, he humbled himself, so much so that we can dare to claim that the humble nature of Jesus is normative to the point of being a mark of an apostolic community. The "greatest as the servant of all" is an identifying characteristic of authentic Christian ministry: it conforms the minister to the way of the Lord Jesus,

> the self-emptying gift of self, rather than self-filling. This notion of Christian ministry is biblically based and well-fortified in the Christian tradition.[19]

The Christian Tradition extends beyond the examples of diaconal ministry mentioned above. Even architecture "documents" some of the deacon's roles. By the eighth century in Rome, popes had established as many as twenty-two *diaconiae* and assigned them to the deacons. One of the remaining *diaconiae* is the beautiful Santa Maria in Cosmedin near the Tiber River. (This is a well-known and popular tourist destination because the ancient *Bocca della Verità*, the "Mouth of Truth," is in the portico, a scene made famous by Gregory Peck and Audrey Hepburn in *Roman Holiday*.) The *diaconiae* were structures for the distribution of food and other necessities for the poor in the area. Over time, this rather rudimentary structure—where charity was done—was developed and expanded to include an oratory where the deacons could assemble in prayer. To this day, this oratory contains the Easter candle as well as the ambo for the proclamation of the Gospel, both principal responsibilities of the deacon. Eventually, a sanctuary was added to the oratory. This three-part design of nave, oratory, and sanctuary is a graphic reminder of the deacon's threefold ministry of Word (the oratory), Sacrament (sanctuary), and Charity (the nave).[20] Furthermore, these three constitutive elements make up one sacred reality. The humble care of the poor is part and parcel of the proclamation of the word and the great thanksgiving that is the Eucharist. In John's Gospel, the *hypodeigma* of the foot washing at the Last Supper is linked to the institution of the Eucharist. None of these things exist in isolation or opposition to each other. In the words of the old standard, it's "all or nothing at all."

In a most interesting development, the *diaconiae* are once again developing in Rome. In a recent address to the deacons of the Diocese of Rome, Pope Francis expressed his delight that "the diocese of Rome has resumed the ancient custom of entrusting a church to a deacon to become a *diaconia*." He referred to the ancient diaconal Churches, "distinct from the parishes and distributed throughout the city's municipalities, in which deacons carried out grass-roots work on behalf of the entire Christian community....That is why in Rome we have tried to recover this ancient tradition with the diaconate in the church of Saint Stanislaus." In a humorous aside, Pope Francis greeted the deacon who had been assigned to take charge of St. Stanislaus and his family, saying, "I hope you do not end up like Saint Lawrence, but keep going!"[21]

Perhaps nothing captures the complex ministry of the deacon more than our Eastern traditions, which describe deacons as fulfilling angelic functions. This is found in Eastern liturgies, spirituality, art, and theology. Eastern liturgy consciously compares and describes deacons as the angels of the earthly liturgy, and Eastern icons depict angels in diaconal vesture and deacons as angels.[22] The roots of this Tradition run deep. Alexander Kniazeff has written,

> The Byzantine deacon mediates between altar and nave. He goes back and forth between celebrant and people. These comings and goings of the deacons in Byzantine celebrations have often led to these ministers being compared to the angels who in Jacob's vision (Gen 28) ascend and descend the ladder that stands on the earth with its top reaching to the heavens, or those other angels who are depicted on the side doors of the iconostasis called "diaconal" doors because the deacon uses them to enter and leave the sanctuary as the parts of the service require.[23]

To appreciate the richness of this association more fully, let us review some of the history behind the role of angels. In classic Greek philosophy, Plato refers to figures such as Hermes and Iris, messengers of the gods, as "divine angels" (ἄγγελοι). They carry messages to earth from the gods, sometimes interpreting those messages or even acting in the name of the gods. The study of biblical interpretation, hermeneutics, owes its name to the same Hermes. Other angels are depicted with the ancient caduceus—the traditional sign of the healing they bring. They are always winged to signify swiftness in executing the gods' will as well as their ability to go anywhere on behalf of the gods.

In the Hebrew Tradition, the Greek ἄγγελοι became מלאכים (*malachim*), messengers. Mentioned in almost every book of the

Hebrew Scriptures, these angels exercise various functions: conveying messages to mortals, interpreting those messages, shielding, rescuing, caring for the people, and smiting Israel's enemies. The apocalyptic Book of Daniel is particularly illustrative. We find angels identified by name, we encounter "guardian" angels, and we find angels arranged hierarchically.

The most familiar examples from Christian Scripture include Gabriel appearing both to Mary and Joseph. Acts 12:11 tells us, "Peter came to himself and said, 'Now I am sure that the Lord has sent his angel and rescued me from the hands of Herod.'" Matthew 11:10: "See, I am sending my messenger ahead of you, who will prepare your way before you." In Acts 6:15, Stephen appears in front of the Sanhedrin. "And all who sat in the council looked intently at him, and they saw that his face was like the face of an angel." This passage is fascinating since Stephen, traditionally held as the protodeacon of the New Testament, is about to begin his address to the Sanhedrin, delivering the prophetic message that ends with his martyrdom.

In Mark and the parallel passage in Matthew, we find something interesting. Mark (1:13) tells us, "And the angels were διηκόνουν to him," and Matthew (4:11) has, "Then the devil left him and behold, angels came and διηκόνουν to him." We generally translate the Greek *diakonoun* as "ministering" to Jesus, with no reference to "deacons." Since *diakon*-words can have the general meaning of service, this is not of concern. What is fascinating, however, is the artistic connection. In several extant murals in Rome and elsewhere, this scene shows the ministering angels vested as deacons.

Protodeacon David Kennedy summarizes the deacon's angelic role in the Eastern liturgy:

> This angelic *topos* is a characteristic way of interpreting the diaconal liturgical role. The angels serve God in diverse manners, through vocal praise and glorification, as well as being his messengers: they are the links between the heavenly realm and the earthly creation. So also the deacons link the bema (the future eschaton manifested in the sacramental actions of the priest) with the nave (the realized eschaton manifested in the assembly of the baptized).

> The deacon carries the gospel book into the nave from the holy table (the throne of God) at the Little Entrance. The deacon again carries the gospel book into the nave to proclaim in the midst of the earthly assembly the gospel pericope proper to that liturgy.
>
> At the Great Entrance, the deacon carries the unconsecrated bread into the nave from the prothesis table.... He will later carry the consecrated body and blood of the Lord from the holy table into the nave as he proclaims, "Approach with fear of God and with faith."
>
> In all these movements between bema and nave, the deacon acts as a messenger and servant in a manner similar to the angels. In services without the deacon, it is much more difficult to see by means of the ritual action the link between future and realized eschatologies. While the priest makes the Little and Great Entrances, the comings and goings between bema (sanctuary/altar area) and nave are not as many and distinctive without a deacon serving. The reason for this distinctiveness is that the deacon chants the litanies from the ambo in the nave, while a priest at Divine Liturgy without a deacon takes them from before the holy table. When a deacon serves, there is considerably more movement between the bema and the nave. As he moves, the deacon's orarion (stole) flutters behind him in the image of an angel's wing.[24]

The iconostasis further associates the deacon with angels. The North and South Doors are often called the Deacons' Doors because the deacons use them frequently. Alternatively, they may be called Angels' Doors. The doors are adorned with icons of sainted deacons or angels, especially the archangels Michael and Gabriel. For example, the deacon icons (of Stephen, for instance) show him in liturgical vestments and angelic wings. If the figure on the door is an archangel (such as Michael), he will be vested as a deacon as well. In the Eastern Tradition, the deacon rearranges his stole across his chest before distributing communion and restores it to its original configuration after communion. The icons almost invariably depict the angel or deacon wearing the stole in the manner of communion, underscoring the strong eucharistic symbolism of the angelic role of the deacon.

The angelic association with the diaconate is not limited to the Eastern Tradition. Archbishop Roberto Octavio Gonzales Nieves, OFM, of San Juan, wrote that the diaconate has been renewed in the Church today "to act as a herald: the angel of evangelization."

In ancient times deacons were sent by bishops with important communications to other Churches; also in Eastern liturgies, the stole is seen as the deacon's angelic wings, and in Western art many angels appear wearing dalmatics. Today we can see the deacon as "the new Gabriel who proclaims"—for us—the good news of salvation. Today the restored diaconate says, "The Holy Spirit will come upon you, and the power of the Most High will overshadow you."[25]

Our Tradition offers us a pantheon of deacon heroes like Stephen, the preacher; Philip, the catechist and baptizer; Lawrence, the advocate for the poor and steward; and Francis of Assisi, visionary and spiritual companion. The Tradition also includes the archangels Raphael, healer, guide, and protector; Michael, defender and champion; Gabriel, herald, teacher, and guardian.

Our quest for an expanded understanding of the scope of *diakonia*, grounded in Scripture, has led us to consider the overwhelming richness and depth of our Tradition, East and West. We conclude this section by turning to Pope Emeritus Benedict XVI. In his wonderful Christmas present, the encyclical *Deus Caritas Est*, he offers this powerful summation of the Church's *diakonia*:

> The Church's deepest nature is expressed in her three-fold responsibility: of proclaiming the word of God, celebrating the sacraments, and exercising the ministry of charity. These duties presuppose each other and are inseparable. For the Church, charity is not a kind of welfare activity which could equally well be left to others but is a part of her nature, an indispensable expression of her very being. (no. 25)

Eyes, Ears, Heart, and Soul: Seeing What's Not Being Done

Deacons are supposed to see things that other people miss and see them as Christ sees them. The deacon's perceptive ability has been a feature of the diaconate from its earliest days, as we hear in the *Didascalia Apostolorum*: "Let the deacon be the hearing of the bishop, and his mouth and his heart and his soul; for when you are both of one mind, through your agreement, there will be peace also in the Church."[26] Regardless of the deacon's specific pastoral assignment from his bishop, the deacon remains on the lookout for needs that are not being met. Once identified, it is the deacon's responsibility to address the need if he can, and refer it to other professionals, lay or clerical, if he cannot.

The connection with the bishop cannot be overstated. The deacon is the eyes, ears, heart, and soul of the bishop. The deacon is not doing any of this on his own authority or as a kind of pastoral project taken on independently. Ordained into the bishop's service, as we have seen in chapter 4, the deacon's ministry is an extension of the bishop, helping him to see and respond. As the *Didascalia* says, "And be you [bishop and deacon] of one counsel and one purpose, and one soul dwelling in two bodies.[27]

A deacon director once spoke with a young pastor about asking the bishop to assign a deacon to the pastor's parish. "Oh, I don't need a deacon here. All our needs are met. There would be nothing for a deacon to do." The director probed. What did Father mean, that all the parish's needs were met? The pastor responded that there were working committees and other groups that handled most of the day-to-day functions of the parish, he had a sizeable staff handling everything from catechesis to maintenance, and he had the services of several other priests either assigned to the parish or living in residence there. After the phone call, the deacon director realized that the pastor was right: all the internal needs of the parish structure were being met.

However, what about other needs of the parish and the community? Were there people going to be poor, homeless, and hungry? Were there gangs in the area, perhaps providing a sense of belonging, however misguided, to vulnerable young people seeking a community? Were there societal outcasts, immigrants, or other people living "on the margins"? Father's focus seemed, justifiably, *ad intra*, concerned primarily with the people who were in the parish, and welcoming new faces when they came into the parish. However, significant needs were not being met, and those needs tended to be *ad extra*, outside the parish walls. And that is where a deacon could be most helpful in this particular place and time. The deacon director called the pastor back.

The future will demand this ability to see what others do not, or cannot, see. The pastor in the story is a good man, a fine priest, and a terrific pastor. Nothing in the story is meant to suggest otherwise. But, in this case, his focus as the pastor is on the parish itself, as it should be. But the complementarity of the priest working with a deacon extends the reach of the parish, invites outsiders in, and helps those who are often "invisible" to be seen and cared for. On this side of heaven, there will always be those in need. "For you always have the poor with you" (Matt 26:11).

One Size Does Not Fit All: *Vive la Difference!*

One of Pope Francis's favorite sayings is that "one size does not fit all!" Over one billion strong, our Church lives across all human cultures, regions, traditions, and languages. The Church in Tonga experiences the Church differently from the Church in Peoria, my hometown. The same can be said of the Church in Buenos Aires compared to the Church in Iceland, Nigeria, or Auckland. United in faith, we are diverse in practice.

Since we are not a cookie-cutter Church, we do not and should not have a cookie-cutter diaconate. In its wisdom, Vatican II left the decision about renewing the diaconate to each national episcopal conference; in the United States and many other countries, the bishops further delegated that decision to each diocesan bishop. Each bishop directs the processes to form deacons for his diocese, using general principles and competencies provided by the conference. The bishop tailors this formation and postordination policies to the particular needs of his diocese. On the one hand, deacons and candidates can encounter problems when they move from one diocese to another due to their secular employment. Those issues aside, however, such subsidiarity is—and will continue to be—essential for the Church and its diaconate in the future.

One area that needs more clarification in the future is the celibate deacon. Most deacons, especially here in the United States, are married. However, a significant number of deacons are unmarried. I was once waiting in the wings of an auditorium, preparing to address a gathering of deacons, candidates, and their wives. One of the candidates approached me and asked me if I would talk about "the married diaconate." He seemed upset, and I asked him what was on his mind. He shared that throughout their formation, speakers and instructors had hammered home the idea of the "dual sacramentality" of the married deacon and what a blessing that was for the Church; he was concerned that I might be there to repeat that same theme. Digging deeper, I found out that this candidate was not married; never had been. "Deacon, I've come to grips with the fact that I will always be thought of as a second-class deacon because I'm not married like so many of my classmates." As a married deacon myself, his comment stung with truth. Far too often, the "permanent diaconate" is equated with a "married diaconate."

Celibate deacons are certainly not second-class deacons. Those of us who are involved with the formation, ministry, and life of deacons need to do a better job of recognizing, affirming, and promoting the gifts of our celibate deacons. We have great concern with the health of the marriages of our deacons and deacon candidates. In some places, similar concern for the healthy celibate lives of our unmarried brothers is not nearly so evident. In addition, as lived in the context of the priesthood, celibacy is not the same as celibacy lived by a deacon still engaged with a secular career and lifestyle.

Turning to married deacons, there remains a great need for more research into the relationship between matrimony and orders. For so long in the Latin West, Catholic men were given a choice: get ordained or get married. That was the binary choice. However, in the Eastern Catholic Churches and now in the Latin Church, we can be ordained and married. Additional critical reflection on the complementarity of these two sacraments is greatly needed and would be very helpful for the formation of future deacons.

Another related issue is the current canon that establishes ordination as an impediment to marriage. In other words, if a widowed deacon would wish to marry again, he is not free to marry because of this impediment of orders (*impedimentum ordinis*). St. John Paul II attempted to reduce the conditions under which a dispensation could be granted. Later, however, Pope Benedict revisited these conditions and reversed course, making the dispensation nearly impossible to receive. I was serving at the USCCB and inquired about the reasons for the change. Cardinal Walter Kasper, who was at that time the president of the Pontifical Council for Promoting Christian Unity, responded that the change was made out of respect for the Orthodox Churches. In the Pontifical Council's discussions with the Orthodox, they had raised this issue—permitting widowed deacons to marry again—citing the ancient custom that, simply stated, holds that "married men may be ordained, but ordained men may not marry." The Orthodox representatives mentioned that this was one axiom all traditions had agreed upon from the beginning. They were concerned that the Catholic Church was moving away from that position. As a result, the required conditions for the dispensation were tightened again.

The issues involved are complex, and this matter will need ongoing study.

As we step into an uncertain future, bishops, deacons, and presbyters need to examine the needs of their time and place and then ask how ministry in general—and diaconate ministry in particular—should be adapted to meet those situations. Perhaps teams of deacons could be assigned for a specific mission. Not long ago, a bishop assigned three of his deacons to support outreach to immigrant day laborers. These laborers had been congregating around convenience stores and coffee shops, approaching customers to ask for work. The diocese owned a small house nearby, and the bishop asked these deacons to convert the house into a safe gathering place for the laborers and prospective employers. Some years ago, the Korean-American deacons of a large archdiocese approached their archbishop for permission to set up a street corner ministry of evangelization and outreach. The archbishop eagerly agreed. A few decades ago, deacons of a large Midwestern archdiocese began a truck-stop ministry, providing counseling and other services for long-haul truckers. This effort spread to neighboring dioceses, and the deacons arranged for priests to come to the truck stop to celebrate Mass for the truckers, especially for those who needed to be on the road, away from their families during the holidays and on Sundays and holy days.

Most often, initiatives like these start from the ground up. As we saw in the previous topic, the deacons involved used their deacon "eyes," found the needs, and mobilized to meet them. However, the point here is that what may work in one location, one diocese, one parish, or one community may not work in another. We need to seek the creative inspiration of the Holy Spirit and respond to the Spirit's urgings. If we don't, there is a danger of being locked up in a box that sees all ministry as the same everywhere and for all time. Remember the words of Pope Francis: "One size doesn't fit all!"

Conclusion

Courage is active. Courage means having the strength to overcome fear and to act. Moral courage, for example, describes a person who takes the right action despite any and all opposition. Courage is not passive, simply enduring something; courage acts to change, defend, and move forward into the unknown. Courage acknowledges fear and then moves beyond it. We sometimes encounter people who say, "Oh, I could never do that; I'd be too afraid." Courage helps acknowledge that fear is not the end of things. Being afraid and freezing in place is overcome by acting with courage.

It takes courage to face the world with humility. A person might understand humility as a way to cower away from the world, but that is not what true humility is about. As we saw in the *Rule of St. Benedict*, authentic and courageous humility can form the basis of communal and ecclesial life, and that has been the thesis of this work. Humility acknowledges who we are in the sight of God. It is realistic, honest, and grounded. It is the basis of love itself. Without humility, St. Paul could not tell the Corinthians, "Love is patient; love is kind; love is not envious or boastful or arrogant or rude. It does not insist on its own way; it is not irritable or resentful; it does not rejoice in wrongdoing, but rejoices in the truth. It bears all things, believes all things, hopes all things, endures all things. Love never ends" (1 Cor 13:4–8).

Courageous humility acknowledges our own ignorance. This is true whether talking about individuals or the Church as the people of God. Courageous humility holds that only God is omniscient and that we are not God. We share our understanding of the truth with others while accepting that only God is Truth and that we, the Church, are not God. We, as a Church, are constantly striving to find better and more effective ways of expressing the Truth that is God.

Courageous humility demands that we honestly examine our ecclesial conscience with regularity. We hold no human institution as exempt from reform and renewal. The role of the Church is to proclaim God's word, to evangelize, to spread the good news that God loves us so much that the Second Person of the Trinity emptied himself into our humanity to be with us on the whole journey of life, suffering, death, and new life. The role of the ordained, including deacons, is to give love, strength, and support to build up the whole Church so it can carry out its mission.

I hope that these personal reflections are helpful in some way to those who read them. Throughout this project, I have offered my opinion about possible changes to canon law, the ordination rite for deacons, and other practices and policies of the Church. I hope some of these ideas may be useful as the Church and the diaconate move ahead. I also hope that these offerings might encourage others to ponder these matters and offer their own recommendations as well.

We close where we began, with St. Paul's instructions to the Christians at Philippi, adding as a final thought, the encouraging words of the First Letter of John.

> Make my joy complete: be of the same mind, having the same love, being in full accord and of one mind. Do

nothing from selfish ambition or conceit, but in humility regard others as better than yourselves. (Phil 2:2–3)

Beloved, we are God's children now; what we will be has not yet been revealed. What we do know is this: when he is revealed, we will be like him, for we will see him as he is. (1 John 3:2)

NOTES

Preface

1. Edward J. Kilmartin, "Lay Participation in the Apostolate of the Hierarchy," in *Official Ministry in a New Age*, ed. James H. Provost (Washington, DC: CLSA, 1981), 94.

2. Pope Francis, *Let Us Dream: The Path to a Better Future* (New York: Simon and Schuster, 2021), 1.

3. This paragraph is drawn from Pope Francis, *Address of His Holiness Pope Francis for the Opening of the Synod*, October 9, 2021.

4. Francis, *Let Us Dream*, 1.

5. Vatican II, *Gaudium et Spes* 4 (hereafter cited in text as *GS*).

6. Richard R. Gaillardetz, "The 'Francis Moment': A New Kairos for Catholic Ecclesiology," CTSA Presidential Address, *CTSA Proceedings* 69 (2014): 63.

7. Gaillardetz, "The 'Francis Moment.'"

8. Yves Congar, *Power and Poverty in the Church: The Renewal and Understanding of Service* (Mahwah, NJ: Paulist Press, 2016), 93.

9. John XXIII, "Allocution for the Opening of the Second Vatican Council," *AAS* 54, no. 14 (1962): 786–96.

10. Paul VI, Address to the Cardinals and the Consultants of the Council for the Code Revision of Canon Law, November 20, 1965: "Nunc admodum mutatis rerum condicionibus…ius canonicum, prudentia adhibita, est recognoscendum: scilicet accommodari debet novo mentis habitui, Concilii Oecumenici Vaticani Secundi proprio, ex quo curae pastorali plurimum tribuitur, et novis necessitatibus populi Dei." *AAS* 57 (1965): 998.

11. Ladislas Orsy, "The Meaning of *Novus Habitus Mentis*: The Search for New Horizons," *The Jurist* 48 (1988): 429–47, at 429.

12. Orsy, "Meaning of *Novus Habitus Mentis*," 431.

13. Paul VI, *Hodie Concilium*, *AAS* 58 (1966): 57–64.

14. St. Augustine, *Epistola* 118, ch. 3, par. 22.

15. *Lumen Gentium* 21 (hereafter cited in text as *LG*).

16. Betsy Johnson-Miller, "A Pilgrim Church: The Unfinished Work of Vatican II, Part Two," interview with Richard R. Gaillardetz, Bearings Online Collegeville Institute, March 3, 2016.

17. See Richard R. Gaillardetz, *An Unfinished Council: Vatican II, Pope Francis, and the Renewal of Catholicism* (Collegeville, MN: Liturgical Press, 2015), 76.

18. John Paul II, *Fides et Ratio*, 93.

19. Pope Francis, Homily for the World Day of the Poor (33rd Sunday of Ordinary Time), November 14, 2020.

20. Pope Francis, Apostolic Visit to Slovakia, Meeting with Bishops, Priests, Religious, Seminarians, and Catechists, September 13, 2021.

Chapter One: A Humble Church as Icon of the Humble Trinity

1. The title of this chapter is drawn from the title of the first chapter ("The Church as Icon of the Trinity") of Veli-Matti Kärkkäinen's *An Introduction to Ecclesiology: Ecumenical, Historical and Global Perspectives*. While his chapter is in specific reference to major elements of Eastern Orthodox ecclesiology, I find his approach equally applicable for the Catholic Church. The Catholic Church, by which I mean all churches *sui iuris* in communion with each other and with the Holy See, is a community of churches from a variety of Eastern and Western traditions. The Eastern Catholic Churches, i.e., share much in common with their Eastern Orthodox counterparts, so what Kärkkäinen says about Eastern Orthodox ecclesiology has applicability to Catholic ecclesiology in general.

2. John Paul II, post-synodal apostolic exhortation *Pastores Dabo Vobis* (March 25, 1992), no. 12: *AAS* 84 (1992): 711, citing John Paul II, post-synodal apostolic exhortation *Christifideles Laici* (December 30, 1988), no. 8: *AAS* 81 (1989): 405; cf. Synod of Bishops, second extraordinary general assembly, 1985.

3. Lucien Richard, *Christ: The Self-Emptying of God* (Mahwah, NJ: Paulist Press, 1997), 84.

4. Johann Baptist Metz, *Poverty of Spirit* (New York: Paulist Press, 1968, 1998), 10–11.

5. Hans Urs von Balthasar, *Love Alone* (New York: Herder and Herder, 1969), 15.

6. Hans Urs von Balthasar, *Mysterium Paschale: The Mystery of Easter*, trans. Aidan Nichols (Edinburgh: T&T Clark, 1990), 29.

7. Hans Urs von Balthasar, *Prayer*, trans. Graham Harrison (San Francisco: Ignatius Press, 1986), 184.

8. John Paul II, *Fides et Ratio*, 93.

9. Richard, *Christ*, 94.

10. Augustine, *Sermo* 160, citing 2 Cor 10:17.

11. Christopher Fry, *The Lady's Not for Burning*, act 1.

12. John Henry Newman, "Preface to the Third Edition," in *The* Via Media *or the Anglican Church*, vol. 1 (London: Longmans, Green, and Co., 1891), xl. http://www.newmanreader.org/works/viamedia/volume1/preface3.html.

13. St. Ambrose, *Psal* 118:14:30: PL 15:1476.

14. St. Augustine, *Sermo* 267, 4: PL 38, 1231D; cf. *CCC*, 797.

15. St. Cyril of Jerusalem, *Catechetical Lectures*, 17.

16. Pope Francis, Homily at the Catholic Cathedral of the Holy Spirit, Istanbul (hereafter Istanbul Homily), Saturday, November 29, 2014.

17. Daniel P. Horan, "The Church Is Suffering from Holy Spirit Atheism," *National Catholic Reporter*, March 20, 2019.

18. Pope Francis, Istanbul Homily.

19. St. Thomas Aquinas, *Summa Theologiae*, III, q. 62, a. 1, ad 1.

20. St. Ignatius of Antioch, *Ad Smyrn.* 8, 2: Apostolic Fathers, II/2, 311.

21. Mary Ann Fatula, "Autonomy and Communion: Paying the Price," *Spirituality Today* 39 (Summer 1987): 164.

22. Cardinal Roger Mahony, "Church of the Eucharist, a Communion for Mission," *Origins* 33, no. 42 (April 1, 2004): 723.

23. Betsy Johnson-Miller, "A Pilgrim Church: The Unfinished Work of Vatican II, Part Two," interview with Richard R. Gaillardetz, Bearings Online Collegeville Institute, March 3, 2016.

24. Cf. Richard R. Gaillardetz, *An Unfinished Council: Vatican II, Pope Francis, and the Renewal of Catholicism* (Collegeville, MN: Liturgical Press, 2015), 76.

Chapter Two: Ecclesial 12-Step Program

1. Cf. Joan Chittister, *The Rule of Benedict: A Spirituality for the 21st Century* (New York: Crossroad, 1992, 2010).

2. Claude J. Peifer, "The Rule of St. Benedict," in *RB 1980: The Rule of St. Benedict in Latin and English with Notes and Thematic Index*, ed. Timothy Fry, Imogene Baker, Timothy Horner, Augusta Raabe, and Mark Sheridan (Collegeville, MN: Liturgical Press, 1981), 91 (hereafter cited in text as *RB 1980*).

3. Joan Chittister, *Radical Spirit: 12 Ways to Live a Free and Authentic Life* (New York: Crown Publishing, 2017), 3–4.

4. Cf. Ansgar Kristensen and Mark Sheridan, "The Role and Interpretation of Scripture in the Rule of Benedict," in *RB 1980*, 475–76.

5. As cited in *RB 1980*, note 7.9, some MSS have *ascendendos*, conveying more a sense of obligation. I am using that alternative translation here.

6. Pope Francis, "Fear of the Lord," General Audience, June 11, 2014.

7. Rudolf Otto, *The Idea of the Holy: An Inquiry into the Non-rational Factor in the Idea of the Divine and Its Relation to the Rational* (Oxford: Oxford University Press, 1968).

8. Chittister, *Radical Spirit*, 25.

9. *RB 1980*, 1, note, p. 56: "*Ausculta* is the spelling of the oldest extant manuscript of RB, Oxford Hatton 48, while *obsculta* is the spelling of Codex Sangallensis 914. Most modern editors have preferred *obsculta* as more authentic."

10. Chittister, *Radical Spirit*, 80.

11. Valerian J. Derlega and John H. Berg, eds., *Self-Disclosure: Theory, Research, and Therapy* (New York: Plenum Press, 1987), 1.

12. Chittister, *Radical Spirit*, 89.

13. Chittister, *Radical Spirit*, 136.

14. Chittister, *Radical Spirit*, 144–45.

15. Richard Gaillardetz, "A Church in Crisis," *Worship* 93 (July 2019): 212.

16. Chittister, *Radical Spirit*, 158.

17. John XXIII, Opening Address, Second Vatican Council, October 11, 1962.

18. Francis, *Fratelli Tutti* (hereafter cited in text as *FT*).
19. John XXIII, Opening Address at Second Vatican Council.

Chapter Three: Renewing Structures for a Humble and Diaconal Church

1. Avery Dulles, *Models of the Church* (New York: Doubleday, 2002), 27–28.
2. Dulles, *Models of the Church*, 27–28.
3. John R. Quinn, *The Reform of the Papacy: The Costly Call to Christian Unity* (hereafter *Reform*) (New York: Crossroad, 1999), and *Ever Ancient, Ever New: Structures of Communion in the Church* (hereafter *Structures*) (Mahwah, NJ: Paulist Press, 2013).
4. Congregation for the Clergy, "Instruction on the Pastoral Conversion of the Parish Community in the Service of the Evangelizing Mission of the Church," July 20, 2020, 1.
5. John Henry Newman, *An Essay on the Development of Christian Doctrine* (Notre Dame, IN: University of Notre Dame Press, 1989), ch. 1, sec. 1, par. 7.
6. Yves Congar, *Vraie et fausse réforme dans l'Eglise* (Paris: Editions du Cerf, 1950, 1968), translated and with an introduction by Paul Philibert, OP (Collegeville, MN: Liturgical Press, 2011), 52, citing J. Leclerq, "Un opuscule inédit de Jean de Limoges sur l'exemption," *Analecta S. Ord. Cisterc.* 3 (1947): 147–54.
7. John XXIII, Opening Address of the Second Vatican Council, October 11, 1962.
8. Paul VI, Encyclical Letter *Ecclesiam Suam* (August 6, 1964), 9–11: *AAS* 56 (1964): 609–59 (hereafter cited in text as *ES*).
9. Paul VI, apostolic exhortation *Evangelii Nuntiandi*, 14, citing the "Declaration of the Synod Fathers," 4, *L'Osservatore Romano* (October 27, 1974): 6.
10. John Paul II, post-synodal apostolic exhortation *Ecclesia in Oceania* (November 22, 2001), 19: *AAS* 94 (2002): 390.
11. Pope Francis, *Evangelii Gaudium* (November 24, 2013) (hereafter cited in text as *EG*).
12. John Paul II, *Ut Unum Sint*, May 25, 1995 (hereafter cited in text as *UUS*).

13. "Vinita Hampton Wright on the Principle and Foundation," IgnatianSpirituality.com, https://www.ignatianspirituality.com/vinita-hampton-wright-on-the-principle-and-foundation/.

14. Pope Francis, "Address to Seminarians."

15. Quinn, *Structures*, 3.

16. Michael Casey, *A Guide to Living in the Truth: Saint Benedict's Teaching on Humility* (Liguori, MO: Liguori/Triumph, 1999, 2001), citing Bernard of Clairvaux, *Treatise on the Steps of Humility and Pride*, 6, and *Sancti Bernardi Opera: The Works of Bernard of Clairvaux*, 3.20.14–15.

17. John Paul II, post-synodal apostolic exhortation *Pastores Dabo Vobis*, March 25, 1992 (hereafter cited in text as *PDV*).

18. Congar, *Vraie et fausse réforme*, 240–41.

19. William T. Ditewig, "The Exercise of Governance by Deacons: A Theological and Canonical Study" (PhD diss., Catholic University of America, 2002).

20. James M. Barnett, *The Diaconate: A Full and Equal Order* (New York: Seabury, 1981, 1995).

21. Quinn, *Structures*, v.

22. Quinn, *Reform*, 178.

23. See *Code of Canon Law*, c. 129 (hereafter cited in text as *CCL*).

24. Quinn, *Structures*, 3–4.

25. Quinn, *Structures*, 3–4.

26. Quinn, *Structures*, 4.

27. Quinn, *Structures*, 5.

28. Francis, apostolic constitution *Episcopalis Communio* (September 15, 2018), citing his Address on the Fiftieth Anniversary of the Synod of Bishops (October 17, 2015).

29. Francis, "Address of Holy Father Francis to the Faithful of the Diocese of Rome," Saturday, September 18, 2021.

30. John Paul II, "Deacons Serve the Kingdom of God," catechesis during general audience, October 5, 1993.

31. For further examination of the kenotic leadership of deacons, see, e.g., William T. Ditewig, "The Kenotic Leadership of Deacons," in *The Deacon Reader*, ed. James Keating (Mahwah, NJ: Paulist Press, 2006).

Chapter Four: Strengthened by Sacramental Grace

1. Paul VI, *motu proprio Ad Pascendum*, August 15, 1972.

2. John Paul II, "Allocution to the Permanent Deacons and Their Wives Given at Detroit, MI" (September 19, 1987): *Origins* 17 (1987): 327–29.

3. William T. Ditewig, *Leading Our Children to God* (South Bend, IN: Ave Maria Press, 1984), and *Lay Leaders: Resources for the Changing Parish* (South Bend, IN: Ave Maria Press, 1990).

4. For a fuller treatment, see William T. Ditewig, *The Emerging Diaconate: Servant Leaders in a Servant Church* (Mahwah, NJ: Paulist Press, 2007), 61–75.

5. Everett Ferguson, "Hippolytus," in Ferguson, *Encyclopedia of Early Christianity*, 531–32; B. R. Suchla, "Hippolytus," in Döpp and Gerrlings, *Early Christian Literature*, 287–89.

6. Ferguson, "Hippolytus," 531–32; Suchla, "Hippolytus," 287–89.

7. R. Hugh Connolly, *Didascalia Apostolorum: The Syriac Version* (Oxford: Clarendon, 1929), 148.

8. Ignatius, *Trallians* 3:1, in *Early Christian Fathers*, ed. Cyril C. Richardson (New York: Collier Books, Macmillan, 1970), 99, and *Magnesians* 6:1, 95.

9. *Didascalia Apostolorum*, III, 13, 2–4, in *Didascalia et Constitutiones Apostolorum*, ed. F. X. Funk (Paderborn, 1906), 214.

10. James M. Barnett, *The Diaconate: A Full and Equal Order* (New York: Seabury, 1981, 1995).

11. In the Middle Ages a question arose whether the subdeacon should receive the stole as part of his ordination, just as the deacon and presbyter were invested with the stole. The consensus was that, even though the subdiaconate was a major order and entitled to wear the sleeved tunicle, the subdeacon should not receive the stole.

12. Augustinus Kerkvoorde, "Theology of the Diaconate," in *Foundations for the Renewal of the Diaconate* (Washington, DC: USCC, 1993, reissued in 2003), 91.

13. Kerkvoorde, "Theology of the Diaconate," 91.

14. Pope Pius XII, apostolic constitution *Sacramentum Ordinis*, November 30, 1947 (hereafter cited in text as *SO*).

15. Latin original: "Emitte in eum, quaesumus, Domine, Spiritum Sanctum, quo in opus ministerii tui fideliter exsequendi septiformis gratiae tuae munere roboretur."

16. Thomas Merton, *Entering the Silence: Becoming a Monk and a Writer*, bk. 2, *The Journals of Thomas Merton* (New York: HarperCollins, 2009), March 15, 1949. Emphasis original.

17. See, e.g, William T. Ditewig, *The Emerging Diaconate: Servant Leaders in a Servant Church* (Mahwah, NJ: Paulist Press, 2007); Otto Pies, "Block 26: Erfahrungen aus dem Priesterleben in Dachau," *Stimmen der Zeit* 141 (1947–48): 10–28; Wilhelm Schamoni, *Familienväter als geweihte Diakone* (Paderborn: Schöningh, 1953). English translation: *Married Men as Ordained Deacons*, trans. Otto Eisner (London: Burns and Oates, 1955); Karl Rahner and Herbert Vorgrimler, eds., *Diakonia in Christo: Über die Erneuerung des Diakonates* (Freiburg: Herder, 1962).

18. See, e.g., Ditewig, *Emerging Diaconate*, esp. ch. 5.

19. *Acta et documenta Concilio oecumінco Vaticano II apparando; Series prima (antepraeparatoria)* (Vatican City: Typis Polyglottis Vaticanis, 1960–1961) (*ADA*), II/II, 128–31.

20. *Acta Synodalia Sacrasancti Concilii Vaticani II* (Vatican City: Typis Polyglottis Vaticanis, 1970) (*AS*), 227–30.

21. *Acta Synodalia Sacrasancti Concilii Vaticani II*, 317–19.

22. *Acta Synodalia Sacrasancti Concilii Vaticani II*, 229.

23. *Ad Gentes* will hereafter be cited in the text as *AG*.

24. Leo Cardinal Suenens, "The Coresponsibility of Deacons," in *Diaconal Reader: Selected Articles from the "Diaconal Quarterly,"* ed. John F. Kinney (Washington, DC: NCCB, 1985), 47.

25. John Paul II, Address to Joint Plenarium, "The Deacon's Ordination," November 30, 1995, 3.

26. Congregation for Catholic Education, *Basic Norms for the Formation of Permanent Deacons* (Vatican City: Libreria Editrice Vaticana, 1998), 7 (hereafter BNFPD). For a more detailed analysis of the language involved, see William T. Ditewig, "The Exercise of Governance by Deacons: A Theological and Canonical Study" (PhD diss., The Catholic University of America, 2002), 162–76.

27. Pope Benedict, apostolic letter *motu proprio Omnium in Mentem*, October 26, 2009.

28. See, e.g., Ditewig, *The Emerging Diaconate*; Pies, "Block 26: Erfahrungen aus dem Priesterleben in Dachau"; Schamoni, *Familienväter als geweihte Diakone*.

29. John Paul II, Allocution to the Permanent Deacons and Their Wives Given at Detroit, MI (September 19, 1987): *Origins* 17 (1987): 327–29.

30. Benedict XVI, *Deus Caritas Est*, December 25, 2005.

31. Paul VI, *Hodie Concilium*, *AAS* 58 (1966): 57–64.

32. Pope Francis, "Address to the Permanent Deacons of the Diocese of Rome with Their Families," June 19, 2021.

33. See, e.g., International Theological Commission Research Document "From the *Diakonia* of Christ to the *Diakonia* of the Apostles," 2002; also, see can. 1 from the Council of Trullo (692).

34. It is interesting to note that internationally the vast majority of diaconate organizations make use of the imagery from the foot washing: bowls, pitchers of water, and towels. Clearly, these images have caught the imagination of deacons and bishops as capturing and communicating the essence of the diaconate.

35. United States Conference of Catholic Bishops, *The National Directory for the Formation, Ministry and Life of Permanent Deacons in the United States of America*, 2nd ed. (Washington, DC: USCCB, 2021), 41, repeating the text of the 2005 first edition, 39, also citing its predecessor document, Bishops' Committee on the Permanent Diaconate, National Conference of Catholic Bishops, *Permanent Deacons in the United States: Guidelines on Their Formation and Ministry, 1984 Revision* (Washington, DC: United States Catholic Conference, 1985), 43.

36. John Paul II, Allocution to the Permanent Deacons and Their Wives.

Chapter Five: The Code of Canon Law, a Servant Church, and Diaconate

1. James A. Coriden, *Canon Law as Ministry: Freedom and Good Order for the Church* (Mahwah, NJ: Paulist Press, 2000), 3.

2. *New Catholic Encyclopedia*, 2nd ed., s.v. "Provost, James H.," by John Beal (Farmington Hills, MI: Gale, 2003), 11:786, https://cvdvn.files.wordpress.com/2018/05/new-catholic-encyclopedia-vol-11.pdf.

3. James H. Provost, "Permanent Deacons in the 1983 Code," in *Canon Law Society of America Proceedings* 46 (1984): 175.

4. John Paul II, *Sacrae Disciplinae Leges*, in *AAS* 75 (1983): 11.

5. John Paul II, allocution to Roman Rota, January 26, 1984: *AAS* 76 (1984): 645–46.

6. Unless otherwise noted, the English translations will be taken from the *Code of Canon Law, Latin-English Edition, New English Translation* (Washington, DC: Canon Law Society of America [CLSA], 1998), and the *Code of Canons of the Eastern Churches, Latin-English Edition* (Washington, DC: CLSA, 1992).

7. "Ecclesiastical laws must be understood in accord with the proper meaning of the words considered in their text and context. If the meaning remains doubtful and obscure, recourse must be made to parallel places, if there are such, to the purpose and circumstances of the law, and to the mind of the legislator."

8. *New Commentary*, 27, citing Jobe Abbass, "The Usefulness of Comparative Studies," in *Two Codes in Comparison* (Rome: Edizioni Orientalia Christiana, 2018), 278–94.

9. Bertram F. Griffin, "The Three-Fold *Munera* of Christ and the Church," in *Code, Community, Ministry: Selected Studies for the Parish Minister Introducing the Revised Code of Canon Law*, ed. James H. Provost (Washington, DC: Canon Law Society of America, 1982, 1983), 19–20.

10. Griffin, "Three-Fold *Munera*," 19.

11. Griffin, "Three-Fold *Munera*," 20. See also J. James Cuneo, "The Power of Jurisdiction: Empowerment for Church Functioning and Mission Distinct from the Power of Orders," *The Jurist* 39, no. 1/2 (1979): 200: "*Potestas iurisdictionis* would not simply mean ruling function. Rather it too would apply to any of the three types of sacred functions [teaching, sanctifying, ruling] in the Church. It also signifies a means to fulfill these types of functions."

12. Robert J. Kaslyn, "Introduction," in *New Commentary on the Code of Canon Law*, ed. John P. Beal, James A. Coriden, and Thomas J. Green (Washington, DC: CLSA, 2000) [hereafter *New Commentary*], 241.

13. John D. Zizioulas, *Being as Communion: Studies in Personhood and the Church* (Crestwood, NY: St. Vladimir's Seminary Press, 1985), 216.

14. Zizioulas, *Being as Communion*, 216.

15. Joseph W. Pokusa, "A Canonical-Historical Study of the Diaconate in the Western Church" (JCD diss., Catholic University of America, 1979).

16. *Catéchisme de l'Église Catholique* (Ottawa: Conférence des Évêques catholiques du Canada, 1993), 875: "De Lui, ils reçoivent la mission et la faculté (le «pouvoir sacré») d'agir *in persona Christi Capitis*."

17. *Catechismus Catholicae Ecclesiae* (Vatican City: Libreria Editrice Vaticana, 1997), 875: "Ab Eo Episcopi et presbyteri missionem et facultatem ('sacram potestam') agendi *in persona Christi Capitis* accipiunt, diaconi vero vim populo Dei serviendi in *diakonia* liturgiae, verbi et caritatis, in communione cum Episcopo eiusque presbyterio."

18. *Acta Synodalia Sacrasancti Concilii Vaticani II* (Vatican City: Typis Polyglottis Vaticanis, 1970–), 82–87 (hereafter cited in text as *AS*).

19. Provost, "Permanent Deacons in the 1983 Code," 175.

20. See, e.g., William T. Ditewig, "The Exercise of Governance by Deacons: A Theological and Canonical Study" (PhD diss., The Catholic University of America, 2002).

21. For example, the popular translation of the documents of Vatican II by Austin Flannery offers no translation of *pro cura animarum*. The translations by Abbott and by Tanner include the phrase.

22. John P. Beal, "The Exercise of the Power of Governance by Lay People: State of the Question," *The Jurist* 55 (1995): 1, 15.

23. James H. Provost, "Ecclesiastical Offices," in *New Commentary*, 207.

24. St. Thomas Aquinas, OP, *Summa Theologiae*, vol. V, Q. 35, art. 2 (Madrid: Biblioteca de Autores Cristianos, 1952), 135.

25. Aquinas, *Summa Theologiae*, vol. V, 136.

26. *The Canons and Decrees of the Council of Trent*, ed. and trans. H. J. Schroeder, OP (Rockford, IL: TAN, 1978), 171.

27. John M. Huels, "The Power of Governance and Its Exercise by Lay Persons: A Juridical Approach," Studia Canonica 35 (2001): 61.

28. Huels, "The Power of Governance," 61n3.

29. Nathan Mitchell, OSB, *Mission and Ministry: History and Theology in the Sacrament of Order* (Wilmington, DE: Michael Glazier, 1982), 301.

30. Huels, "The Power of Governance," 60, citing K. Mörsdorf, "Ecclesiastical Authority," in *Sacramentum Mundi: An Encyclopedia of Theology*, ed. K. Rahner et al., vol. 2 (New York: Herder and Herder, 1968), 133–39.

31. Huels, "The Power of Governance," 65–66.

32. John M. Huels, in email correspondence with William T. Ditewig, July 17, 2001.

33. Huels, email correspondence, July 17, 2001.

34. Edward N. Peters, "Canonical Considerations on Diaconal Continence" *Studia Canonica* 59 (2005): 147–80.

35. Blog exchange: Edward Peters, "Some Thoughts on Dcn. Ditewig's Comments on Diaconal Continence," January 17, 2011, *In the Light of the Law*, http://canonlawblog.blogspot.com/2011/01/some-thoughts-on-dcn-ditewigs-comments.html.

36. *New Commentary* and the *Code of Canons of the Eastern Churches, Latin-English Edition* (Washington, DC: CLSA, 1992), 27, citing J. Abbass, "The Usefulness of Comparative Studies," in *Two Codes in Comparison*, 278–94.

37. Letter from the Pontifical Council on Legislative Texts, Prot. No. 13095/2011, December 17, 2011.

38. Frederick R. McManus, "The Sacrament of the Anointing of the Sick," in *New Commentary*, 1186.

39. John P. Beal, "The Exercise of the Power of Governance by Lay People: State of the Question," *The Jurist* 55 (1995): 1, 15.

40. Beal, "The Exercise of the Power of Governance," 15.

41. Congregation for the Clergy, Instruction "The Pastoral Conversion of the Parish Community in the Service of the Evangelizing Mission of the Church," June 29, 2020, 81.

42. Congregation for Clergy, "Pastoral Conversion," 82.

43. Congregation for the Clergy, *Directory for the Ministry and Life of Permanent Deacons* (hereafter *DMLPD*), February 22, 1998, 41.

44. One commentator remarks, "Canon 1574 of the 1917 *Code* noted that diocesan judges exercised *delegated* power. The present canon has deleted that observation and, in accord with the definitions found in canon 131 §1, a diocesan judge would now seem to be exercising *ordinary* power." Lawrence G. Wrenn, "Processes," in *New Commentary*, 1624.

45. *Communicationes. Pontificium Consilium De Legum Textibus Interpretandis* (Vatican City: Tipografia Vaticana, 1969 et seq.), 24 (1992), 137 (hereafter *Communicationes*). All translations mine.

46. *Communicationes*, 138–39.

47. *Communicationes*, 205.

48. *Communicationes*, 231.

49. *Communicationes* 25 (1993), 201.

50. *Communicationes* 13 (1981), 306.

51. John J. McCarthy, "The *Diakonia* of Charity in the Permanent Diaconate: Its Application to Certain Clerical Offices as Addressed in the *Directory for the Ministry and Life of Permanent Deacons*" (JCD diss., Pontificia Studiorum Universitas a S. Thoma Aq. in Urbe, 2000), 114.

52. Pontifical Commission for the Revision of the Code of Canon Law, *Relatio complectens synthesim animadversionum ab Em.mis atque Exc.mis Patribus Commissionis ad Novissimum Schema Codicis Iuris Canonici Exhibitarum, cum responsibus a Secretaria et Consultoribus datis* (Vatican City: Typis Polyglottis Vaticanis, 1981). (Hereafter *Relatio.*)

53. *Relatio*, 123.

54. *Relatio*, 123.

55. *Relatio*, 123.

56. McCarthy, "*Diakonia* of Charity," 118.

57. Congregation for the Clergy, et al., *Ecclesiae de Mysterio* (August 15, 1997) in *AAS* 89 (1997): 852–76; English translation in *Origins* 27 (November 27, 1997): 397–409.

58. Congregation for the Clergy, *Ecclesiae de Mysterio*, art. 4.

59. *DMLPD*, 41.

Chapter Six: Ordaining Deacons in a Humble Church

1. Ditewig, *The Emerging Diaconate: Servant Leaders in a Servant Church* (Mahwah, NJ: Paulist Press, 2007), ch. 8.

2. In the Latin rite of ordination, the ordinand is called forward to the bishop from the assembly. A deacon or priest presents the ordinand to the bishops, asking that he be ordained. The bishop asks, "Do you know him to be worthy?" to which the representative responds, "After inquiry among the Christian people and upon the recommendation of those responsible, I testify that they have been found worthy." The bishop responds, "Relying on the help of the Lord God and our Savior Jesus Christ, we choose these, our brothers, for the Order of the Diaconate." In the Eastern Catholic Churches, during the postordination investiture with sacred vestments and the instruments of office, the

full assembly repeatedly affirms their worthiness (in the Byzantine tradition, e.g., the bishop, presbyters, and assembly repeatedly proclaim, ἄξιος!).

3. Ditewig, *Emerging Diaconate.*

4. David N. Power, OMI, "Appropriate Ordination Rites: A Historical Perspective," in *Alternative Futures for Worship*, vol. 6, *Leadership Ministry in Community*, ed. Bernard J. Lee (Collegeville, MN: Liturgical Press, 1987), 131.

5. General Instruction of the Roman Pontifical (GIRP), 1.

6. Pierre Jounel, "Ordinations," in *The Church at Prayer*, vol. 3, *The Sacraments*, ed. A. G. Martimort (Collegeville, MN: Liturgical Press, 1988), 144.

7. GIRP, 11.

8. GIRP, 11.

9. GIRP, 11.

10. John Henry Newman, *An Essay on the Development of Christian Doctrine* (Notre Dame, IN: University of Notre Dame Press, 1989), I.7. Emphasis added.

11. See also *AA* 1: "[The laity's] part in the church's mission has already been mentioned as proper to them and indispensable. The Church can never be without the apostolate of lay persons, deriving as it does from their very vocation as a Christian."

12. Joseph A. Komonchak, "The New Diaconate Guidelines," in *Proceedings of the 1986 Convention of the National Association of Permanent Diaconate Directors in Baltimore, MD, April 28–May 1, 1986* (Chicago: National Association of Permanent Diaconate Directors, 1986), 7.

13. John Paul II, Allocution to the Permanent Deacons and Their Wives Given at Detroit, MI (September 19, 1987): *Origins* 17 (1987): 327–29.

14. Joseph Bernardin, "The Call to Service: Pastoral Statement on the Permanent Diaconate" (Chicago: Archdiocese of Chicago, 1993), 5. Emphasis in the original.

15. St. Paul VI, following the recommendations of the Council, eliminated the rite of tonsure (by which a seminarian became a cleric) and suppressed the minor orders of porter and exorcist and the major order of subdeacon in the Latin Church. The former minor orders of lector and acolyte were retained, but as lay (i.e., not ordained) ministries.

16. *The Pontifical of Egbert, Archbishop of York*, printed from a tenth-century manuscript in the Imperial Library, Paris, published for

the Surtees Society (London: Whittaker & Co.; Edinburgh: Blackwood & Sons, 1853), 18–21.

17. *Pontifical of Egbert of York*, 21.

Chapter Seven: Recurring Questions on the Diaconate

1. Leo Cardinal Suenens, "The Coresponsibility of Deacons," in *Diaconal Reader: Selected Articles from the "Diaconal Quarterly,"* ed. John F. Kinney (Washington, DC: NCCB, 1985), 47.

2. USCCB Complementary Norms, accessed February 25, 2022, https://www.usccb.org/committees/canonical-affairs-church-governance/complementary-norms#tab--canon-284-clerical-garb.

3. USCCB, *The National Directory for the Formation, Ministry, and Life of Permanent Deacons in the United States of America*, 2nd ed. (Washington, DC: USCCB, 2021), 94, citing *CIC*, c. 288.

4. Pope Celestine I, "Epistola II ad Episcopos Provinciæ," in *Sacrorum Conciliorum Nova et Amplissima Collectio*, ed. Ioannes Mansi, vol. 4 (Graz: Akademische Druck-U. Verlagsanstalt, 1960), 465.

5. Congregation for the Doctrine of the Faith, "Note on the Minister of the Sacrament of the Anointing of the Sick," February 11, 2005, http://www.vatican.va/roman_curia/congregations/cfaith/documents/rc_con_cfaith_doc_20050211_unzione-infermi_en.html.

6. "Note on the Minister of the Sacrament of the Anointing of the Sick."

7. See, e.g., Sacred Congregation for the Doctrine of the Faith, Declaration *Inter Insigniores* on the Question of Admission of Women to the Ministerial Priesthood (October 15, 1976): *AAS* 69 (1977): 98–116 and John Paul II, Apostolic Letter *Ordinatio Sacerdotalis* (May 30, 1994) in *Origins* 24, no. 4 (June 9, 1994): 50–52.

8. International Theological Commission, "From the Diakonia of Christ to the Diakonia of the Apostles: An Historico-Theological Research Document" (London: Catholic Truth Society, 2003), 100.

9. Consider, e.g., the groundbreaking work of Phyllis Zagano, who served on the first commission appointed by Pope Francis, especially in her *Holy Saturday: An Argument for the Restoration of the Female Diaconate in the Catholic Church* (New York: Crossroad, 2000).

She has published several other works on various aspects of the question since. For example, Phyllis Zagano, ed., *Women Deacons? Essays with Answers* (Collegeville, MN: Liturgical Press, 2016). Another survey is Gary Macy, William T. Ditewig, and Phyllis Zagano, *Women Deacons: Past, Present, Future* (Mahwah, NJ: Paulist Press, 2012).

10. Canon Law Society of America, "The Canonical Implications of Ordaining Women to the Permanent Diaconate: Report of an *Ad Hoc* Committee of the Canon Law Society of America" (Washington, DC: CLSA, 1995).

11. CLSA, "Canonical Implications." For the question of the deacon and governance, see William T. Ditewig, "The Exercise of Governance by Deacons: A Theological and Canonical Study" (PhD diss., Catholic University of America, 2002).

12. John Paul II, Post-Synodal Apostolic Exhortation *Pastores Dabo Vobis*, March 25, 1992, 17, citing *PO* 7–9.

13. It should go without saying, but just for clarity, we should emphasize that for a married deacon, his prime relationship is with his wife and family. What we are speaking of in this section are those relationships established by the deacon's ordination.

14. United States Conference of Catholic Bishops, *National Directory for the Formation, Ministry and Life of Permanent Deacons in the United States of America* (hereafter *National Directory*) (Washington, DC: USCCB: 2021), 54.

15. Congregation for the Clergy, *Directory for the Ministry and Life of Permanent Deacons*, February 1998, 40.

16. *National Directory*, 45, citing BNFPD, 16, and 1984 Guidelines, 51.

17. John Paul II, "Deacons Are Active Apostles of the New Evangelization: Address to Permanent Deacons and Their Families during the Jubilee Celebration for Deacons, February 19, 2000."

18. *National Directory*, 41.

Chapter Eight: Concluding Reflections

1. United States Conference of Catholic Bishops, *National Directory for the Formation, Ministry and Life of Permanent Deacons in the United States of America* (Washington, DC: USCCB, 2005), 54.

2. James M. Barnett, *The Diaconate: A Full and Equal Order*, rev. ed. (Valley Forge, PA: Trinity Press, 1995).

3. The predecessor organization, along with the United States Catholic Conference, to the United States Conference of Catholic Bishops.

4. Reginald Fuller in Barnett, *The Diaconate*, xii.

5. John St. H. Gibaut, *The Cursus Honorum: A Study of the Origins and Evolution of Sequential Ordination* (New York: Peter Lang, 2000), 331–32.

6. Gibaut, *Cursus Honorum*, 331–32.

7. *The Canons and Decrees of the Council of Trent*, ed. and trans. H. J. Schroeder, OP (Rockford, IL: TAN, 1978), 174.

8. *Concilium Tridentinum: Diariorum, actorum, epistularum, tractatuum nova collectio*, ed. Georresian Society, 13 vols. (Freiburg: Herder, 1901–), 9:601.

9. *Concilium Tridentinum*, 9:558–59.

10. Edward P. Echlin, *The Deacon in the Church: Past and Future* (Staten Island, NY: Alba House, 1971), 100.

11. *The 1917 Pio-Benedictine Code of Canon Law*, Edward N. Peters, curator (San Francisco: Ignatius Press, 2001), 61.

12. Francis, Apostolic Letter *motu proprio Antiquum Ministerium*, instituting the Ministry of Catechist, May 10, 2021.

13. Herman Beyer, "διακουέω, διακουία, διάκουος," in *Theological Dictionary of the New Testament*, trans. Geoffrey W. Bromiley (Grand Rapids, MI: Eerdmans, 1964–76), 2:81–93; Wilhelm Brandt, *Dienst und Deinen in Neuen Testament* (Gütersloh: Bertelsmann Verlag, 1931).

14. For a more detailed discussion, see Ditewig, *The Emerging Diaconate: Servant Leaders in a Servant Church* (Mahwah, NJ: Paulist Press, 2007).

15. Beyer, "διακουέω, 82, cited in W. Shawn McKnight, *Understanding the Diaconate: Historical, Theological, and Sociological Foundations* (Washington, DC: Catholic University of America Press, 2018), 5–6.

16. Bishops' Committee on the Permanent Diaconate, National Conference of Catholic Bishops, *Permanent Deacons in the United States: Guidelines on Their Formation and Ministry*, 1984 revision (Washington, DC: United States Catholic Conference, 1985), 43.

17. John N. Collins, *Diakonia: Re-interpreting the Ancient Sources* (New York: Oxford University Press, 1990).

18. W. Shawn McKnight, *Understanding the Diaconate: Historical, Theological, and Sociological Foundations* (Washington, DC: Catholic University of America Press, 2018).

19. McKnight, *Understanding Diaconate*, 28.

20. See, e.g., Frances J. Niederer, "Pagan Monuments Converted to Christian Use: The Roman 'Diaconiae,'" *Journal of the Society of Architectural Historians* 12, no. 3 (1953): 3–6, https://doi.org/10.2307/987593.

21. Pope Francis, "Address to the Permanent Deacons of the Diocese of Rome, with Their Families," June 19, 2021.

22. It should be noted that even in some medieval art and architecture of the Latin Church, angels are frequently clothed as deacons. For example, in certain depictions, the angels descending to minister to Jesus after his temptations in the desert are clearly depicted in the vestments of the deacon.

23. Alexander Kniazeff, "The Role of the Deacon in the Byzantine Liturgical Assembly," in *Roles in the Liturgical Assembly: The Twenty-Third Liturgical Conference of Saint Serge*, ed. Matthew J. O'Connell (New York: Pueblo Publishing, 1981), 172.

24. David Kennedy, "The Diaconate and Theologia Prima: Part VI," *Diaconate in Christ*, April 18, 2019, https://diaconateinchrist.typepad.com/diaconate-in-christ/.

25. Roberto Octavio Gonzalez Nieves, OFM, Diaconate Ordination Homily, citing Luke 1:35.

26. R. Hugh Connolly, *Didascalia Apostolorum: The Syriac Version Translated and Accompanied by the Verona Latin Fragments* (Eugene, OR: Wipf and Stock, 2010), 109.

27. Connolly, *Didascalia*, 148.

ADVANCE PRAISE FOR *COURAGEOUS HUMILITY*

"Pope Francis's great reform in response to a new era seeks a Church that convinces through humble witness, a Church of service rather than power, a Church that is credible by its dependence on God's strength. As Bill Ditewig shows us, this is not only just a matter of urgent structural and institutional transformation, but of a conversion of mindset and a renewal of the heart. In *Courageous Humility*, he gives us a compelling vision of that conversion, as well as guidance and suggestions to enable it in law and liturgy, by drawing on the wisdom of the ancients as well as his many years of service as a deacon. Bold, hopeful, and compelling, *Courageous Humility* is about *diakonia* in its broadest sense, and deserves to be read wherever there is ministry in the Church."

—Austen Ivereigh

"Deacon William Ditewig, hands down, is the most articulate exponent of the diaconate in today's Catholic Church, and this book is Ditewig at his very best. His image of deacons as 'icons of the Church's humility' is destined to become the defining treatment of the subject in Catholic literature, and it's not just a slogan but a Magna Carta for the diaconate. This is a book that not just every deacon, but every Catholic who cares about the future of the Church, ought to read."

—John L. Allen Jr., editor of *Crux* and senior Vatican analyst for CNN

"*Courageous Humility* is nothing less than a masterwork. This may be Deacon Ditewig's most important and enduring book. Here is a beautiful and bold reflection on living our faith in the twenty-first century by fulfilling a call that goes back to the first century—a call to courage, humility, and hope. With intelligence, passion, and profoundly personal insight, Deacon Ditewig offers us a portrait of a church that is one, holy, catholic, apostolic—and diaconal! Take and read. You are holding in your hands a modern classic."

—Deacon Greg Kandra, blogger and author, *A Deacon Prays*

"At a time when many people's confidence in the Catholic Church has reached a dismal low, Pope Francis has called for a listening and synodal church. William Ditewig has responded to both this crisis and the pope with a clear vision of the Church based in diaconal service. *Courageous Humility*, with its thorough and creative understanding of the diaconate and its implications for the whole Church, should be required reading for all involved in ministry: lay ecclesial ministers, deacons, priests, and bishops."

—Susan Ross, professor emerita of theology,
Loyola University Chicago

"The diaconate plays a crucial role in the ongoing discussions on clericalism and the future of ministry in the Catholic Church. These essays by Ditewig provide much needed pastoral and ecclesiological perspective, grounded in decades of experiences as a deacon and a scholar."

—Massimo Faggioli, professor of theology and religious studies,
Villanova University

"In *Courageous Humility*, Deacon William Ditewig provides us with a new lens through which we can take a fresh look at the Church and its diaconal ministry. Drawing from his varied experiences and decades of ministry, Doctor Ditewig offers pragmatic possibilities for reforming and revising the Church's understanding of authority, holy orders, canon law, and liturgical rites. Finally, *Courageous Humility* addresses contemporary questions surrounding the diaconate in the hope that the search for answers will facilitate the full potential of deacons and the Church."

—Michael J. Tkacik, PhD, associate professor, Department of
Philosophy, Theology, and Religion, Saint Leo University, Florida